COUNCIL
OF EUROPE

CONSEIL
DE L'EUROPE

The Challenge
of
Human Rights Education

Edited by Hugh Starkey

CASSELL

Published in Great Britain by Cassell Educational Limited
Villiers House, 41/47 Strand, London WC2N 5JE, England

First published 1991

British Library Cataloguing in Publication Data
The challenge of human rights education. – (Cassell Council of Europe Series)
  1. Human rights study and teaching
  I. Starkey, Hugh
323.07
ISBN 0–304–31943–0

Phototypeset by Input Typesetting Ltd, London
Printed and bound in Great Britain by
Page Bros, Norwich

Contents

Foreword

On 4 November 1950, ministers of 15 countries met in Rome and signed the European Convention for the Protection of Human Rights and Fundamental Freedoms. The Convention, which established the first international machinery for the protection of human rights, was inspired by the belief that human rights and fundamental freedoms are 'the foundation of justice and peace in the world' and that they are best maintained by an effective political democracy.

Just over 40 years later, all of the Council of Europe's 25 member states have signed the Convention, which has also influenced efforts to guarantee human rights in other continents.

The Council is convinced that education too can make a vital contribution to the protection and promotion of human rights. For example, it can help to:

- make young people aware of their common heritage of political ideals and traditions, in particular freedom and the rule of law;
- equip them with the knowledge, skills and attitudes that they will need if they are to play an active part in the operation and development of our democratic institutions.

The Council of Europe has, therefore, worked with teachers, specialists and non-governmental organizations like Amnesty International to define how education systems, especially schools, can help to promote an active commitment to human rights and the principles of pluralistic democracy. Through its meetings of experts and its teachers' seminars, the Council has brought about a rich sharing of ideas, experience and innovation in human rights education, and this information is being used as the basis for audiovisual material for schools and publications for teachers like the present handbook.

The editor of this book, Hugh Starkey, and many of the other authors have been closely involved in the Council of Europe's work on human rights education. I would like to pay a warm tribute to their commitment and expertise, and to the enthusiasm of the hundreds of European teachers who have contributed to our reflections on this important subject.

The development of human rights education in Europe has been informed and enriched by contacts and exchanges of experience and ideas with many other areas of the world, most notably with the United States and Canada. This fruitful relationship is acknowledged and celebrated in the four North American chapters of this volume.

This publication is most timely because there is a keen interest in education for democratic values throughout Europe at present. Most countries in Central and Eastern Europe are preparing new programmes of education for democratic citizenship to replace the heavily ideological civic education courses which are no longer in force. At the same time, a serious reflection is under way in Western Europe about the role of education in overcoming political apathy and combating such challenges to democratic values as intolerance, xenophobia, racism, violence and terrorism.

As contributions to this handbook show, human rights education is a much wider concept than the study of legal and constitutional texts and mechanisms. Human rights should permeate the whole of school life – the ethos and organization of the school, as well as the content of the curriculum. Schools should, therefore, show respect and consideration for all their members, encourage solidarity and promote dialogue. They should also provide young people with opportunities for meaningful participation in the running of their school community.

Approaches to human rights education will obviously differ in primary and secondary schools, but they should lead to an understanding of, and sympathy for, the concepts of democracy, justice, equality, freedom, solidarity, peace, dignity, and rights and responsibilities.

Twenty-nine states take part in the Council of Europe's education programme, and the content of human rights education varies from country to country and, in some cases, from school to school. Nevertheless, the Council recommends that there should be a common core consisting of:

- the main categories of human rights, duties, obligations and responsibilities;
- the various forms of injustice, inequality and discrimination, including sexism and racism;
- people, movements and key events in the historical and continuing struggle for human rights;
- the main international declarations and conventions on human rights, e.g. the Universal Declaration of Human Rights and the European Convention for the Protection of Human Rights and Fundamental Freedoms.

Among the skills needed for understanding and supporting human rights, the Council of Europe attaches special importance to:

- skills associated with language development, such as written and oral expression and the ability to discuss and listen;
- skills involving judgements – the collection and analysis of material from various sources (including the mass media); the detection of bias, preju-

dice and stereotypes; and the ability to arrive at fair and balanced conclusions;

- social skills, including the recognition and acceptance of differences and the ability to establish positive and non-oppressive personal relationships;
- action skills such as solving conflict in a non-violent way, taking responsibility, participating in group decisions, and understanding and using the mechanisms for the protection of human rights that exist at local, national, European and world level.

The importance of equipping young people with critical and analytical skills for understanding and interpreting the messages of the mass media was stressed recently by the Standing Conference of the European Ministers of Education. Media education can have an important political function because it can help to form citizens who cannot be swayed or manipulated by biased information.

The effectiveness of human rights education depends, of course, on the commitment, quality and skills of the individual teacher who will need both training and support. On the other hand, there have been so many demands on teachers in recent years that there is a danger that human rights education may be perceived as just another passing fashion, and not as an essential part of preparation for life in a pluralistic democracy.

The Australian educator, Ralph Pettman, has spoken of human rights education as 'an education in moral literacy'. I also see it as an education in civil courage. Our societies will need both of these qualities if they are to withstand the intolerance and the tensions generated by unemployment and by continuing poverty and inequality in the world.

Maitland Stobart
Deputy Director of Education, Culture and Sport
Council of Europe

Cassell Council of Europe series
This series is the result of a collaboration between the Council of Europe and Cassell. It comprises books on a wide range of educational material, drawn largely from seminars and research which have been initiated and sponsored by the Council of Europe.

TITLES IN THE SERIES

M. Eraut: *Education and the Information Society*
C. Pilley: *Adult Education, Community Development and Older People*
M. Shennan: *Teaching about Europe*
H. Starkey: *The Challenge of Human Rights Education*
G. Weiner: *The Primary School and Equal Opportunities*

Contributors

Martine Abdallah-Pretceille is Directrice of the École Normale, Amiens.

Francine Best is a former Director of the Institut National de Recherches Pédagogiques, France.

Philippa Bobbett is Project Worker at Oxford Development Education Centre.

Margaret Branson is Administrator in the Division of Instructional Services for Kern County, California.

Jeremy Cunningham is Head of Carterton Comprehensive School, Oxfordshire.

Patricia Dye is at the Plymouth–Carver School, Massachusetts.

Derek Heater was formerly at Brighton Polytechnic.

Peter Leuprecht is Director of Human Rights at the Council of Europe.

Ian Lister is Professor of Education at the University of York.

Pauline Lyseight-Jones is Inspector for Primary Education for the London Borough of Ealing.

Keith McLeod is Professor of Education at the University of Toronto.

Margherita Rendel is Reader in Human Rights and Education at the University of London, Institute of Education.

Micheline Rey is a consultant for the Council of Europe's Programme on Intercultural Education, and lecturer at the University of Geneva, Switzerland.

Robin Richardson is Director of the Runnymede Trust, London.

Caroline Roaf is Head of Education for Special Needs at Peers School, Oxford.

David Shiman is Professor of Education at the University of Vermont.

Hugh Starkey is Principal Lecturer at Westminster College, Oxford.

Maitland Stobart is Deputy Director for Education, Culture and Sport at the Council of Europe.

Introduction

A VISITOR YET A PART OF EVERYBODY –
THE TASKS AND GOALS OF HUMAN RIGHTS EDUCATION

'I'd come back to school with the story,' starts Maxine, a London schoolgirl in the tale *A Thief in the Village* by James Berry. It is a true story which she tells, about happenings, discoveries and insights some years ago in the Jamaican village where her father was born, and where she herself has recently spent three happy holidays:

> I was a visitor yet I was a part of everybody. The people treated me like their long lost village princess. And they had no doubts about how their village language and voices thrilled me something big. Each time, my holiday was just brilliant with all sorts of fresh fun. (Berry, 1987)

'A visitor yet a part of everybody': there is a fine shorthand image here of the just society, the just community. The right tension and balance between individual separateness ('a visitor') and corporate rootedness ('a part of every-body') depend in their turn on a right tension and balance between differentiation and equality: 'Equality without differentiation', runs an ancient maxim in Zen Buddhism, 'is bad equality'; differentiation without equality is bad differentiation' (Sekida, 1975). It is a powerful maxim for reflecting on the nature of human rights, and, therefore, and more specifically, on the nature of education about and for human rights.

Maxine in *The Thief in the Village* has the good fortune, by the sound of it, to be taught by a teacher committed to human rights education. What this means in practice, or might mean, is the subject of this chapter, and of this book. But before enumerating and discussing a few of the main features of sound human rights education, and before returning in due course to Maxine and the tale she tells from her father's Jamaican village, I should like to introduce the overall topic of human rights education with a simple story about an imaginary situation, an imaginary search, an imaginary debate. It is at first sight a story which is, as they say in certain parts of Africa, terribly one-handed:

> Well a tale is not a tale
> Without a word or two on how it fares:

I

My ears are opened to the ground
For what errors you may find.
It is simple and plain
That one hand cannot wash a story clean;
It needs the help of the other. (Mapanje and White, 1983)

A one-handed story is a story without a living and breathing audience immediately present, a tale without a listening community which tells the storyteller at every turn how the tale is faring, and what errors it may contain and what aspects of it may be speaking past the hearers and, as it were, may be falling to the ground. But that is the nature of stories on a printed page. At least this is a story *about* pairs of hands, the hands of tellers and the hands of listeners, as they move to and fro in dreams and discussions. It goes like this:

It's about this family. Through the illest of ill fortunes, the members of this family suddenly found themselves to be refugees from their homeland. They had no geographical, social, cultural or political space to dwell in or to return to: they could only move onwards, outwards, could only be footloose migrants now for the rest of their lives. The family consisted of an old grandmother, close to the end of her days; her three grown-up children and their partners; and about a dozen grandchildren, including a tiny infant, a few weeks old.

What was to become of them? They knew that in practice they were at the mercy of the international community – various formal legal arrangements and procedures for dealing with stateless and directionless persons such as themselves. But nevertheless they debated and deliberated: nevertheless, in the very heart of the trauma they were experiencing, they shared their dreams and hopes concerning the kind of new country they would most like to settle in.

The six adults had between them six main threads to weave into the fabric of the debate.

'Basically,' said the first, 'everything depends on luck. Obviously we must look after ourselves as well as we can, and we must keep ourselves strong. But at the end of the day what matters is luck, either good luck or bad luck. So let's stop talking and dreaming about this matter. There's absolutely no profit in it, talk is pointless.'

'Well yes I do agree in many ways,' said the second. 'But good luck comes in some countries more easily than in others. In particular let's remember that the best things in life are free. What we need is sunny weather, warm and full of blessings nearly every day, and always predictable. And beautiful scenery and landscape. I don't care where we go providing the climate is warm and comforting, and the scenery marvellous.'

'That's all very well,' said the third, 'but the quality of life depends not just on the sun and the scenery but on whether we are left alone to be ourselves, and to stay exactly as we are. We must be able to continue to speak our own dear language, to tell our children our own special tales and truths, and to be protected in all our ways by our own dear God. Nothing, after all we have gone through, is more important than continuity and stability, an assured future through the cherishing and preservation of our past.'

'Yes of course,' said the fourth, 'that is quite right. But in what kind of society are we most likely to be left free? We must be very realistic and blunt about this. The most important things are race and culture. Let us go to a country where the people are as similar as possible to ourselves in their physical appearance, and in the way they live their everyday lives. Then we ourselves will be almost invisible, we shall fit in easily, and people will be kind to us, and let us do what we want.'

'That's all very well,' said the fifth, 'but there's no point in preserving our traditions if we can't eat, and if we can't have decent health, and if we don't feel that we are valuable to our new country, not just tolerated. So for these reasons we have got to have jobs, and money, and a sense of belonging. The most important thing is to go to a country which will guarantee us useful and reasonably well-paid employment, both now and in the future.'

'Of course it is important,' said the sixth, 'that we should go to a place where there are jobs, and where we are accepted as playing a valuable part in society, and where people treat us well. But this depends primarily on law and statute. Let us go to a country with a really good human rights record, and a written constitution, and where they really do believe in the rule of law, not just talk about it. A country which takes justice seriously, and in which the government is bound by the same laws as everyone else – that is the kind of country in which we are most likely to be free, and to be happy, and to be fulfilled.'

The six of them turned to the old grandmother, each of them wanting and expecting her to support their own views. She happened at that moment to be holding the infant, the youngest and the newest of the whole extended family. She stroked the child's face gently, and gazed into the depths of the child's eyes. 'Let us go,' she said, 'to the country where the power and the energy in this child will have the best chance of unfolding into a human being fully alive.' And she added: 'And the education most likely to produce a human being fully alive, I would say, having listened to the views which you have all expressed, is an education which is based on, and which is continually about, and which is planned and nourished by, concepts of human rights.'

The child in her arms smiled. But was the smile grateful and approving, or was it ironic and resigned? – No member of the family could at that stage tell.

The story invites us to consider in detail what the main features of sound human rights education are likely to be, and I will shortly turn to this. But first, I have three more general points. The first of these is that the genre to which this story belongs, that of a group of people debating together the kind of society they would ideally like to live in, echoes one of the twentieth century's most powerful metaphors relating to the concept of human rights: the 'original position' imagined by John Rawls in his *A Theory of Justice* (Rawls, 1971).[1] Rawls imagines a group of human beings constructing a society in which they do not know what their own interests and their own positions will be, and he argues that the formal features of such a society would be those of a liberal democracy, with a real, not rhetorical, commitment to the rights of minorities, and to a continual redistribution of power and wealth towards the most disadvantaged. It is a metaphor which readily lends itself to classroom discussions and role-plays in schools. For example, a discussion game has been devised which imagines a group of human beings on a spaceship heading for a new planet.[2] They have been put into a kind of hibernation for the duration of the trip, during which none of them have any notion of their own gender or ethnicity, nor of their own abilities, personalities and talents in relation to each other. Not knowing, therefore, what will be in their own best interests as individuals or as members of groups, their task is to devise a legal system and educational system for the new planet, and to plan arrangements relating to – for example – gender roles, and the treatment of minorities.

Rawls's emphasis on formal principles of justice is reminiscent of the work of Lawrence Kohlberg on moral reasoning and development (Kohlberg, 1984). Teachers running classroom discussions based on Rawls's metaphor can therefore usefully bear Kohlberg's typology in mind. This story about the extended family, for example, reflects through its six main characters some of the six main perspectives which Kohlberg identified, including fatalism, hedonism and self-interested pragmatism. The sixth of the characters begins to represent Kohlberg's concepts of abstract justice.

A third general point arising from the story is that its central metaphor of migration is particularly relevant in virtually all countries in the world at the present time. A society's attitude to its own visitors and migrants, and also to its indigenous cultural and racial minorities, is a very reliable litmus test for its system of justice and human rights. For there is an important sense in which all of us are migrants, and in which the plight of the migrant is the plight of us all. Salman Rushdie has written:

> If *The Satanic Verses* is anything, it is a migrant's-eye view of the world. It is written from the very experience of uprooting, disjuncture and metamorphosis (slow or rapid, painful or pleasurable) that is the migrant condition, and from which, I believe, can be derived a metaphor for all humanity . . . . *The Satanic Verses* celebrates hybridity, impurity, intermingling, and transformation that comes from new and unexpected combinations of human beings, cultures, ideas, politics, movies, songs. It rejoices in mongrelisation and fears the absolutism of the Pure. Melange, hotchpotch, a bit of this and a bit of that is *how newness enters the world*. It is the great possibility that mass migration gives the world. (Rushdie, 1990)

Rushdie in effect outlines the context here in which human rights education in the 1990s will happen, or will fail to happen. In one country after another there are now glorious possibilities of greater differentiation and greater equality, leading to the greater likelihood of 'newness entering the world'. In Europe the potentialities will be fulfilled insofar as governments safeguard and extend the human rights and entitlements, in education in particular but also more generally through the whole range of social policy and at all levels of political systems, of their black and other ethnic minority citizens.

Other chapters in this book have very many proposals and suggestions about what the main features of sound human rights education might be. Indeed, the whole book can be read as a detailed unpacking of the concerns in the grandmother's proposal in the story at the start of this chapter. I should like to select – rather arbitrarily, I acknowledge – five features which seem to me to be particularly important. But my list is definitely not intended to be exhaustive or comprehensive, I must warn, and I wish to emphasize that there are many essential and crucial ideas in other parts of this book which are not included in this particular list. I will write under five brief headings: (1) pressure groups; (2) encounters with the 'real' world'; (3) holism and interdependence; (4) the school as a just community; and finally, at which point I shall return to Maxine in James Berry's tale, (5) the stories of learners. Throughout I shall be taking as axiomatic that the basic concepts of human rights education are those which are set out in the Council of Europe Recommendation of May 1985.

PRESSURE GROUPS

All five points can valuably be introduced with some extracts from writings by 15-year-old secondary school students who had taken part in a project entitled 'Save Our Earth'.[3] The project had been organized as a cross-curricular enterprise within the framework of the Technical and Vocational Education Initiative (TVEI), and had included an opportunity for students to interview – indeed, to interrogate – the representatives of various pressure groups. One can readily sense from these extracts the main kinds of learning which were involved:

THE BLACK ENVIRONMENTAL NETWORK

I was immensely interested in interviewing this group . . . because I wanted to know why an environmentalist group was founded primarily for black people I couldn't see how colour had anything to do with the state of the earth. Naturally, that was the first question I wanted to ask. The Network representative . . . was very pleasant . . . he answered effectively by explaining that black people are usually the ones who aren't represented on issues like pollution, which is an international problem. He also said black people are usually the ones who suffer because of debts owed to European banks . . . . Probably the biggest achievement the group has made so far is gaining two useful Members of Parliament to act as the Network's link with parliamentary affairs. Already they have succeeded in getting a very important question asked in Parliament . . . . He talked to us on our level without dictating to us or making it all too formal. He explained everything clearly without patronising us or underestimating our knowledge. Also he didn't overcram us with too many facts – which was very helpful. (*Report by Lesley Mullings.*)

FRIENDS OF THE EARTH

The organisation was formed 17 years ago. It was originally the Americans who thought of the idea and organised the campaign . . . . Mostly people volunteer and there are 270 groups scattered all over the world, campaigning on different issues. Also, local groups go around and look over and examine things for the Friends of the Earth. They deal with national issues as well as international issues, which are all examined when people go around to shops and see whether people should buy the items which are sold! . . . The pressure groups help the environment by sending petitions, lobbying MPs and sending leaflets . . . I think it's important to involve young people because as we grow up we will fight even more for the preservation of our children. (*Report by Bhavna Patel.*)

WOMEN'S ENVIRONMENTAL NETWORK

In the past WEN has put pressure on the government to produce unbleached paper instead of using chlorine in paper – they have been successful . . . . They got their initial funding from membership and donations, the money goes towards running the group. It pays for the office, meetings, bills, and printing of leaflets. They also received a grant to do some research. International links were formed after the group had established itself . . . . The group is an all women group because there are some issues that only affect women. (*Report by Manjula Patel.*)

WORLD WILDLIFE FUND

The WWF changes government attitudes by paying people to do scientific research and compile reports . . . . The WWF is campaigning for the Brazilian government to stop cutting down miles and miles of tropical rainforests . . . . The problem is that the people don't know about rotational farming, and so the nutrition the trees need is used up much too fast for it to be replaced. There is hope in Cameroon and Nigeria, because both governments have decided to reserve big sections of their rainforest . . . . We hope that the government of Britain and the governments of the world can change their attitudes to the destruction of the rainforests and by acting now save the future of our earth. (*Report by Mansukh Hirani.*)

These extracts show that very many key concepts in human rights education were being learnt and absorbed, and that the learning was happening naturally and experientially through interaction with representatives of the 'real' world, not through conventional classroom instruction. And they show in particular that the concepts were being made manageable because it was being shown that politics itself is manageable: governments are made and maintained by ordinary citizens, and ordinary citizens for their part can and do make a difference. The world is not unchangeably monolithic, but on the contrary is malleable. The appropriate attitude is not of fatalism and resignation, and of denial of one's own resources and resourcefulness, but on the contrary of hope and determination, and trust and confidence in one's own capacity, and in the capacity of other members of one's generation too, to make an impact on what happens. It is not easy to organize a project such as this, and the students' writings pay great tribute to the considerable imagination and energy of their teachers as well as to themselves. Nevertheless they inspire us to consider a crucial touchstone: human rights education should, amongst other things, be teaching that the world is malleable, not immutable, and should be teaching how in practice human beings can unite and mobilize, and fight to get things changed.

ENCOUNTERS WITH THE 'REAL' WORLD

As mentioned earlier, this project involving pressure groups was arranged within the framework of TVEI, an initiative in British education aiming to make education more immediately relevant and accountable to the 'real' world beyond schools, and to do this by breaking down traditional and elitist distinctions between 'knowledge' and 'activity', 'education' and 'training', 'school' and 'work', and thus orientating the curriculum towards new paradigms of learning and schooling.[4] A distinctive feature of TVEI projects at their best is that school-age students meet and interact with adults who are not full-time teachers.

The nature of really fruitful contacts with adults was shown very clearly in one of the extracts about the work with pressure groups. 'He talked to us,' wrote one girl, 'on our level without dictating to us or making it all too formal. He explained everything clearly without patronising us or underestimating our knowledge.' This kind of experience is of course available from full-time teachers also! But the conventions and customs of schooling are such that dependency, and therefore a kind of fatalism and denial of one's own capacities, are more frequent attitudes amongst the young in their relationships with teachers than the kind of resourceful self-confidence expressed by the girl after her meeting with the pressure group.

Such interactions between 'school' and 'work' are valuable not only for young people, and for young people's perceptions of themselves as responsible and valuable members of society, but also for the adults from the world of work whom they meet. The latter too become more aware of their responsibilities for welcoming and empowering the young in the mainstream of society, and are less inclined to leave education to 'professionals', with all the ambivalence which then develops and festers. At best, human rights education leads not only to greater knowledge, commitment and resourcefulness amongst young people, and not only to greater justice within schools and classrooms, but also to a release of energy and commitment in the wider world, and to procedures of greater justice. There is a 'stored fertility'[5] in many sectors and strata of society, and human rights education has a key role in exploring this, and releasing it.

HOLISM AND INTERDEPENDENCE

The extracts about the pressure groups showed over and over again that human rights issues have many interconnections and linkages with each other, and cannot effectively or sensibly be addressed in isolation from each other. The project held together local issues and global, governmental and non-governmental action for change, the political world and the natural world, and it incorporated, as a natural taken-for-granted assumption, issues of race and gender equality. One of the campaigns with which the students became more familiar was in relation to the Brazilian rainforests, and it is particularly apt therefore to quote here from a speech about holism and interdependence by a campaigner in Brazil. Ailton Krenak is a member of a small tribe of the Krenak Indians, also known generically as the Botocudos. He is introducing here his argument that action to save the physical environment in Brazil (and for that matter anywhere else in the world) is inseparable from issues of human rights and social justice. We will not follow him here into the political arguments, but will take only (so to speak) his basic metaphor:

> When talking about native science it's impossible to separate it out of its context. If I pull one of the shells off a bracelet, the entirety is less beautiful, and the shell itself, however beautiful, has less meaning. We can miss so much of what a shell actually is if we cut it away from myths, practices, the people who discovered and named the shell and other similar shells, and the rituals and stories and secrets of that shell. That's only one part of the shell and that shell – let's say it's agriculture – is only one part of the special knowledge we have about nature. There are strands of life and history and nature and what it means to be an Indian that tie that shell to the others. (Hecht and Cockburn, 1989)

The concepts of holism and interdependence require not only that we see all or many apparently disparate phenomena as all linked together, all part of the same system, but also that we see ourselves as part of the total reality, not apart from it. This too is empowering and liberating.

THE SCHOOL AS A JUST COMMUNITY

Children and young people can change the mental pictures which they have of the world beyond the school gates, and can thus derive a sense of their own responsibilities and resourcefulness. But there is a real limit, of course, to what they can objectively do to affect that world directly. (Not that they are often allowed, in most schools, even to approach the limit, let alone to explore and extend it.) But within their own schools they can most certainly, in principle, be involved in courageously fashioning, and vigilantly maintaining, structures and procedures of justice. In her choice of a country for her family to adopt, the grandmother in our story would be passionately interested not only in national educational systems but also in individual schools. If pressed, she might well prefer her grandchildren to grow up in a just school in an unjust society, rather than in an unjust school in a society with a splendid constitution, strong rule of law, and public commitment to human rights.

A school is not a family, where everyone knows everyone else, and where most things can be done through mutual one-to-one relationships; it is, however, a community – a gathering of relative strangers who have to struggle and work together to create procedural machinery for protecting and enhancing each person's freedom and fulfilment:

> In school, one must come to realise that there is more to morality than being friendly with your friends; there is more to morality than showing love to those you think are lovable; there is more to morality than being generous and affectionate to those who turn you on. If schools do not help students understand that morality goes beyond personal affection of family and friends, then schools will have failed in moral education and in preparing students to live in the larger society.[6]

THE STORIES OF LEARNERS

It is important, yes, that students should learn experientially about the importance of rules and regulations, about the inevitability and rightness at times of impersonal roles, about the essential value of formal constitutions and procedural arrangements. However, the purpose of all such structures is to provide the best possible chance for people to be, in the grandmother's phrase in our story, 'human beings fully alive'.[7] Maxine's teacher in *The Thief in the Village*, for example, is concerned with formalities; in this instance with pressing and driving Maxine to write out her story, to choose all her words with precision and searching, to reflect through inner struggle on the meaning of the tale which she has been told, to share the fruits of her searching and reflecting with the rest of the class in her London school; his underlying purpose is to release qualities of courage and resourcefulness within Maxine herself, and in her own family and community, and to enable her to contribute thus to the learning and growth of others. When the stories of the learners are welcomed and shared in the everyday classroom situation, human rights education is happening in one of its purest and most valuable forms.

Maxine's aunt Nenna, when she was a child of much the same age as Maxine is now, found herself in the middle of a grave injustice in the village where she lived – a local eccentric known to the villagers as Big-Walk was falsely accused of theft through a process of community scapegoating, and was arrested and taken into custody. The truth was fortunately discovered, however, and Big-Walk was released. Nenna had made a crucial if indirect contribution to the discovery of the truth, and after the real culprit had been apprehended she went with another character, Taata Raphael, to talk with Big-Walk:

> 'Big-Walk. Why you t'ink people don't like you?'
> Big-Walk swung his head round like a surprised bull, then hesitated. Looking at Nenna he sighed, then said, 'I do not like them. Not like them. I me. I the way I is. I – jus' me.'
> 'Know this, young Nenna Willow,' Taata Raphael said. 'Folks like when

everybody else is like theyself. But the worl' not like that an' folks not wise to that yet.' (Berry, 1987)

Maxine is learning that to be a human being fully alive is to be both a visitor and a part of everybody. And she is learning that the conditions for such living are very fragile, and that therefore the conditions require eternal vigilance and eternal struggle. In this learning she is a challenge and an inspiration to us all.

Robin Richardson

NOTES

1 There are several valuable commentaries in Daniels (1975).
2 The spaceship metaphor is taken from Wren (1975), and the discussion exercise referred to here was developed by staff based at Maidenhead Teachers' Centre and is published within a pack of materials concerned in particular with gender equality issues (Maidenhead Teachers' Centre, 1986).
3 The project described here took place in the London Borough of Brent, and was planned and organized by the LEA's TVEI team, led by Lesley Hall and Jane Quigley. The extracts from students' writings are reprinted with grateful acknowledgement to the individuals concerned.
4 The terms here are from the Grubb Institute's document *Technical and Vocational Education Extension: Towards a Paradigm for Total Learning* (Grubb Institute, 1989).
5 The term 'stored fertility' is from an article about Paulo Freire (Hyde, 1978), quoted in a paper by the Grubb Institute (1987).
6 Kohlberg's notions of the school as a just community are introduced here by Rest (1989).
7 The term 'a human being fully alive' is associated with St Irenaeus, Bishop of Lyons, *c.* AD 130–200.

REFERENCES

Berry, J. (1987) *A Thief in the Village*, Hamish Hamilton, London, p. 8.

Daniels, R. (1975) *Reading Rawls: Critical Studies of a Theory of Justice*, Basil Blackwell, Oxford.

Grubb Institute (1987) *Goals for Our Future Society*, Grubb Institute, London.

Grubb Institute (1989) *Technical and Vocational Education Extension: Towards a Paradigm for Total Learning*, Grubb Institute, London.

Hecht, S. and Cockburn, A. (1989) *The Fate of the Forest*, Verso, London, p. 211.

Hyde, D. (1978) 'Liberating the powerless ones', *The Month*, November, p. 390.

Kohlberg, L. (1984) *Essays in Moral Development: the Psychology of the Moral Development*, Harper & Row, San Francisco.

PART I

KEY HUMAN RIGHTS TEXTS AND THE CHALLENGE TO EDUCATION

Preface

This section of the book reminds us of two things. Firstly, that modern concepts of human rights first found expression in the late eighteenth century in Europe and in America and have been restated constantly in succeeding years as individuals and groups test their limitations. Secondly, that one essential feature of rights is their codification in texts. The force of the texts depends on the judicial apparatus which accompanies them. A text such as the Universal Declaration of Human Rights which has no court to support it must rely on moral pressure for its effect.

For texts to have any force whatsoever requires that they be known. Education is thus an indispensable complement to human rights as well as to democracy. Margaret Branson quotes Justice Thurgood Marshall: 'Education directly affects the ability of a child to exercise his First Amendment interests . . .' Peter Leuprecht cites Crenière in 1789: 'a right is the effect of an agreement through which one acts'. Action, in this sense, presupposes knowledge, and knowledge, education.

Even where, as with the European Convention on Human Rights, there is an enforcement mechanism and a court, education is still vital, as René Cassin saw clearly: 'Legal force of itself is only a secondary safety valve: it is the education of young people and even of adults that constitutes the primary and real guarantee for minority groups faced with racial hatred that leads so easily to violence and murder.' Speaking of teachers, he continued: 'When they speak about human rights, when they convey to their pupils the notion of their rights, their dignity and their duties as citizens and as human beings, then they are carrying out a task that complements wonderfully the work we have achieved at the highest level.' In other words human rights conventions rely on education. The legal and the educational are essential partners in the protection of fundamental freedoms.

The chapters in Part 1 also remind us of the importance of a historical perspective. A human-rights-based curriculum looks to the future. The preamble to the European Convention refers to human rights and fundamental freedoms as 'the foundation of justice and peace in the world'. As the world is not yet totally just and peaceful we assume that justice and peace in the world are aims rather than achievements. Their realization lies in the future. It is, nonetheless, the past that shows us the ways to achieving these ends, namely by struggle, challenge and individual and collective effort. Human rights education looks at the past to prepare the future. It also, of course, attempts to engage with the present. Chapter 3 includes examples of activities undertaken by schools working in and with their local communities. Young people need to gain first-hand experience of democracy, of co-operative working with others, of social mechanisms for helping people to achieve their rights. Research and interviews, helping young children, older people or people with disabilities, are some ways in which students in full-time education encounter and work with others in society. The school is no longer simply the information-rich action-poor isolated institution that Torsten Husen described.

Finally, these chapters bring to our attention the unfinished nature of the work of human rights. Even where written conventions or constitutions are in force there is constant pressure to improve and update them. It is important for citizens to know the principles of human rights and to use this knowledge to challenge injustice. Human rights is not a rigid and static system, it is a dynamic concept implying on the one hand the preservation of freedoms and on the other an impulse towards justice. Armed with the principles of human rights and a knowledge of the struggles involved in their achievement, citizens of all ages can debate what it is they want to hold on to and what it is that needs changing. The past and the future are in creative tension around the notion of human rights.

CHAPTER 1

Human Rights 1789 to 1989

Peter Leuprecht

The anniversaries of the great human rights proclamations are following each other in rapid succession: at the end of 1988 there was the fortieth anniversary of the Universal Declaration of Human Rights, this year will see the tricentenary of the Bill of Rights and the bicentenary of the Declaration of the Rights of Man and of the Citizen, while next year will mark the fortieth anniversary of the European Convention on Human Rights.

It is tempting to compare these texts. I intend to point out some features shared by two of them which are separated by more than a century and a half – the 1789 Declaration and the European Convention on Human Rights, which transformed at European level some of the principles expressed in the Universal Declaration into definite legal obligations binding on Contracting Parties. I have chosen four of these common features which are unlikely to receive much attention in the official commemorative speeches.

INCOMPLETE PROCLAMATIONS

The 1789 Declaration and the European Convention on Human Rights have in common not only undeniable historical success but also an incompleteness. Of this their respective authors were perfectly aware: on the day after the adoption of the Declaration, that is on 27 August 1789, the French National Assembly voted through a text which recognized that it was incomplete: similarly, the preamble of the European Convention on Human Rights refers to '*first* steps for the collective enforcement of *certain* of the Rights stated in the Universal Declaration'.

It is therefore contrary to historical truth and the intentions of the authors of the Declaration and the Convention to represent them as complete and transform them into museum pieces. They are in fact stages – albeit important and even decisive stages – in a process whose dynamic character was clearly indicated by the authors of the Statute of the Council of Europe, when they defined one of the objectives of the organization as 'the maintenance and *future realization* of human rights'.

LIMITS TO UNIVERSALITY

In principle, the rights of man and of the citizen proclaimed in 1789 were valid for all citizens; but was this citizenship truly universal, i.e. did it cover all human beings without exceptions and without restrictions?

In his *Reconnaissance et exposition raisonnée des droits de l'homme et du citoyen* read on 20 and 21 July 1789 to the Constitutional Committee, Sieyès, drawing a distinction between 'active rights' and 'passive rights', states 'Not everyone is an active citizen. Women, at least in the present circumstances, children, foreigners and those who contribute nothing to the common weal, must not actively influence public affairs.'

Condorcet had to fight hard after the adoption of the 1789 Declaration to ensure that human rights were not only proclaimed but effectively guaranteed for all: he campaigned for recognition of the civil rights of Jews and women and against black slavery and the slave trade. The *Code Noir* after all, was formally repealed only in 1848.

Article 1 of the European Convention on Human Rights affirms the principle of its universal application *rationale personae*: Contracting States undertake to 'secure' to everyone within their jurisdiction the rights defined in the Convention. However, does the Convention really guarantee the human rights of everyone in Europe? Even the text of the Convention does not keep all the promises of universality contained in Article 1. For example, Article 16 permits Contracting States to impose restrictions on the political activity of aliens; Article 2 of the Fourth Protocol guarantees the right to liberty of movements and freedom to choose one's residence only to those 'lawfully with the territory of a state'. Lastly, the legal instruments of the Council of Europe in the field of economic and social rights are not based on the principle of universality, but on those of nationality and reciprocity.

The universality principle in the field of human rights in Europe is even more limited in practice than in these texts. There is an enormous amount of work still to be done to make these rights fully and equally accessible to all, without any more exclusions. As early as 1789 Seconds wrote: 'For as long as this human nature, which is so weak . . . is not protected, and all members of society defended by law . . . for as long as a single person remains deprived of the rights of man and of the citizen, there will be . . . no reason, no wisdom and no humanity in these laws.'

SOCIAL RIGHTS POSTPONED

The social dimension of human rights is missing from the 1789 Declaration and almost absent from the European Convention on Human Rights. However, this subject was covered in the discussions which preceded and prepared the way for both documents. Contrary to what has often been written, civil and political rights and social rights appear side by side in draft versions of the 1789 Declaration. Similarly, the drafters of the European Convention on Human Rights had to deal with both categories of rights.

The social dimension of human rights was to be taken into account in the 1793 Declaration and in the European Social Charter. Nevertheless, is it not true that we have made much less progress along the road to 'social democracy' than along the road to 'political democracy', to quote the terms used by Pierre-Henri Teitgen back in 1949?

FORGOTTEN MINORITIES

Lastly, the 1789 Declaration and the European Convention on Human Rights are both silent about the rights of minorities and exposed and vulnerable groups.

I think it is safe to say that never before has so much been done to ensure the protection, at both national and international levels, of certain 'individual' rights as has been done in Western Europe since the end of the Second World War. Should not this guarantee of individual rights be complemented by the protection of the rights of exposed and vulnerable groups and minorities? This would no doubt help to secure truly universal human rights without any exclusions. Incomplete proclamations, limits to universality, the postponement of the guarantee of social rights and forgotten minorities all provide food for thought and especially reasons for action. As Crenière, a delegate to the Constituent Assembly, wrote in 1789, 'a right is the effect of an agreement through which one acts'. Let us tackle the job in that spirit of 'practical idealism' suggested by Jacques Maritain in the aftermath of the Second World War which saw the birth of the Universal Declaration and the European Convention on Human Rights.

This text was first published in the Council of Europe's magazine *Forum* and is reproduced by permission.

CHAPTER 2

The Council of Europe Recommendation on the Teaching and Learning of Human Rights in Schools

Hugh Starkey

Official texts can provide strong support and guidance for schools and teachers. 'A right is the result of a convention on which one acts' said Crenière in 1789. Texts remain dead letters unless and until they are known and acted upon. The challenge for human rights educators is to ensure that useful official texts are known and that they are accompanied by sufficient practical help for them to be acted upon.

Human rights is, in some senses, a field dominated by lawyers. There are written texts in abundance, but few focus directly on education or even make direct reference to it. One recent European text, the Recommendation of the Committee of Ministers of the Council of Europe on 'Teaching and Learning about Human Rights in Schools' (Recommendation R (85) 7), does, however, try to make explicit what schools can do to promote the teaching and learning of human rights. The present chapter gives some background to the text and suggests ways in which teachers can use it as a starting point for their actions.

The School Education Division of the Council of Europe, 30 years after the Universal Declaration of 1948, saw the need for help for teachers beyond copies of official texts. In 1978, following a Resolution 78 (41) of the Committee of Ministers on 'The teaching of human rights', a five-year programme of research and consultation was initiated. The final symposium of this project, held in Vienna in 1983, brought together experts from both sides of the Atlantic and representatives of the member states. Their deliberations resulted in a series of recommendations which were then submitted to governments for modification. A revised draft was adopted by the Committee of Ministers of the Council of Europe on 14 May 1985.

This text, known as Recommendation R (85) 7 on 'Teaching and Learning about Human Rights in Schools', has been widely disseminated by governments and non-governmental groups. The text and its appendix express agreed positions about what schools could and should be doing to promote knowledge of and awareness of human rights issues. The challenge is to make this text a basis on which teachers can act and to enlist further support from governments for its full implementation.

THE RECOMMENDATION

The text consists of a formal motion or Recommendation followed by an appendix. The Recommendation notes that the aim of the Council of Europe is *'to achieve a greater unity between its members for the purpose of safeguarding and realising the ideals and principles which are their common heritage'*. It then refers to human rights as important *'ideals and principles'* and recalls a number of commitments to human rights and human rights education made collectively by member states. These are given an urgency by the context of the mid-1980s. The Ministers are:

'Conscious of the need to reaffirm democratic values in the face of:
intolerance, acts of violence and terrorism;
the re-emergence of the public expression of racist and xenophobic attitudes;
the disillusionment of many young people in Europe, who are affected by the economic recession and aware of the continuing poverty and inequality in the world.'

The key commitment to human rights education follows:

'Believing, therefore, that, throughout their school career, all young people should learn about human rights as part of their preparation for life in a pluralistic democracy;'

This statement is in the tradition of human rights texts in its stress on the universality of the entitlement. It is for all young people for all of their time in school. The member states of the Council of Europe are committed to systems of pluralistic democracy. The foundations of the survival of and development of democracy are laid in schools.

Finally, the Ministers express their faith in the potential of the school itself to be a microcosm of a society based on the principles of human rights:

'Convinced that schools are communities which can, and should, be an example of the respect for the dignity of the individual and for difference, for tolerance, and for equality of opportunity.'

Human rights education, as a number of chapters in this book maintain, is to be based on a whole-school project. The aim of such an enterprise is to develop a participative and just community. This entails a teaching programme specifically designed to convey the human rights values on which the project is based and to explore the implications of these standards for life in a community. Human rights values will also, importantly, inform the school community in its relations with the community at large and with the wider world.

THE APPENDIX

The appendix is entitled '**Suggestions for teaching and learning about human rights in schools**'. It is divided into six main sections as follows: Human rights in the school curriculum; Skills; Knowledge to be acquired in the study of human rights; The climate of the school; Teacher training; International Human Rights Day.

1. Human Rights in the School Curriculum

1.1 The understanding and experience of human rights is an important element of the preparation of all young people for life in a democratic and pluralistic society. It is part of social and political education, and it involves intercultural and international understanding.

In a democracy, human rights are the basis of relationships within and between groups. Meetings, for instance, are conducted on the basis of respect for others and tolerance of divergent views. Preparation for life in society therefore requires an understanding of these customs and procedures. An understanding of human rights is only effectively achieved through experience of them in action. Ideally, young people's experience of school will provide this. Nonetheless there also needs to be opportunity for students to study these values systematically and to learn about issues where human rights come to the fore.

Wherever values are specifically examined, such as in civic, social or religious education, human rights should be a point of reference. Where values are implicit, as is usually the case with textbooks and most teaching, human rights is a touchstone. This may be particularly important in those areas of the curriculum which cover relations between groups and nations.

Schools may wish to formulate policy goals such as the following:

- Teachers have an understanding of human rights and the way this can be applied to the life and the curriculum of the school.
- Human rights are accepted as the basis of relationships in the classroom and the school.
- Human rights concepts are taught systematically.
- School rules and disciplinary procedures are on the basis of fair treatment and due process.
- The school has policies to promote equality and avoid unjust discrimination such as on the basis of gender, race or disability.
- Teachers are encouraged and enabled to develop a global perspective.

1.2 Concepts associated with human rights can, and should, be acquired at an early stage. For example, the non-violent resolution of conflict and respect for other people can already be experienced within the life of a pre-school or primary class.

Much of early childhood education is about socialization and is thus almost by definition about learning to live harmoniously in a community. Respect for others comes from a feeling of self-respect. Human rights educators thus set store by *affirmation activities*. The United Nations Convention on the Rights of the Child includes the right to a name in Article 7. Affirmation activities assert the importance of the name. Even non-readers can be given colourful cardboard name-cards which they can recognize as their own. On entering the class they can take their card to the place where they want to work.

Children need to be helped to say their own name confidently and clearly. A first step is for children to stand in a circle and in turns move forward and say their own name. With practice and confidence they can jump into the circle, adding a gesture.

Reciprocally, children learn the names of others: teachers, helpers, children. There are games to help children to learn each other's names. For instance, they stand in a circle. One of them is given a soft ball. The child rolls the ball to another across the circle, whilst calling the name of the intended recipient. The child receiving rolls it to another, also calling their name, and then sits down. The game is over when everyone is seated. A stop-watch can be used and best performances noted. Children can help each other by whispering when names are not known.

An English junior school for 8–11-year-olds reports an improved atmosphere since the introduction of daily 'circle time' (White, 1989). Teacher and class sit on the floor in a circle. Everyone is given a chance to contribute and to listen to others. For instance, the teacher starts a sentence going round the circle which is completed by each pupil. 'My favourite television programme is . . .' or 'Today I'm feeling . . .' or 'Today I'm looking forward to . . .' News and information can also be exchanged in the circle and each day a child (with scrupulous fairness, of course) is designated 'special'. This is marked by a badge with an affirming statement and a card made up of positive remarks by the other children noted by the teacher. 'We think . . . is special because . . .'

It is also important for children to experience being part of different groups. This can be done by games or by co-operative tasks. (For further examples see McLeod (1984), Peace Education Project (1985) and Masheder (1987).)

1.3 *Opportunities to introduce young people to more abstract notions of human rights, such as those involving an understanding of philosophical, political and legal concepts, will occur in the secondary school, in particular in such subjects as history, geography, social studies, moral and religious education, language and literature, current affairs and economics.*

This section refers to knowledge of human rights texts themselves. The very concept of a text that protects is an abstract notion, so it is important to illustrate it with examples. One key distinction is that between a *Declaration*, such as the Universal Declaration of Human Rights, which is a statement of intent with no legal force, and a *Convention*. Conventions, such as the European Convention or the new Convention on the Rights of the Child, include legal mechanisms for guaranteeing rights. All inhabitants of the 25 member states of the Council of Europe are protected by the European Convention. The UN Convention on the Rights of the Child covers over half of the world's population (all those under 18).

Another important concept is that of *universality*, or non-discrimination in rights. Article 14 of the European Convention and Article 2 of the UN Convention on the Rights of the Child spell this out: 'ensure the rights to each child . . . without discrimination of any kind, irrespective of the child's or his or her parents' or legal guardian's race, colour, sex, language, religion, political or other opinion, national, ethnic or social origin, property, disability, birth or other status.'

Rights protected under these Conventions include the right to:

- life, survival and development;
- a name, nationality and an identity to be preserved;
- liberty and security of person;
- not to be a slave;
- not to be tortured;
- the protection of the law;
- a fair and public hearing in the courts;
- privacy in home and correspondence;
- an adequate standard of living;
- education;
- leisure, play and artistic and cultural activities;
- marry and found a family;
- own property.

and these *fundamental freedoms*:

- freedom of thought, conscience and religion;
- freedom of opinion and expression;
- freedom of peaceful assembly and to join a trade union;
- freedom from unlawful attacks on honour and reputation;
- freedom of movement and residence.

These rights, and situations in which they are denied, can be illustrated in the study of school subjects, for example:

History

- The origins and growth of democracy.
- Slavery. Colonialism. Imperialism.
- Revolutions, their ideals and their impact.
- The suspension of human rights in wars.
- The United Nations.

- European unity.
- The growth of trade unions.
- Social and educational legislation and development.
- Communications and the mass media.

Geography

- Movements of people.
- Explanations of poverty and starvation.
- Migrant workers.
- Apartheid.
- Colonialism and neo-colonialism.
- Minorities.
- Protection of the environment.

Social studies/civic education

- Political and legal systems.
- Social inequalities and their causes.
- The police.
- Trade unions.
- Education.
- The mass media.

In fact there is virtually no area of the curriculum where a human rights dimension is unhelpful or inappropriate. One school, in Scheibbs in Austria (Starkey, 1984), organized a human rights week during which every teacher was asked to include the theme of human rights during their teaching. Scientists considered biological myths about race or the applications of technology. Maths teachers looked at some statistics of inequality. Foreign language teachers developed social and language skills and studied themes in literature and cases from the foreign language press. This experiment points the way to a whole-school curriculum policy on human rights.

> 1.4 *Human rights inevitably involve the domain of politics. Teaching about human rights should, therefore, always have international agreements and convenants as a point of reference, and teachers should take care to avoid imposing their personal convictions on their pupils and involving them in ideological struggles.*

Pupils and their parents may hold strong views which they may feel are threatened when controversial issues are raised at school. Human rights education should be explicit and mention made of this in school handbooks or prospectuses.

In dealings with parents, politicians and the community, the following considerations may be helpful:

- It is useful to adopt specific policy statements, reflecting human rights values. Schools may draw up their own policies or they may use those of teacher unions or local education authorities.
- Students who do not have the opportunity to learn about democracy and rights may more easily adopt simplistic racist or authoritarian views.

This is a danger for schools and for society. There is likely to be more danger in schools failing to prepare pupils to participate in political life in a democracy than there is in them discussing and examining issues involving controversy at appropriate points in the curriculum.

- The use of materials from a variety of sources will demonstrate an attempt to deal objectively with complex issues.

Fears are sometimes expressed that teachers may impose their own political convictions on students by indoctrination. Since indoctrination requires students to believe a proposition without question, a teaching style that involves discussion and leaves room for questions should be above reproach.

On the other hand it is quite right for schools to transmit and attempt to foster those attitudes that are agreed to be desirable in a democratic society. To be in favour of human rights is, by definition, to be against indoctrination, which is coercive and limiting of freedom of thought.

2. Skills

The skills associated with understanding and supporting human rights include:
i. intellectual skills, in particular:
— skills associated with written and oral expression, including the ability to listen and discuss, and to defend one's opinions;

Communication skills are basic education. They are essential for participation in society at any level, but they are particularly important in democratic systems where debate and discussion are inherent. Since human rights issues often provoke strong feelings, they are particularly good subjects for discussion, as students wish to contribute.

Listening carefully to the views of others is, however, an equally important skill. Active listening conveys respect for the speaker. Teachers should try to be models as good listeners. This present volume contains a number of suggestions for discussion activities. Further examples can be found in Pike and Selby (1988).

— skills involving judgement, such as:
the collection and examination of material from various sources, including the mass media, and the ability to analyse it and to arrive at fair and balanced conclusions;
the identification of bias, prejudice, stereotypes and discrimination;

Bias occurs where one view is expressed or image presented at the expense of others. Prejudice is thinking badly of others without reason. A stereotype is a generalized view of a group that is static and inflexible. It serves to perpetuate myths. A combination of these distortions, which are to be found widely in schoolbooks, literature and the media, may help to perpetuate racism and sexism and the discrimination and inequality which result from these. In any case, a view of an individual or group founded on prejudice, biased information or stereotype, is partial and will not reflect the whole truth. Such partial views deny to those thus considered the respect and dignity to which they are entitled as human beings.

Many educational groups involved with minorities, with women's issues, or with multicultural or intercultural education have devised activities to increase students' capacities to develop more accurate and perceptive views of others. One approach to combating bias and stereotyping is to use checklists of questions. After an introduction to the idea, students can make up their own.

Here are some sample questions:

Are women and men shown in a variety of occupations, including non-traditional ones? When women are depicted as full-time homemakers are they depicted as competent and decisive? (The English Centre, 1985)

How are the working class portrayed?: subservient, brutal, stupid, crude, sexist, lethargic, drunkards . . . etc? (McFarlane, 1986)

All or some? Does the book speak of, for example, 'the French' when it really means 'the French government' or 'many French people' or 'some French people' etc.? Does it similarly make a blanket use of terms such as 'rich countries', 'developing countries', 'third world countries'? (World Studies project, 1979)

ii. social skills in particular:
– recognizing and accepting differences;

It is the essence of human rights that differences, physical or cultural, should have no bearing on a person's entitlement to freedom, equality and dignity. Society, however, often gives a negative or positive value to physical and cultural characteristics and students should be made aware of this.

At any age it is important for students to get to know each other and value each other as unique individuals, each with much to contribute. It is important that students have opportunities to explore and share their own and each other's background and cultural traditions. This can be done by making displays including items and photographs brought from home. Children also gain much from the occasional involvement of parents with their class.

Themes chosen for study or project work can emphasize similarities at a general level whilst exploring differences at a particular level. Festivals, for instance, implies similarity, whereas Diwali, Eid, Easter or Hanukkah are particular examples.

– establishing positive and non-oppressive personal relationships;

Where students are enabled to get to know each other and respect each other, and where fairness is part of the climate of the class, students have the conditions under which they can create positive and non-oppressive personal relationships. Affirmation activities and group work are important ingredients.[1]

– resolving conflict in a non-violent way;

As many conflicts arise because of poor communications, all language development activities, including developing listening skills, have a part to play in this education.

Conflicts should, in any case, be resolved within a framework of law or rules, as Jeremy Cunningham describes in Chapter 6. Classes can devise their own charters or codes of behaviour.

The following sequence is suggested by the Australian educationalist Rosemary Milne (Milne, 1984) for dealing with serious conflicts:

1 Stop any physical or verbal aggression.
2 Start to ascertain the real problem by asking those involved and those witnessing for brief statements.
3 Allow children to speak quietly in turn and give physical reassurance to upset children.
4 Ask the children for suggestions for resolving the conflict and be prepared to contribute one or two ideas.
5 Discuss the alternatives on the basis of searching for a fair solution.
6 Agree on a course of action and follow it. If there is unhappiness after a trial period, try another solution.
7 Follow up the incident with a discussion, a story, puppet work, role play or artwork. Explore comparable incidents.

A simpler formulation involving the evaluation of the causes of conflict is proposed by Anne Halvorsen, of Norway (Lyseight-Jones, 1985).

- What happened?
- What will the consequences be and what does it lead to?
- What do we have to do to prevent this happening again?
- Why did this happen?

Both these sets of advice can be used as discussion starters by students following the viewing of a television programme depicting conflict, or reading a passage of literature, a comic strip or a story in the newspaper.

- *taking responsibility;*
- *participating in decisions;*

Living in a democracy is not just about voting occasionally in adult life. It is about participating actively in various forms of the life of the community one lives in. An important aspect of organizations in society is that they attempt to mould the future. They take decisions about the direction of resources and about structures and policies. Participating in such decisions is playing a part in creating the future. It is one way of taking responsibility.

There are many ways in which even young children can take responsibility at school. For instance:

- caring for animals;
- watering plants;
- tidying the book corner;
- choosing a story;

- creating and caring for a nature area.

Older children can help younger children by:

- reading to them or hearing them read;
- performing plays or providing entertainments;
- organizing special celebrations or parties;
- helping with craft work.

An ambitious project at the Istituto Tecnico Commerciale 'Luigi di Savoia' in Rieti, Italy, involved a selected group of older secondary school students discussing school life and health issues with 11- and 12-year-olds in small groups. The older pupils were timetabled to visit the younger ones in their classes once a month throughout the school year, visiting each first-year class in turn. The project, which is still continuing, aims to influence the younger pupils to adopt healthy lifestyles, in particular to avoid harmful substances such as tobacco, alcohol and other drugs. The older students are selected for their ability to communicate with and their potential to influence the younger ones. They receive some training and they keep a logbook of their conversations. Amongst the positive results reported are an improved atmosphere in the school and particularly an improved sense of confidence and security in the younger pupils; the circulation of ideas for improving school life which are taken up by the democratic school council structure; greater sensitivity to questions of health and harmful substances (Cresta, 1985).

There are also opportunities to take responsibility within the wider community. Many schools arrange for older secondary students to undertake work experience or community service, for example:

- visiting elderly or mentally handicapped people;
- helping in nursery schools;
- involvement with conservation and environmental projects;
- working with disabled people.

Within a school students can be responsible, on a rota, for receiving and welcoming visitors. Some community schools invite pensioners to use the school canteen, in which case students can sit at table with them with the responsibility to make them welcome and talk to them.

All these activities require and develop the skills of planning and decision-making. In many schools there is also a formal democratic structure, with elections to class and school councils. Such schools should provide training for potential representatives, which means, of course, all students.

– understanding the use of the mechanisms for the protection of human rights at the local, regional, European and world levels.

These mechanisms are essentially rules, codes, charters and laws together with a policing and investigative system and courts and tribunals. Where there is a formal course of civic education it is expected that these topics will be covered.

In practice, students need to know how to get protection or redress at school, how to get help from the police, how to contact local government departments and how to seek help from elected representatives. By far the most effective way to learn is through actually working the system.

For example, a class of 10-year-olds in a school in England (Bishop Kirk Middle School, Oxford) identified certain improvements to the school to which they felt they were entitled as part of their right to health and their right to education (more hygienic conditions in the cloakrooms, better decoration of the classrooms, changes to the play area). They prepared their case carefully and put it to the Head, who was sympathetic but explained that there was inadequate funding from the local school authority. The class then wrote to a councillor who was also a school governor. He came and discussed the case with them. Certain changes were made. The students learnt about structures, democratic processes and constraints in a very vivid way (Holden and Starkey, 1988).

In France a class of 10-year-olds in a primary school in Vitré, Brittany discovered that their museum contained an Egyptian mummy which was not on display because its sarcophagus was in the museum of a neighbouring town. They set themselves the task of getting the mummy displayed with its sarcophagus. The project involved interviewing museum officials and councillors, enlisting the support of parents and obtaining the interest of the local press. They also studied Egypt and France's involvement in colonialism.

Such projects may seem, at first sight, far from human rights education as such. They are both, however, vehicles for enabling students to gain a real understanding of democratic processes and power structures.

As far as understanding international mechanisms for protecting human rights is concerned, the social skill is in appreciating the appropriate level at which a problem should be dealt with. The European or United Nations machinery can only be invoked after all national recourse has been exhausted. In practice, few concerns of young people will need to go beyond the school itself or the local administration. However, it is important to give students opportunities to explore both the scope and limitations of local remedies and ensure that they are aware of the possibility of taking their concerns further if this is appropriate.

Students may also be encouraged to act on behalf of others, through school Amnesty International groups or by voluntary involvement with the campaigns of non-governmental organizations. In these cases they may well feel it appropriate to cite international human rights texts as the justification for their intervention.

3. Knowledge To Be Acquired in the Study of Human Rights

3.1 *The study of human rights in schools will be approached in different ways according to the age and circumstances of the pupil and the particular situations of schools and education systems. Topics to be covered in learning about human rights could include:*

   i. *the main categories of human rights, duties, obligations and responsibilities;*

Human rights are sometimes divided into categories, although many specialists maintain that the concept of indivisibility rules out any categorization that implies a hierarchy of rights. Given that all rights are essentially derived from the notion of human dignity, human rights is a total package that is not to be divided (e.g. Marie, 1985). Since, however, reference is frequently made in discussions of human rights to categories, it may be helpful to be familiar with the following terms:

- Economic rights
- Social rights
- Cultural rights
- Civil rights
- Civil liberties
- Political rights
- Individual rights
- Collective rights

The main rights that are internationally recognized as such are those found in the International Bill of Human Rights which consists of the Universal Declaration of 1948 and the two United Nations Covenants on Human Rights of 1966 which came into force in 1976. These rights have passed into international law through conventions signed by a large number of states. These conventions are of four types:

1. GENERAL CONVENTIONS

which concern all, or a large proportion of, human rights and have been adopted at world or regional level.

2. SPECIFIC CONVENTIONS

which are intended to protect particular human rights and which concern: genocide, war crimes and crimes against humanity; slavery, traffic in persons, forced labour; torture; asylum; freedom of information, private life; social security.

3. CONVENTIONS ON GROUP PROTECTION

which correspond to the special needs of distinct groups; refugees, stateless persons; migrants; workers; women; children; combatants, prisoners and civilian persons in time of armed conflict.

4. CONVENTIONS CONCERNING DISCRIMINATIONS

which seek to prevent discrimination based on race or sex and discrimination in education, in employment and in occupation.[2]

ii. the various forms of injustice, inequality and discrimination, including sexism and racism;

Many students, female students for instance, and members of minority groups, will be only too familiar with injustice, inequality and discrimination at first hand. Schools need to provide space for the expression and discussion of such experience and work towards justice and equality in the areas for which they are directly responsible. This experience can then help students to understand injustice in the wider world.

iii. people, movements and key events, both successes and failures, in the historical and continuing struggle for human rights;

Each country and each people will have its own perspective on what constitute inspiring and noteworthy events and who are the key actors. A French education project includes the following in its list of landmarks prior to the twentieth century:[3]

1215 Magna Carta (England)
1598 Edict of Nantes (France)
1628 Bill of Rights (England)
1679 Habeas Corpus (England)
1776 Declaration of Independence (US)
1789 Declaration of the Rights of Man and of the Citizen (France) revised 1793 and 1795

This is, of course, a very selective list, and examples could also be taken from other parts of the world. For example:

1839 Sultan Abdul-Mejid's Ottoman Imperial Rescript 'The Hatt-i Sherif of Gulhane' (Laqueur and Rubin, 1979).

In the twentieth century the French list includes:

1918 Declaration of working and exploited people (USSR)
1919 League of Nations and International Labour Organisation
1941 Atlantic Charter
1945 United Nations Charter
1948 Universal Declaration of Human Rights
1950 European Convention
1959 UN Declaration on the Rights of the Child
1961 European Social Charter
1966 International Covenant on economic, social and cultural rights
1966 International Covenant on civil and political rights
1969 American Convention on human rights
1975 Helsinki final act
1981 African Charter on human and peoples' rights

Additional landmarks might include:

1955 African National Congress Freedom Charter
1989 UN Convention on the Rights of the Child

The lives and struggles of individuals and movements make inspiring stories for young people of any age.[4] More analytical studies of events can be made in history classes.

Twentieth-century examples from Europe could include:

Anne Frank (1929–1945)
Danilo Dolci (b. 1924)
Pastor Niemöller
Mairead Corrigan (b. 1944) Nobel Peace Prize 1976
René Cassin (1887–1976) Nobel Peace Prize 1968

iv. the main international declarations and conventions on human rights such as the Universal Declaration of Human Rights and the Convention for the Protection of Human Rights and Fundamental Freedoms.

Teachers have a problem in bringing texts to life and making them interesting and accessible to their students. There are a number of activities for exploring texts that can engage students, for example:

- *Rewriting.* Students are asked to rewrite selected articles in a simpler form.
- *Keywords.* Select a key word for each article (e.g. underline it). Alternatively the teacher selects key words and asks students to predict the content of the article.
- *Examples.* Students look for or imagine examples of rights in action for each article.
- *Illustration.* Articles are illustrated and a display or poster made.
- *Appendix.* What additional rights could justifiably be appended to this text?
- *Application.* Students attempt to apply the rights to their life at school and in the community
- *Cases.* Study some of the cases and the judgments from the European Court of Human Rights, e.g. the right to access to justice (Airey case 1979), right to privacy (Klass case 1978), right to freedom of expression (Handyside case 1976, Sunday Times case 1979).
- *Opinion.* Given that the Declaration and the Convention on the Rights of the Child were drafted by adults, students can be asked to give their opinion of these texts. What parts seem especially important to them? In what ways are the texts disappointing, perhaps? A number of simplified versions of the Universal Declaration are now available.[5]

3.2 The emphasis in teaching and learning about human rights should be positive. Pupils may be led to feelings of powerlessness and discouragement when confronted with many examples of violations and negations of human rights. Instances of progress and success should be used.

In some respects the term 'human rights' is strongly linked in the public mind with prisoners of conscience and inhuman and degrading treatment. This tends to put the focus of human rights at a point far removed from most young people in Europe and North America. There are many reasons why torture, for example, although a matter of great public concern, is not a topic that should be dwelt on in schools.

The successful struggles for the abolition of slavery, for trade unions, for women's suffrage, and for national freedom from colonialism are examples

33

of topics which are important historically, but which also have important implications today.

> 3.3 *The study of human rights in schools should lead to an understanding of and sympathy for, the concepts of justice, equality, freedom, peace, dignity, rights and democracy. Such understanding should be both cognitive and based on experience and feelings. Schools should, thus, provide opportunities for pupils to experience affective involvement in human rights and to express their feelings through drama, art, music, creative writing and audiovisual media.*

Many human rights struggles have been accompanied by songs, some of which are well known to young people. Listening to and performing such songs is given added interest when they are placed in context.

Human rights themes often inspire young people to their best efforts in painting, poetry, drama or working in media such as tape-slide or video which demand hours of work beyond the scope of the school timetable.

4. The Climate of the School

> 4.1 *Democracy is best learned in a democratic setting where participation is encouraged, where views can be expressed openly and discussed, where there is freedom of expression for pupils and teachers, and where there is fairness and justice. An appropriate climate is, therefore, an essential complement to effective learning about human rights.*
>
> 4.2 *Schools should encourage participation in their activities by parents and other members of the community. It may well be appropriate for schools to work with non-governmental organizations which can provide information, case studies and first-hand experience of successful campaigns for human rights and dignity.*
>
> 4.3 *Schools and teachers should attempt to be positive towards all their pupils, and recognize that all of their achievements are important – whether they be academic, artistic, musical, sporting or practical.*

The implications of this section are covered in Part 2 of this book and in Chapter 14.

5. Teacher Training

> 5.1 *The initial training of teachers should prepare them for their future contribution to teaching about human rights in their schools. For example, future teachers should:*
>   i. *be encouraged to take an interest in national and world affairs*
>   ii. *have the chance of studying or working in a foreign country or a different environment*
>   iii. *be taught to identify and combat all forms of discrimination in schools and society and be encouraged to confront and overcome their own prejudices.*
> 5.2 *Future and practising teachers should be encouraged to familiarize themselves with:*
>   i. *the main international declarations and conventions on human rights*

ii. the working and achievements of the international organizations which deal with the protection and promotion of human rights, for example through visits and study tours.

5.3 All teachers need, and should be given the opportunity, to update their knowledge and to learn new methods through in-service training. This could include the study of good practice in teaching about human rights, as well as the development of appropriate methods and materials.

The implications of this section are covered in Chapter 8.

6. International Human Rights Day

Schools and teacher training establishments should be encouraged to observe International Human Rights Day (10 December).

The 10 December is the anniversary of the adoption of the Universal Declaration by the General Assembly of the United Nations in 1948. This anniversary can provide an opportunity to mobilize the whole school or a part of it and to involve parents and community groups.

Such an event can help to introduce the notion of human rights in school to teaching colleagues and parents. If the day is set aside for special events, teachers can be asked to prepare their classes and to undertake work on a human rights theme appropriate to their subject or age range.

Rather than use such a broad theme as human rights in general it is probably better to focus on one aspect, such as:

- minority rights;
- racial equality;
- rights of the disabled;
- celebration of cultural diversity within the school;
- liberation struggles;
- women's rights;
- solidarity with another country or group within a country;
- a Third World theme;
- a peace theme;
- community twinning.

Although in some areas a political theme may represent the concerns of the parents and the community, an intercultural approach emphasizing celebration can, perhaps, better combine education, enjoyment and an opportunity to build the school community. Parents and others will wish to be involved. For instance, a school international evening can be based on sharing food and drink from the cultures represented in the school.

It is well to have a special event such as a dramatic performance or concert, or even a speaker or a film which will encourage parents to come to the school. The school can then also provide exhibitions and displays prepared by various classes as well as appropriate refreshments.

The experience of teachers and schools that have contributed to the Council of Europe's study of human rights and education has shown that a human rights dimension can be a part of work with young people at any age and in any curriculum subject. A school celebration of International Human Rights Day provides an opportunity to demonstrate the richness and diversity of this rewarding work within a unifying framework.

Experience from several European countries suggests that a special human rights day or week can be a remarkable catalyst for mobilizing staff, students, parents, community organizations, education officials and civic authorities. The initiative for such a project can come from a single teacher, a group of students, a headteacher, a parents' group, a voluntary group or any other body. Once a small group has been formed which is prepared to support the initiative, other groups will often lend their support and produce a snowball effect.

A secondary school in Lisbon, Portugal (Starkey, 1987), celebrated 10 December with an exhibition involving students aged 15–17. Classes studying French, English, history, geography, art, biology and civics contributed, working on their exhibits for several weeks beforehand. The exhibition included posters, tape-slide sequences, sculpture and displays of information. The topics included peace, world development, the United Nations, the Council of Europe, democracy in Portugal, the exploitation of child labour in nineteenth-century England, child labour in the twentieth century, and food growing and distribution.

The exhibition was held in a school hall. It was opened formally by an official of the Ministry of Education. Students, parents and local people were invited to visit the exhibition. The exhibition was, to those visitors, a bold institutional statement about the democratic values of the school and of Portugal. For the students and their teachers who had prepared it, it was an opportunity to focus on the human rights dimension of the subject they were studying, whatever it was.

A more ambitious approach from a local authority in France started as a community initiative, but involved schools. The Conseil Général du Gard organized a human rights week in Nîmes in the week after 10 December 1987. An exhibition space in the centre of the city was given over to exhibitions on the theme of human rights. Some of these were provided by United Nations organizations (UNESCO, UNICEF, WHO), and some by human rights and humanitarian organizations (Amnesty, Médecins sans Frontières). The boldest and most colourful statements came from the posters of 16-year-old students from a local school. The exhibitions were open to the public throughout the week. Those visiting could also watch videos and purchase books from the special display put on by a local bookshop. Local interest was aroused and maintained by press coverage and also by a nightly series of lectures from visiting specialists. Each talk was of general interest, but also targeted a specific section of the community (doctors, teachers, members of solidarity groups). A further group of students aged 13–14 was involved by writing and illustrating poems on human rights themes which were reproduced and made available to visitors to the exhibitions. The civic authorities showed their approval by attending a public reading of the poems by their young authors.

Other days and anniversaries can also be opportunities for similar celebrations. National days often celebrate important steps on the road to democracy. Other international days include:

January 15 Martin Luther King Day
March 8 International Women's Day
April 7 World Health Day
June 1 International Children's Day
June 5 World Environment Day
August 6 Hiroshima Day
October 24 United Nations Day

NOTES

1 Many suggestions are contained in Kingston Friends Workshop Group (1987).
2 This classification is that used by Jean-Bernard Marie of the International Institute of Human Rights in Strasbourg. See his annual list of signatories to international conventions in the *Human Rights Law Journal*.
3 The project is described by Francine Best in Chapter 8. This list can be found in the annotated bibliography *Pour une éducation aux droits de l'homme* (1985).
4 See also, for example, Ferguson (1989), which contains 100 short accounts of historical and contemporary events and people showing the effectiveness of non-violent social action.
5 The original simplified version in French by Professor Massarenti is in Massarenti and Veyrat (1984). A version grouped into ten statements under keywords is published in Richardson (1978). An English version inspired by Massarenti's text is published in Amnesty International (1983).

REFERENCES

Amnesty International (1983) *Teaching and Learning About Human Rights*, Amnesty International (British Section), London.
Cresta, M. (1985) *Progetto Giovani 85*, Movimento Federalista Europeo, Rieti.
Ferguson, J. (1989) *Give Peace a Chance*, Gooday, East Wittering.
Holden, C. and Starkey, H. (1988) 'The right to privacy and dignity', in Pike, G. and Selby, D. (eds) *Global Teacher, Global Learner*, Hodder and Stoughton, London.
Kingston Friends Workshop Group (1987) *Ways and Means: An Approach to Problem Solving*, KFWG, Kingston upon Thames.
Laqueur, W. and Rubin, B (1979) *The Human Rights Reader*, Meridian, New York.
Lyseight-Jones, P. (1985) *Human Rights Education in the Primary School*, Council of Europe DECS/EGT (85) 46, Strasbourg.
McFarlane, C. (1986) *Hidden Messages: Activities for Exploring Bias*, Development Education Centre, Gillett Centre, Selly Oak Colleges, Birmingham.
McLeod, K. A. (1984) *Multicultural Early Childhood Education*, Faculty of Education, Guidance Centre, University of Toronto, Canada.

Marie, J.-B. (1985) *Human Rights or a Way of Life in a Democracy*, Council of Europe, Strasbourg.

Masheder, M. (1987) *Let's Cooperate*, Peace Education Project, London.

Massarenti, L. and Veyrat, O. (1984) *L'École des droits de l'homme*, Faculté de psychologie et des sciences de l'éducation, Université de Genève, Geneva.

Milne, R. (1984) *Moral Development in Early Childhood*, PhD Thesis, University of Melbourne. Cited in Pettman, R. (1990) *Teaching for Human Rights*, United Nations Economic and Social Council, Commission on Human Rights.

Peace Education Project (1985) *PEP Talk No. 7: Cooperative Games*, Peace Education Project, London.

Pike, G. and Selby, D. (1988) *Human Rights. An Activity File*, Mary Glasgow, London.

Pour une éducation aux droits de l'homme (1985) Références Documentaires 30, CNDP, Paris.

Richardson, R. (1978) *Fighting for Freedom*, Nelson, London.

Starkey, H. (1987) *Teaching and Learning about Human Rights in Secondary Schools*, Council of Europe DECS/EGT (87) 20, Strasbourg.

The English Centre (1985) *The English Curriculum: Gender*, The English Centre, London.

White, M. (1989) 'Magic circle', *Times Educational Supplement*, 30 June, p. 24.

World Studies Project (1979) *Learning for Change in World Society*, 2nd edn, One World Trust, London.

CHAPTER 3

From the Bill of Rights (1791) to the Universal Declaration: The American Tradition of Education for Democracy

Margaret Branson

That there is an intimate relationship between education and constitutional government is something Americans have never doubted. In recent years the highest court in the land has seen fit on several occasions to point to that nexus. In 1954 Chief Justice Earl Warren used these oft-quoted words to announce the United States Supreme Court's unanimous decision in *Brown* v. *Board of Education*:

> Today education is perhaps the most important function of state and local governments. Compulsory school attendance laws and the great expenditures for education both demonstrate our recognition of the importance of education in our democratic society. It is required in the performance of our public responsibilities, even services in the armed forces. It is the very foundation of good citizenship. (*Brown* v. *Board of Education* 347 US 483, 493 (1954))

Twenty years later when the Court was called upon to decide a case initiated by Mexican-American parents who alleged that the Texas system of financing public education violated their children's right to equal protection under the Fourteenth Amendment, it again seized the opportunity to enunciate the essential role of education in a constitutional government. Speaking for the majority in *San Antonio Independent Schools District* v. *Rodriguez*, Justice Lewis F. Powell, Jr acknowledged that 'education, of course, is not among the rights afforded explicit protection under our Federal Constitution'. Nonetheless, he went on to say, 'Nothing this Court holds today in any way detracts from our historic dedication to public education. We are in complete agreement . . . that the grave significance of education both to the individual and to our society cannot be doubted.' (*San Antonio Independent School District* v. *Rodriguez* 411 US 1 (1973)) 'The grave significance of education' to democratic society was spelled out even more explicitly in Justice Thurgood Marshall's dissent in *San Antonio Independent School District* v. *Rodriguez*, with which Justice William O. Douglas concurred. As Marshall explained:

> The fundamental importance of education is amply indicated by the prior decision of this court, by the unique status accorded public education by our society, and by the close relationship between education and some of our most basic constitutional values . . .
>
> Education directly affects the ability of a child to exercise his First Amendment interests, both as a source and as a receiver of information and ideas, whatever interests he may pursue in life . . .
>
> Of particular importance is the relationship between the essential function of instilling in our young an understanding of and appreciation for the principles and operation of our governmental processes. Education may instill the interest and provide the tools necessary for political discourse and debate. Indeed, it has frequently been suggested that education is the dominant factor affecting political consciousness and participation. (*San Antonio Independent School District* v. *Rodriguez* 411 US 1 (1973))

By 1982, the United States Supreme Court was ready to assert that its previous findings regarding the interrelationship of education and a democratic government were now 'well-settled principles'. When Justice William Brennan delivered the majority opinion in *Plyler* v. *Doe*, a case in which Mexican children who had entered the United States illegally sought injunctive and declaratory relief against exclusion from public schools pursuant to a Texas statute and school district policy, he saw fit to review the many instances in which the Court had enunciated those principles.

> Public education is not a 'right' granted to individuals by the Constitution. But neither is it merely some governmental 'benefit' indistinguishable from other forms of social welfare legislation. Both the importance of education in maintaining our basic institutions, and the lasting impact of its deprivation on the life of the child, mark the distinction. The American people have always regarded education and [the] acquisition of knowledge as matters of supreme importance. We have recognized the public schools as the most vital civic institution for the preservation of our democratic system of government, and as the primary vehicle for transmitting the values on which our society rests. [As] . . . pointed out early in our history . . . some degree of education is necessary to prepare citizens to participate effectively and intelligently in our open political system if we are to preserve freedom and independence. And these historic perceptions of the public schools as inculcating fundamental values necessary to the maintenance of a democratic political system have been confirmed by the observations of social scientists. In addition, education provides the basic tools by which individuals might lead economically productive lives to the benefit of us all. In sum, education has a fundamental role in maintaining the fabric of our society. We cannot ignore the significant social consequence borne by our Nation when select groups are denied the means to

absorb the values and skills upon which our social order rests. (*Plyler* v. *Doe* 102 S. Ct. 2382 (1982))

Although Chief Justice Warren Burger dissented in *Plyler* v. *Doe*, neither he nor Justices White, Rehnquist, and O'Connor who joined him, disputed 'the well-settled principles'. In fact, the Chief Justice asserted that 'the importance of education is beyond dispute'. His dissent, he explained, was based on the belief that the 'political processes' rather than the courts should be used to remedy the problem at hand. Even so, he continued, 'Were it our business to set the Nation's social policy, I would agree without hesitation that it is senseless for an enlightened society to deprive any children – including illegal aliens – of an elementary education. . . . Denying a free education to illegal alien children is not a choice I would make were I a legislator. Apart from compassionate considerations, the long-range costs of excluding any children from the public schools may well outweigh the costs of educating them.' (*Plyler* v. *Doe* 102 S. Ct. 2382 (1982))

SCHOOLS AS BULWARKS OF FREEDOM

What are now 'well-settled principles' regarding the importance of education in a democratic society are, in fact, confirmations of sentiments which have been voiced by thoughtful Americans throughout their nation's history. Those who had waged a successful revolution against England were eager to conserve and consolidate their gains. From their reading of history they were convinced that republics were 'as evanescent as fireflies on a summer evening'. They also were aware of just how weak the new nation they had helped to bring to birth really was. They looked, therefore, for some means of protecting the liberty that had been hard won. Schooling for all seemed to them to be the most appropriate vehicle.

Three American intellectuals were in the forefront of the early effort to promote schools as bulwarks of freedom: Benjamin Rush, physician, politician and signer of the Declaration of Independence; Noah Webster, lexicographer, attorney and author who served in the Revolution against Burgoyne; and Thomas Jefferson, author of the Declaration of Independence, founder of the University of Virginia and third President of the United States. Although the three men differed to some degree in their motivations and in other particulars, they held five important beliefs about education in common:

1　Education should be systematic, useful and republican in aim.
2　Diffusion of knowledge among the people was essential because knowledge was 'our best guard against corruption' and 'the instrument of vast progress'.
3　Democratic instruction for all members of society was more important than higher education of an elite.
4　Republican leaders did require a special education, one that was more

concerned with abstract principles and one that would imbue them with civic virtue.

5 The United States was a great experiment and it was important that it succeed, not only for the sake of Americans but for the sake of all the world's people.

Even before the United States Constitution was written, Benjamin Rush was advising his countrymen that 'the form of government we have assumed has created a new class of duties to every American'. Those duties, Rush insisted, made it necessary to establish 'nurseries of wise and good men' and a system of education from common schools through colleges to ensure the survival of the republic.

Noah Webster was even more assertive. He proclaimed education to be 'the most important business in civil society'. In despotic governments, the people had no need for education, 'except for what tends to inspire them with a servile fear'. Education, Webster contended, 'is fatal to despotism'. But in a republican government 'the whole power of education is required. Here every class should know and love the laws.' Webster expanded his ideas in his essay 'On the Education of Youth in America', written in 1790. In that essay Webster asserted:

> In our American republic, where government is in the hands of the people, knowledge should be fully diffused by means of public schools. Of such consequence is it to society, that the people who make laws, should be well-informed, that I conceive no legislature can be justified in neglecting proper establishments for this purpose. . . . Education in great measure, forms the moral character of men, and morals are the bases of government. Education should, therefore, be the first care of a legislature; not merely the institution of schools, but the furnishing them with the best men for teachers. (Webster, 1790)

The third member of this intellectual triumvirate, Thomas Jefferson, was passionately committed to the need for education. He often spoke and wrote of its importance. In a letter to his long-time friend and co-signer of the Declaration of Independence, George Wythe of Virginia, Jefferson confided that 'I think by far the most important bill in our whole code is that for the diffusion of knowledge among the people. No other sure foundation can be devised, for the preservation of freedom and happiness.' Jefferson then went on to urge Wythe to use his persuasive skills on behalf of education.

> Preach, my dear Sir, a crusade against ignorance; establish and improve the law for educating the common people. Let our countrymen know that the people alone can protect us against these evils (contamination from the Old World), and that the tax which will be paid for this purpose is not more than the thousandth part of what will be paid to kings, priests and nobles who will rise up among us if we leave the people in ignorance. (Ford, 1904)

Jefferson forcefully restated his belief in widespread education on numerous other occasions. He once declared 'I know of no safe depository of the ultimate powers of the society but the people themselves; and if we think them not enlightened enough to exercise their control with a wholesome discretion, the remedy is not to take it from them, but to inform their discretion by education.' He also warned his fellow citizens that 'If a nation expects to be ignorant and free . . . it expects what never was and never will be.'

Rush, Webster and Jefferson were not the only advocates for education in the young republic. John Adams, James Madison, George Washington and many other leaders also called for a commitment to education as a safeguard for freedom. In his Farewell Address as President of the United States, Washington exhorted his fellow Americans to 'promote then as an object of primary importance, institutions for the general knowledge. In proportion as the structure of a government gives force to public opinion, it is essential that public opinion should be enlightened.' Washington and the five presidents who immediately followed him all urged the creation of a national university to ensure the education of future leaders, but the Congress declined to establish one. Other colleges and universities were already in existence, of course, and many more were to be founded in the ensuing years.

Support for education and belief in its importance as a bulwark of democracy was not confined to intellectuals and political leaders. James MacGregor Burns points to William Manning, a farmer and tavern keeper in North Billerica, Massachusetts, as one example of the kind of commitment to education that existed among the common people (Burns, 1983). Little is known about Manning other than that he marched to Concord on that famous day in April but arrived too late to fight at the bridge. Later he served two terms as a Billerica selectman, and he wrote one of the most prescient tracts in American history, 'The Key of Liberty'. He submitted his manuscript with its countless misspellings to the *Independent Chronicle*, the only pro-Jefferson newspaper in Boston, but the newspaper did not publish it. By chance Manning's papers survived, and they give us some insight into what some of the common people of the time thought. The 'ondly Remidy' against existing evils, he wrote, 'is by improveing our Rights as freemen in elections', as long as 'we are posesed of knowledge enough to act rationally in them'.

In his homely but insightful prose, Manning showed himself to be as eager as Rush, Webster, and Jefferson that the great experiment in republican government succeed. He also showed himself to be aware of the challenges which lay ahead, challenges which Rush, Webster and Jefferson understood well. As David Tyack explains them:

> Experience could give no guarantee that citizens would be loyal to the principles and situations which made them free; yet, at the same time, only if individuals could dissent with impunity from the most fundamental convictions of society would they know that they were indeed free. From this clash of necessary consensus and of freedom to dissent stemmed the paradoxical nature of the educational theories of the three intellectuals.

> Determined to preserve the heritage of the Revolution, to unify the nation, and to inculcate proper principles of government, they advocated a kind of republican indoctrination, hoping that the ensuing enlightenment would bring a salutary uniformity. (Tyack, 1967)

The dreams of Rush, Webster, Jefferson and other early American advocates of a national, uniform, systematic education dedicated to the fulfilment of republican aims were not immediately realized. One important reason was that education then as now was seen as the responsibility of the states. State constitutions acknowledged that responsibility. Those adopted subsequent to the ratification of the Constitution were especially explicit. Consider the language used in North Dakota's constitution of 1889. That language illustrates the kind of ideological connection between schooling and the well-being of the republic asserted in many state constitutions.

> A high degree of intelligence, patriotism and integrity and morality on the part of every voter in a government by the people being necessary in order to insure the continuance of that government and the prosperity and happiness of the people, the legislative assembly shall make provisions for the establishment and maintenance of a system of public schools which shall be open to the children of the State of North Dakota and free from sectarian control. This legislative requirement shall be irrevocable without the consent of the United States and the people of North Dakota. (American Political Science Association, American Historical Association, 1986)

Unfortunately space limitations prevent examination here of other state constitutions and their relevance to education in the democratic tradition. Our attention must be directed instead to the addition of the Bill of Rights to the United States Constitution. The first ten amendments or the original Bill of Rights and the 'extended Bill of Rights' including the fourteenth Amendment have proved to be of even greater significance to American education.

THE BILL OF RIGHTS

The United States Constitution as originally written did not mention education nor did it include a bill of rights, or a formulation of natural rights that could be recognized and enforced against the government. But the ink had scarcely dried on the document before questions began to arise about the neglect of such a bill. Those who were opposed to the ratification of the new Constitution for a variety of reasons called themselves Anti-Federalists. The Anti-Federalists were a loose coalition of men and women whose primary concern was states' rights, not civil rights. They sensed, however, that the lack of a bill of rights was their most popular argument, and they proceeded to use it, as Leonard Levy says, 'as an Anti-Federalist mace with which to smash the Constitution' (Levy, 1985).

The framers of the United States Constitution were civil libertarians, and, as George Washington informed Lafayette, 'There was not a member of the

Convention, I believe, who had the least objection to what is contended for by the advocates of a bill of rights.' Why then did the framers not include a specific enumeration of rights? The framers and supporters of ratification, who became known as Federalists, deemed such action unnecessary. They agreed with the position taken by Alexander Hamilton in *The Federalist* no. 84 'that the Constitution is itself, in every rational sense, and to every useful purpose, a Bill of Rights'. Hamilton then went on to argue that such a bill would be 'dangerous' as well as unnecessary, because it

> would contain various exceptions to powers not granted; and, on this very account, would afford a colorable pretext to claim more than were granted. For why declare that things shall not be done which there is no power to do? Why, for instance, should it be said that the liberty of the press shall not be restrained, when no power is given by which restrictions may be imposed? (Chadwick, 1987)

James Wilson, a distinguished jurist, signer of the Declaration of Independence and Pennsylvania delegate to the Constitutional Convention, concurred with Hamilton's reasoning. Wilson believed that a formal declaration of freedom of press or religion over religion over which Congress had no powers whatsoever, could imply that some degree of power had been granted because of the attempt to define its extent. 'If we attempt an enumeration, everything that is not enumerated is presumed to be given.' The consequence, Wilson said, would be that 'an imperfect enumeration would throw all implied powers into the scale of the government and the rights of the people would be rendered incomplete'.

Hamilton and Wilson may have reasoned well, but James Madison realized that both statecraft and political expediency required a switch in the Federalists' position. Popular sentiment was running against them. Madison, therefore, pledged the voters of Virginia, whose support he sought in his bid for election as their Representative to the First Congress, that he would introduce amendments to the Constitution which would secure 'the great rights of mankind'. On 8 June 1779, he made a long, memorable speech to the House of Representatives in which he fulfilled that promise. He introduced amendments culled mainly from state constitutions and state ratifying convention proposals, especially those of Virginia. But he went even further. Madison used the mandatory words 'shall' and 'shall not', which no state constitution had employed and no state ratifying convention had recommended, instead of the words 'ought' or 'should'. A bill of rights, Madison declared, limited the powers of government, thus preventing legislative as well as executive abuse, and, above all, preventing abuses of power by 'the body of the people, operating by the majority against the minority'. He admitted that while it was true that 'paper barriers' might fail, they would raise a standard to educate the majority against acts to which they might be inclined (Schwartz, 1971).

Congress did not accept all of the amendments which Madison proposed, but it finally did agree to submit 12 articles to the states. The first two articles dealing with pay and apportionment of Congress were not accepted, but the ten amendments which were to constitute the Bill of Rights became the 'supreme law of the land' on 15 December 1791. The Bill of Rights thus became a part of the United States Constitution rather than a specific legal enactment, a part of the fundamental law of the land which provides a genuine limit to state power. The Bill of Rights enunciates rights which can be fought over in open court, whatever the authority of the power which seeks to deny them. And, in recent years, the Bill of Rights has proved to be of critical importance to education.[1]

THE SUPREME COURT, THE BILL OF RIGHTS AND THE SCHOOLS

The Bill of Rights, which was added to the Constitution in 1791, constitutes the basis of modern civil liberties law. Initially the prohibitions in the first ten amendments applied only to the federal government. The respective states, however, in their own constitutions adopted similar prohibitions guaranteeing their people against interference in their rights to freedom of speech, press, assembly and religious worship and guaranteeing their lives, liberty and property against arbitrary action by the government.

After the Civil War, the Fourteenth Amendment was added to the United States Constitution. Under this amendment, no state could 'deprive any person of life, liberty or property without due process of law; nor deny to any person within its jurisdiction the equal protection of the laws'. Gradually, the 'due process' and 'equal protection' clauses of the Fourteenth Amendment came to include most of the prohibitions of the Bill of Rights, so that the Constitution, in time, became complete protection for the people against the actions of both state and federal governments.

While many people in the formative years of the nation regarded the judiciary as the least important of the three branches of government, Madison, who has been called the 'Father of the Bill of Rights', correctly foresaw its importance. He expected the federal courts in general and the Supreme Court in particular to play a major role in implementing the guarantees of the Bill of Rights. In a prophetic statement, Madison declared:

> Independent tribunals of justice will consider themselves in a peculiar manner the guardians of those rights; they (the courts) will be an impenetrable bulwark against every assumption of power in the Legislative or Executive; they will naturally be led to resist every encroachment upon rights expressly stipulated for in the Constitution by the declaration of rights. (Brant, 1965)

While Madison's prediction was correct, his timing was awry. Not until World War I did the federal judiciary play an important role in civil liberties matters. The Supreme Court began to evolve the modern law of civil liberties that includes selective incorporation of the Bill of Rights through the Fourteenth Amendment against the states after 1917. The most explosive period of civil liberties decision-making began with the (Franklin) Roosevelt Court and was continued by its successors. Justices began to demonstrate less concern with the kinds of economic cases which previously had preoccupied them and more concern for issues involving individual rights. Henry Abraham, who has made special studies of the Supreme Court's record in civil rights and liberties cases, reports:

> Since 1937 the overwhelming majority of judicial vetoes imposed upon the several states and almost all of those against the national government have been invoked because they infringed personal liberties, other than those of 'property', safeguarded under the Constitution. This preoccupation with the 'basic human freedoms' is amply illustrated by the statistics of the docket of the Supreme Court and the application of its power of judicial review. Well more than half of all cases decided by the Court now fall into this category of basic human freedoms. Whereas in the 1935–36 term only two of 160 written opinions had done so, in the 1979–80 term the ratio had increased to 80 out of 149. (Abraham, 1988)

It is especially important to note that an increasing number of those basic human freedom cases have been concerned with education. Why the Supreme Court should give such careful attention to cases touching on schooling is well explained by one constitutional scholar.

> Basic to any discussion of the role of courts in educational decision-making is the primacy of education in American ideology. Americans believe that education is central to the realization of a truly democratic and egalitarian society. It is through education that the skills necessary to exercise the responsibilities of citizenship and to benefit from the opportunities of a free economy will be imparted, no matter how recently arrived or previously disadvantaged the individual. Thus courts are concerned with protecting access to education. Moreover, since decision-making by those charged with the administration of public education is seen as one of the most significant areas of law in terms of its effects on the lives of individuals and groups in our society, courts are inevitably drawn into reviewing the legitimacy of those decisions. (Levin, 1977)

The scope of cases concerning education is impressive – and sobering. The courts have heard cases concerning compulsory schooling, religious socialization, academic freedom, due process rights for students and teachers, equal opportunity and race, sex-based discrimination, the right of aliens to education at public expense, the rights of language minorities – and more. In adjudicating these cases, the courts, and the Supreme Court justices in particular, have made it a point to serve a pedagogical role as well as a juridical role. Time and again the justices have proved to be 'schoolmasters for the nation', instructing their fellow citizens in their rights and responsibilities. Time and again their opinions have served to remind Americans of the great tradition of rights on which their government is premised. Here are but a few of the more eloquent and telling reminders which have flowed from the courts in recent years in the course of deciding cases concerned with education.

The very purpose of a Bill of Rights was to withdraw certain subjects from the vicissitudes of political controversy, to place them beyond the reach of majorities and officials and to establish them as legal principles to be applied by the courts. One's right to life, liberty, and property, to free speech, a free press, freedom of worship and assembly, and other fundamental rights may not be submitted to vote, they depend on the outcome of no elections. . . .

If there is any fixed star in our constitutional constellation, it is that no official, high or petty, can prescribe what shall be orthodox in politics, nationalism, religion, or other matters of opinion or force citizens to confess by word or act their faith therein. If there are any circumstances which permit an exception, they do not now occur to us . . . (Justice Robert Jackson. *West Virginia Board of Education* v. *Barnette* 319 U.S. 624)

We come then to the question presented: Does segregation of children in public schools solely on the basis of race, even though the physical facilities and other 'tangible' factors may be equal, deprive the children of the minority group of equal educational opportunities? We believe that it does . . .

We conclude that in the field of public education the doctrine of 'separate but equal' has no place. Separate educational facilities are inherently unequal. (Chief Justice Earl Warren. *Brown* v. *Board of Education* 347 U.S. 483)

Our Nation is deeply committed to safeguarding academic freedom, which is of transcendent value to all of us and not merely the teachers concerned. That freedom is therefore a special concern of the First Amendment, which does not tolerate laws that cast a pall of orthodoxy over the classroom. (Justice William J. Brennan. *Keyishian* v. *Board of Regents* 385 U.S. 589)

It can hardly be argued that either students or teachers shed their constitutional rights to freedom of speech or expression at the schoolhouse gate. This has been the unmistakable holding of this Court for almost 50 years . . .

In order for the State in the person of school officials to justify prohibition of a particular expression of opinion, it must be able to show that its action was caused by something more than a mere desire to avoid the discomfort and unpleasantness that always accompany an unpopular viewpoint . . .

The principle of these cases is not confined to the supervised and ordained discussion which takes place in the classroom . . . A student's rights, therefore, do not embrace merely the classroom hours. When he is in the cafeteria, or on the playing field, or on the campus during the authorized hours, he may express his opinions, even on controversial subjects like the conflict in Vietnam, if he does so without 'materially and substantially interfer[ing] with the requirements of appropriate discipline in the operation of the school' and without colliding with the rights of others. (Justice Abe Fortas. *Tinker* v. *Des Moines* 393 U.S. 503)

The First Amendment proscription against any law abridging freedom of expression, perhaps more than any other constitutional guarantee, frequently brings into sharp focus the inexorable tension between enduring concerns for individual freedom and the authority required to preserve the democracy so crucial to realizing that freedom. . . .

The Supreme Court has more than once instructed that '[t]he vigilant protection of constitutional freedoms is nowhere more vital than in the community of American schools.' . . .

Rightly called the 'cradle of our democracy', our schools bear the awesome responsibility of instilling and fostering early in our nation's youth the basic values which will guide them throughout their lives.

Recently, this country enfranchised 18-year-olds. It would be foolhardy to shield our children from political debate and issues until the eve of their first venture into the voting booth. Schools must play a central role in preparing their students to think and analyze and to recognize the demagogue. (Irving R. Kaufman, Circuit Judge, United States Court of Appeals, Second Circuit. *James* v. *Board of Education*, 461F. 2d 566 (1972))

Taken as a whole, the excerpts just quoted from five landmark cases in education are testimony to the tradition of support for rights of students and teachers which the United States courts have provided.

THE UNIVERSAL DECLARATION OF HUMAN RIGHTS

Concern about rights is in the American tradition and at the core of the American creed. The government of the United States was founded on the belief that the primary purpose of government is to secure and protect the rights of the people. The Declaration of Independence, and the United States Constitution and its Bill of Rights make that commitment abundantly clear. So, too, do hundreds of court decisions.

The United States has also evinced its concern for rights in the international arena. The United States has played a key role in helping to establish, maintain, and support the United Nations. The Charter of that organization commits its members to the promotion of 'universal respect for the observance of human rights and fundamental freedoms for all'. Americans, most particularly Eleanor Roosevelt, figured prominently in the drafting of the Universal Declaration of Human Rights. Every American president who has served since the Declaration came into being on 10 December 1948 has declared his support of it. Every American president has also drawn an analogy between the Declaration and fundamental documents on which the United States government is based. President Ronald Reagan, therefore, was following tradition when he issued this proclamation on the eve of the fortieth anniversary of the Universal Declaration:

The second week in December commemorates two important dates. December 10 marks the 40th anniversary of the signing of the Universal Declaration of Human Rights, and December 15 also marks the date almost

200 years ago, when in 1791, the first 10 amendments to the United States Constitution – our Bill of Rights – were ratified.

The human rights we regard today as inherent and unalienable were by no means universally accepted two centuries ago. Such rights as freedom of worship, speech, assembly, and the press were just beginning to be asserted by popular movements that would sweep Europe and elsewhere in the next century. The United States thus foreshadowed and fostered a powerful drive to improve the lot of mankind everywhere . . .

Now, 200 years later, the Universal Declaration, enshrining many of the principles of our Founders, has become that worldwide Bill of Rights . . .

The Universal Declaration, like our own Bill of Rights, starts from the premises that civil liberties and political freedom are the birthright of all mankind and that all of us are equal in the eyes of the law. Like our own Declaration of Independence, it also makes the inescapable connection between freedom, human rights, and government by the consent of the governed. (US Department of State, Bureau of Public Affairs, 1989a)

Noticeable in the proclamation is the emphasis on civil and political rights and the absence of any mention of economic, social or cultural rights. That is not surprising, because the official position of the United States is that the latter are 'goals of sound policy' rather than 'true human rights'. Richard S. Williamson, Assistant Secretary of International Organization Affairs in the Department of State, made that very clear in an address to the United Nations at ceremonies commemorating the fortieth anniversary of the Universal Declaration.

We [the United States government] view human rights as limitations upon the power of the state. Based on the principles set forth in the Bill of Rights of the U.S. Constitution, our view of human rights is centered on defenses from the state, accorded every individual and protected by an independent judiciary. These rights are timeless, unalterable, and not subject to the intellectual or political fashions of the day. They establish the state as the servant of the people and not the other way around . . .

The past 25 years have seen a tendency to redefine human rights to include a new category of 'social and economic rights', such as the right to education, the right to food, or the right to housing . . .

In contrast to our notion of human rights as limitations upon the power of the state, these 'rights' would augment the power of the state, make individuals more dependent, and could not be enforced by an independent judiciary.

The United States sees these socioeconomic 'rights' as the goals of sound policy rather than as true human rights. (US Department of State, Bureau of Public Affairs, 1989b)

A similar policy statement came from Paula Dobriansky, Deputy Assistant Secretary for Human Rights and Humanitarian Affairs in the Department of State. Speaking on behalf of the Reagan and Bush administrations, she said 'We [the United States government] define human rights as the respect for the integrity of the individuals and the observance of political/civil rights.' Dobriansky then went on to attack what she called the 'myth' that 'economic and social rights constitute human rights'.

> There have been efforts to obfuscate traditional civil and political rights with 'economic and social rights'. We believe that traditional political rights provide a vital foundation for any democratic society . . .
> We believe that under present conditions 'economic and social rights' are really more in the nature of aspirations and goals than 'rights'. (US Department of State, Bureau of Public Affairs, 1988, pp. 1–2)

Dobriansky insisted that the semantic distinction the United States government was drawing was highly important, because economic and social entitlements are not rights if most governments are not able to provide them. 'In contrast, any government can guarantee political and civil rights to its citizens. Obfuscating a goal with fundamental rights promotes not only conceptual confusion but often is used to justify actual human rights violations.' (US Department of State, Bureau of Public Affairs, 1988, pp. 2–3)

Despite the fact that the current United States government views political and civil rights as 'true human rights' and economic and social rights as 'aspirations and goals', it acknowledges that the decade which lies ahead 'poses some real dilemmas and challenges for US human rights policy'. One of the most important challenges in the decade ahead is how 'to educate not only our citizens at home but international audiences as well about what human rights are, how one can improve human rights conditions, and what role individuals and non-governmental organizations can play in the process'.

That is indeed a challenge. And it is a challenge educators should try to meet.

APPENDIX: CIVIL RIGHTS AND LIBERTIES IN THE UNITED STATES CONSTITUTIONS

I. PROVISIONS FROM THE ORIGINAL CONSTITUTION

Article I
  Section 9 . . .
    2. The privilege of the writ of habeas corpus shall not be suspended, unless when in cases of rebellion or invasion the public safety may require it.
    3. No bill of attainder or ex post facto law shall be passed.
  Section 10.
    1. No State shall . . . pass any bill of attainder, ex post facto law, or law impairing the obligation of contracts . . .
Article III
  Section 2 . . .
    3. The trial of all crimes, except in cases of impeachment, shall be by jury . . .

Section 3.

1. Treason against the United States shall consist only in levying war against them, or in adhering to their enemies, giving them aid and comfort. No Person shall be convicted of treason unless on the testimony of two witnesses to the same overt act, or on confession in open court.

Article IV

Section 2.

1. The citizens of each state shall be entitled to all privileges and immunities of citizens in the several States.

Article VI

3. . . . no religious test shall ever be required as a qualification to any office or public trust under the United States.

FIRST TEN AMENDMENTS (ADOPTED IN 1791)

Amendment I

Congress shall make no law respecting an establishment of religion, or prohibiting the free exercise thereof; or abridging the freedom of speech, or of the press; or the right of the people peaceably to assemble and to petition the Government for a redress of grievances.

Amendment II

A well-regulated militia being necessary to the security of a free state, the right of the people to keep and bear arms, shall not be infringed.

Amendment III

No soldier shall, in time of peace, be quartered in any house without the consent of the owner, nor in time of war but in a manner to be proscribed by law.

Amendment IV

The right of the people to be secure in their persons, houses, papers, and effects against unreasonable searches and seizures, shall not be violated, and no warrants shall issue but upon probable cause, supported by oath or affirmation, and particularly describing the place to be searched, and the persons or things to be seized.

Amendment V

No person shall be held to answer for a capital, or otherwise infamous crime, unless on a presentment or indictment of a Grand Jury, except in cases arising in the land or naval forces, or in the militia, when in actual service in time of war or public danger; nor shall any person be subject for the same offense to be twice put in jeopardy of life or limb; nor shall be compelled in any criminal case to be a witness against himself, nor be deprived of life, liberty or property, without due process of law; nor shall private property be taken for public use, without just compensation.

Amendment VI

In all criminal prosecutions, the accused shall enjoy the right to a speedy and public trial, by an impartial jury of the State and district wherein the crime shall have been committed, which districts shall have been previously ascertained by law, and to be informed of the nature and cause of the accusation; to be confronted with the witnesses against him; to have compulsory process for obtaining witnesses in his favor, and to have the assistance of counsel for his defense.

Amendment VII

In suits at common law, where the value in controversy shall exceed twenty dollars, the right of trial by jury shall be preserved, and no fact tried by a jury shall be otherwise reexamined in any court of the United States, than according to the rules of the common law.

Amendment VIII

Excessive bail shall not be required, nor excessive fines imposed, nor cruel and unusual punishments inflicted.

Amendment IX

The enumeration in the Constitution of certain rights shall not be construed to deny or disparage others retained by the people.

Amendment X

The powers not delegated to the United States by the Constitution, nor prohibited by it to the States, are reserved to the States respectively, or to the people.

THE EXTENDED BILL OF RIGHTS

Amendment XIII (Ratified in 1865)

Section 1. Neither slavery nor involuntary servitude, except as a punishment for crime whereof the party shall have been duly convicted, shall exist within the United States, or any place subject to their jurisdiction.

Section 2. Congress shall have power to enforce this article by appropriate legislation.

Amendment XIV (Ratified in 1868)

Section 1. All persons born or naturalized in the United States, and subject to the jurisdiction thereof, are citizens of the United States and of the State wherein they reside. No State shall make or enforce any law which shall abridge the privileges or immunities of citizens of the United States; nor shall any State deprive any person of life, liberty, or property, without due process of law; nor deny to any person within its jurisdiction the equal protection of the laws . . .

Section 5. The Congress shall have power to enforce by appropriate legislation the provisions of this article.

Amendment XV (Ratified in 1870)

Section 1. The right of citizens of the United States to vote shall not be denied or abridged by the United States or by any State on account of race; color, or previous condition of servitude.

Section 2. The Congress shall have power to enforce this article by appropriate legislation.

Amendment XIX (Ratified in 1920)

Section 1. The right of citizens of the United States to vote shall not be denied or abridged by the United States or by any State on account of sex.

Section 2. Congress shall have power to enforce this article by appropriate legislation.

Amendment XXIV (Ratified in 1964)

Section 1. The right of citizens of the United States to vote in any primary or other election for President or Vice-President, for electors for President or Vice President, or for Senator or Representative in Congress, shall not be denied or abridged by the United States or any State by reason of failure to pay any poll tax or other tax.

Section 2. The Congress shall have power to enforce this article by appropriate legislation.

Amendment XXVI (Ratified 1971)

Section 1. The right of citizens of the United States, who are 18 years of age or older, to vote shall not be denied or abridged by the United States or by any State on account of age.

Section 2. The Congress shall have power to enforce this article by appropriate legislation.

NOTE

1   See the original and extended Bill of Rights appended to this chapter.

REFERENCES

Abraham, H. J. (1988) *Freedom and the Court: Civil Rights and Liberties in the United States*, 5th edn, Oxford University Press, New York, pp. 7–8.

American Political Science Association, American Historical Association (1986) *This Constitution: Our Enduring Legacy*, Congressional Quarterly, Inc., Washington, DC, p. 193.

Brant, I. (1965) *The Bill of Rights*, Bobbs-Merrill Company, Indianapolis, pp. 49–50.

Burns, J. M. (1983) *The Vineyard of Liberty*, Vintage Books, New York, pp. 139, 144.

Chadwick, M. L. (ed.) (1987) *The Federalist*, Springfield, VA, p. 465.

Ford, P. L. (ed.) (1904) *The Works of Thomas Jefferson*, G. P. Putnam's Sons, New York, pp. 153–154.

Levin, B. (1977) 'Education and the Constitution', *Encyclopedia of the Constitution*, Durham, NC, *Duke Law Journal*, Vol 2, p. 608.

Levy, L. (1985) *Emergence of a Free Press*, Oxford University Press, New York, pp. 220–282.

Schwartz, B. (ed.) (1971) *The Bill of Rights: A Documentary History*, Vol. 2, Oxford University Press, New York, pp. 1023–1034.

Tyack, D. B. (ed.) (1967) *Turning Points in American Educational History*, Blaisdell Publishing Company, Waltham MA, p. 92.

US Department of State, Bureau of Public Affairs (1988) Current Policy No. 1091. An address by Paula Dobriansky, Deputy Assistant Secretary for Human Rights and Humanitarian Affairs, 3 June.

US Department of State, Bureau of Public Affairs (1989a) Selected Documents No. 34 (January 1989) 'Human Rights Day, Bill of Rights Day and Human Rights Week, 1988', Proclamation by President Reagan, 8 December, p. 10.

US Department of State, Bureau of Public Affairs (1989b) Selected Documents No. 34 (January 1989), Remarks by Richard S. Williamson, Assistant Secretary for International Organization Affairs at the United Nations, 8 December, p. 2.

Webster, N. (1790) *A Collection of Essays and Fugitive Writings on Moral, Historical, Political and Literary Subjects*, I. Thomas and E. F. Andrews, Boston.

STAGES IN HUMAN RIGHTS EDUCATION

Preface

Part 2 describes approaches to human rights education as they have been developed in and for the various age-specific phases of formal education. Whilst the Recommendation of the Committee of Ministers of the Council of Europe acknowledges that 'concepts associated with human rights can, and should, be acquired at an early stage', it is also a fact that some of the more abstract concepts can only usefully be approached in later years of schooling.

Part 2 brings together contributions from specialists working with different age-groups, from nursery or pre-school education to high school. There is also an important chapter on teacher education, both initial and in-service. It is fascinating to note what unites these chapters as well as what is specific to them. One unifying theme is that of contract. Schools should express their mission explicitly and expect parents and pupils/students to adhere to the common goals. The mission statement, it goes without saying, should be drawn up in partnership with the school community and the community served by the school. The legal notion of contract is, of course, itself an important concept in human rights.

The mission statement or contract means that the school needs to express its values publicly. Needless to say the writers of these chapters recommend human rights documents as useful starting points in the drawing up of such statements. Not only do human rights documents contain useful phrases that can be borrowed, but they have the status to command widespread adherence. The concept of contract or charter can also be extended to a cluster of schools or a school district, even to a national or state education system. The London Borough of Ealing, as Pauline Lyseight-Jones mentions in her contribution, has produced a document for parents and teachers spelling out the entitlements of children in the borough's schools. The document acknowledges its debt to notions of human rights in its title: *Ealing, every child is given space to grow: Towards a Charter for all Children in School*.

Giving children space to grow is a further unifying theme of this Part. The ecological connotations of the metaphor are appropriate to the 1990s. The concept implies, as Martine Abdallah-Pretceille puts it, that children are the subjects of education, not the objects. 'Subjects' is used here in the grammatical sense of actor or initiator and not in the feudal sense of dutiful hierarchical inferior. As subjects they must be able to exercise choices, to take responsibility and to see themselves as important individuals in the context of a social system whose other members are also individuals with rights and entitlements. Individuals will thus have space, but on a crowded planet such as ours the space will be defined as that which does not adversely impinge on the growing and living space of others. For this reason Pauline Lyseight-Jones suggests that, where there are conflicting rights, the teacher's role is to protect the most vulnerable and least powerful. One instance of such conflicting rights is an everyday struggle of conscience for many teachers; it is the rights of the teacher's family and dependants to time and attention when the entitlements of the students and the school are also pressing.

The early years of education have a tradition of nurturing and caring. Post-primary education has often been a much harsher environment. Educators have increasingly come to realize the advantages of a caring and community-based approach to secondary education and this is exemplified in the contributions of Jeremy Cunningham and Patricia Dye. Both stress the crucial importance of the climate of the school and the classroom. Jeremy Cunningham describes some practical approaches to achieving a human rights school. In particular he stresses the need to make the values of the school explicit and to use disputes constructively as learning points which can 'nurture effective moral development'.

Of course, a helpful school climate is not sufficient in itself to promote human rights education. There is, at secondary level, a need for, as Patricia Dye says 'a sequenced and meaningful' programme of study. Such a programme does not have to be based purely on knowledge. Patricia Dye stresses the need for affective objectives and for action. 'It is almost better,' she asserts, 'for teachers to never address the inequities of our world than to have students believe they can do nothing to change those inequities.'

The transformation of schools and teaching that is occurring with the human rights in education movement necessitates the preparation and training of teachers, both those already in post and those preparing for a teaching career. Francine Best points out that such training must include knowledge of human rights, a commitment to human rights values and democratic schools and a co-operative approach to teaching. The model of the French action-research project which she initiated has the advantage of enabling teachers to work co-operatively and to reflect on their practice. The research and curriculum development can and should involve the wider community, particularly those organizations involved in aspects of human rights. The model proposed is one that gives teachers space to grow.

Human rights education will occur where schools and education authorities make a commitment to it and where there is recognition that all those involved in the process, students, parents, teachers, advisers and administrators, have a need for the space to examine their values, to share with others and have opportunities for action. As human beings, all educators and learners are entitled to space to grow. All involved in the education process should also be committed to protecting and enhancing the growing space of others, children or adults.

CHAPTER 4

Human Rights in the Nursery School

Martine Abdallah-Pretceille

The idea of teaching human rights in pre-primary schools begs two questions:

- What is pre-primary education?
- What is human rights education?

There is by no means a consensus in Europe on the form this education should take or on the manner in which it should be dispensed. The very need for schools to provide such education is contested in some quarters and advocated in others. Furthermore, amongst member States 'there are as many patterns of pre-school organization as there are terms to describe them' (Woodhead, 1979, p. 2). They cater for different ages, operate in different ways, employ different categories of staff, have different educational requirements and use different types of facilities. This great diversity calls for caution and flexibility in analysing the situation and making proposals. Whatever the structures, however, there are certain general principles which may be identified:

- the non-compulsory nature of pre-primary education;
- the need for liaison between the different institutional and other parties jointly responsible for educating children: parents, teachers, educators, medical and welfare staff;
- a vision of pre-school education which is neither a carbon copy nor a scaled-down version of primary schooling, its distinguishing feature being that it treats a child as the subject rather than the object of education.

But the same themes recur in writings about pre-school education irrespective of their country of origin. The importance of recognizing childhood as having special qualities which must be respected; the principle of encouraging children to develop naturally through play; the significance of the senses and activity-based learning at this age; a belief in giving children freedom to explore and experience a wide range of learning environments in the interests of encouraging overall personal development, physical, social, cultural, emotional as well as cognitive; the potential of pre-school education to overcome the harmful effects on development of unhygienic living conditions, a restricted environment, family poverty and other hardships. (Woodhead, 1979, p. 9)

It is on this basis, therefore, that we shall consider the problem of human rights education for children of pre-school age, whatever the type of establishment involved.

If defining pre-school education raises difficulties, defining human rights education is an even more complex matter. Viewed in terms of the mere assimilation of facts (dates, texts, charters, international organizations concerned with defending human rights, etc.), human rights education amounts to a fairly simple teaching exercise independent of the education philosophy adopted by this or that country.

On the other hand, the transition from simple teaching to an education presupposing adherence to specific individual, and collective social, values, to a given ethic, raises sharper issues which are difficult to avoid as human rights education requires reasonable responses and stances – in short, commitments. It is not enough to pay lip-service to the principles governing human rights or to proclaim one's personal convictions; it is necessary to imbue young children with the 'sap', the very essence of human rights. And this means rationalizing and objectivizing what for most adults is more in the nature of innermost feeling, a vague aspiration, than a clear-minded grasp of the values underlying human rights.

The third step in our analysis will be to try to define some methodological approaches and propose some fundamental principles for the educational process. There will be no attempt at exhaustiveness but rather at formalization (as opposed to modification) of the different possibilities. Since educators and adults in general have no past experience of human rights education to go on, and as human rights education for children of pre-school age has scarcely ever been envisaged as such, innovation and anticipation are called for (Abdallah-Pretceille, 1989).

By eliminating all recourse to cognitive and intellectual learning, human rights education of pre-school age becomes a threefold concept marked by three key terms: socialization, ethics and human rights. The fundamental question is whether human rights education can be provided regardless of the type of socialization and education and whether it is incompatible with all reference systems. Do human rights imply certain orientations and choices? Can the universality of human rights be reconciled with absolute relativism, for example? Educators, teachers, parents and local authorities must gauge the scale of the task and, above all, of the choices to be made. Educating people in human rights means trying to train them on both the individual and the social plane. It is not, therefore, any neutral or ordinary educational process, but a campaign. It is thus the duty of the individuals and institutions responsible to make the terms of the contract clear.

HUMAN RIGHTS BETWEEN MORALS AND ETHICS

Does incorporating human rights into pre-school education amount to discovering, or rediscovering, a certain form of moral education? What educational methods might be used for the purpose?

One approach consists of imposing a set of values and demanding compliance therewith. Here, education is asking to inculcate references classified by degrees of good and evil. Human rights then become the yardstick by which all other systems of values are measured. This approach involves the teacher and the educator in the transmission of a moral code, that of human rights. However, a paradox lies in this reduction of the universality of human rights to a specific moral code which, logically, is liable to be rejected in the very name of the right to be different. What is more, the coexistence of several moral codes (social, religious, civic, human rights, etc.) would deny human rights any claim to transcendency.

On that basis, human rights education would be conceived of as the transmission of model attitudes and values and would be reliant on a certain form of physical and moral compulsion. This is a highly prescriptive approach which goes perfectly with a particular kind of moral and/or religious education but is scarcely compatible with human rights education, opposed as it is to any form of coercion. The fact is, then, that human rights cannot be reduced to any form of moral code, even of a secular nature.

The opposite approach consists of education and socialization based on interpersonal relations and exchanges between the individual and his or her environment. Placed at the centre of the educational process, the child is elevated to the status of actor and subject. The child, an individual in the making, is confronted on the one hand by the adult, a person riddled with contradictions, and on the other hand by his or her cultural background, also charged with meanings and marked by values which may indeed be contradictory now and then, but are nonetheless significant.

Considered in this light, human rights education is no longer a matter of dictates, orders or imposed standards but a project, an evolving educational dynamic.

The debate underlying these considerations concerns the relations between the individual and society. The above reference to approaches was not intended as a formality but was designed to show exactly what is at stake: human rights education is not merely a question of introducing human rights into the school curriculum as an additional subject; it denotes a specific educational philosophy aimed at making individuals the active participants in their own development rather than the passive products of an educational process. It would be deceitful not to clarify the paradox and dilemma of this human rights education at the very outset. Choices need to be made, and educational practices fitted into a pattern. The younger the children are, the more teachers should be aware of this need if their efforts are not to result in mutual or uncomprehending rejection.

In any event, one of the ways in which children learn is by following examples (not to be confused with the mere imitation of models). Since intellectualization, objectivization and verbalization cannot serve as a basis for educating young children, the adult (educator, parent, teacher, etc.) is an important point of reference. As a potential vehicle of identity, adults speak as much with their bodies and silences, attitudes and implications as with actual words. Consequently, if human rights education is to be more than a mere lecture on human rights, teachers will need to give as much consideration to what they are and what they do as to what they say.

It must be stressed that educating very young children in human rights does not involve any teaching of objectivization; it is a matter of distilling tiny doses of experience. It entails no spectacular actions directly aimed at human rights but a daily routine, a network of relations and contacts deliberately imprinted with the ethics of human rights. The paradox of human rights education for this age group lies in the very impossibility of basing it on any well-defined corpus of knowledge. Teachers and educators must therefore gear their educational methods to the values inherent in human rights. Yet it is precisely there that a consensus is clearly lacking and differences of opinion emerge. As long as it is simply a question of learning facts, dates, conventions and so on, it is easy to agree. But once educating young children requires more than formalistic adherence, discursive demonstrations or declarations of intent, divergences immediately become apparent. Human rights education for the very young is of necessity dependent on an awakening to values. Being a more fundamental and complex kind of education, it is more difficult to put into practice.

Introducing human rights education at pre-primary level raises again the question of the nature and role of the schools in relation to society. It imposes on schools an obligation to abandon their practice of neutralizing and relativizing values as far as possible and to define their aims and methods in terms of a secular doctrine of an active and positive kind. In short, they must put forward an ethical project.

The concept of 'one must' – which is 'the epitome of the neutral, as a rule that has become alien to my project of freedom and even to my intention to recognize the freedom of others' (Ricoeur, 1985, p. 45) – should be replaced by the ethical intention of an individual 'who can present himself as the person responsible for a moral agent' (Ricoeur, 1985, p. 44). Human rights education clearly presupposes recognition of the concept of person. However, this concept varies according to time, place and culture. The whole outcome of a human rights education depends on the solving of this dilemma.

SOCIALIZATION, ACCULTURATION AND EDUCATION IN HUMAN RIGHTS

In addition to the difficulties connected with defining operational objectives, there is the fact that young children are the focal point of a variety of educational influences, both individual (parents, teachers, nurses, educators and doctors) and collective (families, schools, nurseries and local authorities), who all contribute in their own way, but sometimes at cross-purposes. How can educational coherence be ensured between such diversified parties who do not necessarily share the same values? The problem becomes more complex still in the case of a pluralistic society where different social and ethnic groups whose cultural references and values may violently conflict with one another live side by side.

A child's human environment is characterized by plurality and diversity from the outset; education is no longer the prerogative of families. The values subscribed to by the various social, cultural, occupational, economic, religious, regional and other groups are a source of maximum diversification – not homogenization, as some prefer to believe. Values nowadays follow a spectral rather than a monadic pattern, i.e. they are no longer simple monolithic units. This synchronous proliferation of values is accompanied by dissonances or even discordances which hamper the drawing up of an educational project (as distinct from a teaching project) common to partners not sharing the same cultural references, leading to the accumulation of potential conflicts. Thus education is trapped between the need to base the educational project on a consensus and the difficulty of achieving this harmony without imposing one model on another.

What role do and will human rights play in this scheme? Are they an option? An extra? An atheistic form of new religion and/or ideology? The question is an important one, for it will not admit of a plural answer. Human rights can but subsume the registers constructed on the basis of particular moral codes (religious, political). Education in human rights, therefore, is a matter of deliberate choice and is unable to accommodate any 'perhapses' and 'maybes'. Each system must declare its options and everyone must stand by their commitments. There is no room for uncertainty or ambiguity. European education and/or educational Europe cannot content itself with being a patchword or a mosaic. The various lines of force must be clearly affirmed. This may seem axiomatic, but daily realities are proof enough that this 'axiom' is far from unanimously accepted, let alone put into practice.

Socialization, acculturation and education are diverse processes. True, the family remains their pre-eminent locus, but the question is: how do children react to these multiple competing values? What place is occupied by the values inherent in human rights? It would be naive to believe that these different levels of education operate in total symbiosis. To avoid any social schizophrenia and/or behaviour of a syncretic nature, therefore, certain values should be objectivized, affirmed and proclaimed. It is not possible to advocate respect for human rights and, in the same breath, a certain anomy of values due to their excessive profusion.

It may thus be seen that socialization and acculturation, which used to be experienced and acquired in an implicit and natural way, should be approached in a more explicit and objective manner. The increasing complexity of the social order is undeniably resulting in education being reoriented towards these processes of socialization and acculturation. And in the case of the very young it is only at this level and with a maximum of coherence in terms of values that human rights education can be envisaged. It would be illusory to suggest that one has merely to talk about human rights for agreement to be achieved. This is illustrated by the following anecdote from a nursery school in the Paris suburbs: when the mistress started to initiate her young pupils in the notion of respect for others on the basis of a children's book entitled *Saïd and Sophie*, many parents complained that this type of problem was none of her business but was a matter for family upbringing.

The adoption of human rights as a leitmotiv of values is not compatible with all types of education and socialization. Naivety and irresolution in this field are sources both of conflict and failure; how can objectives be attained which have not been either declared or accepted? Let us have done with hypocrisy and fear, therefore!

Human rights education is inconceivable as part of an authoritarian form of socialization. Normative and normalizing teaching based on inculcation rather than education is a form of imposition which makes no allowance for the processes by which norms and values are interiorized. The only type of socialization compatible with human rights education is that which treats the subject as a social being and as a dynamic, not just passive, agent of their own socialization.

Pre-school education in human rights is thus part and parcel of education, socialization and even acculturation. It cannot therefore be regarded as an adjunct, supplement or option tacked on to principles dispensed by the family. It accordingly calls for close collaboration between teachers and families. But there may still be conflicts of values. The role of violence, the acceptance of force as a means of settling inter-individual and/or inter-group disputes, the weight of obedience and authority in relations between adults and children, the importance attached to autonomy and personal initiative – all these are subjects of controversy and hence disagreement. In a context of multipolarization of values, the creation of an educational platform is a highly delicate undertaking. If we exclude extreme eventualities of total incomprehension or mutual intolerance, the educational contract may be drawn up either by seeking a common core ('lowest common denominator') between the various conceptions or by elucidating the points of divergence while learning to respect and, above all, understand them. Striving for homo-genization makes any consensus, even a minimum one, highly problematical. On the other hand, reciprocal clarification of references and refuge values will facilitate mutual understanding without requiring any acceptance of the other point of view. Dialogue and listening are the best safeguards against adamancy and its degeneration into intolerance. Indifference and negation invariably lead to extremist attitudes and reciprocal intolerance. Communi-cation and negotiation between the different partners responsible for the education of young children are therefore a prerequisite for any educational process.

In conclusion, we may fairly safely say that the first requirement regarding human rights education for the very young is respect for children, which in the present context means respect for all children's need for unity and har-mony. It will scarcely be necessary to stress how easily children can be affected by breaches, conflicts and contradictions between parents and schools, schools and nurseries, parents and child minders, etc.

The main idea to be noted is the concept of *educational project*, which by no means signifies a catalogue of educational activities but is a project agreed on between the principal parties which precisely demarcates the framework of the values adopted. This is not merely an objective but a very condition of education, for without some minimum references – such as those inherent in human rights – there can be no individual or collective structuring of identity. Consequently, the fact that a school or a pre-school establishment provides for human rights education, even on the best possible terms, is not enough in itself to ensure that the education will become a tangible reality and not remain a dead letter.

Thus, the first piece of advice to be given to teachers wishing to dispense a human rights education would be to enter into negotiations with the different partners involved in their pupils' education at this or that level and stage. Strangely enough, the teacher's first educational act takes place outside the school proper. Respect for a child demands actual marks of respect, not discourses on respect for children. Human rights and children's rights require deeds, not words.

PROPOSALS FOR ACTION

Since human rights education for children of pre-school age should avoid factual knowledge, three types of action at three levels may be envisaged:

- school life or life in the institution responsible for pre-school education outside the family unit;
- the values conveyed by human rights;
- the educational project as agreed with the children's families.

The last point has already been dealt with at some length and need not be dwelt on any further. Major difficulties are nevertheless posed by the conduct of such negotiations. By what procedure should they be conducted? On whose initiative? What is each partner's room for manoeuvre? The difficulties are compounded by the fact that it is easier to achieve agreement on the occupational and/or educational activities proposed than on the values they underpin both by their content and by the approaches adopted. Despite these obstacles, however, it should be clearly recognized that no human rights education is possible for the very young without the participation of their parents.

For reason of convenience the two other levels of action will be treated here separately though they are in fact mutually enriching.

Impregnation and examples are the two mainstays of education for young children. Rather than long speeches, it is an atmosphere, a daily routine marked by respect for everyone, that is needed. C. Schauder demonstrated at a Council of Europe seminar (Schauder, 1989) that human rights education ultimately depends on preparatory efforts, i.e. not so much on human rights *per se* as on the creation of conditions ensuring that human rights are respected long before a specific type of education is dispensed.

How should this educational approach be applied? It is accepted that '*early relationships induce a suffering that cannot be expressed and so must be suppressed, fostering the inoffensive or even outright secret development of the seat where hatred of others can blossom*' (Schauder, 1989, p. 13); a teacher's style should be based on listening, communication, attentiveness and alertness towards others so that a child may, in her own personal way, speak and above all express herself. Nowadays children are in contact not only with their parents: many people outside the family circle also play a part in their lives. Unfortunately this proliferation of educational influences makes for dispersal, as each part believes or prefers to believe that others are responsible for looking after the child. Educational responsibility is, as it were, being watered down, not because of any lack of qualified educators but, on the contrary, because there are so many, indeed too many in some cases. It follows that forestalling in early relations all disorders by ousting all forms of violence and suffering inflicted directly or indirectly on children – 'those outrages which are seen and heard and which produce "abused children", but also those which, though unobtrusive and insidious, permeate our educational and pedagogical methods' (Schauder, p. 15) – makes a contribution to human rights education by seeking to prevent racism, and not just cure or remedy it. Human rights education is often seen as a means of counteracting impulses of intolerance, xenophobia and racism. With very young children, however, a deliberately preventive approach should be adopted.

Teachers, educators and parents should be taught to detect all signs of suffering in children before they assume any dramatic or even pathological character, as well as identify any aspect of educational methods and personal relations that is liable to be a source of violence. It is not so much teachers' activities that should be developed as their ability to analyse the implicit level of communication systems – the verbal level, but also the non-verbal level (silences, attitudes, sighs and smiles, gestures and facial expressions, etc. are all meaningful indicators in the case of children). Being attentive to oneself and to others does not mean adopting a moralizing attitude; it requires an expertise that does not necessarily come naturally. There can scarcely be any need to emphasize that pre-school education depends more on know-how than on factual knowledge. Unfortunately, however, nursery schools still sometimes tend to ignore this truth and make a determined effort to dispense knowledge on the pretext that a child's brain is more receptive at that age.

It is also important to bear in mind various measures that have been taken to socialize children and make them more responsible and self-sufficient. Applied with a certain rigour and lucidity, the principles on which schools and children's education have been based for many years are consonant with human rights. The problem is not therefore one of defining new objectives but of pursuing them with the necessary discernment. Although it is unfortunately obvious that not all education is synonymous with human rights education, it would be wrong to think that human rights education can be defined only in terms of specific objectives. This implies that, in teacher training, analysis is more important than content. Teachers should be addressed in their capacity as individuals and human beings rather than in a professional capacity. Admittedly, this is no easy proposition, but it is an essential way of ensuring that human rights education is not reduced to being yet another subject on the curriculum.

Since it is not possible to give an exhaustive list, I shall choose one or two aspects of human rights that could serve as a basis for an education: an education in relations and diversity maybe regarded as a priority theme in so far as respect for human rights necessarily means respect for others and for their right to be different.

It is by no means a question of teaching children to be different but of teaching them to live their own identities amid a variety of other identities. This heterogeneity may be responded to in one of two ways: either by denying all other possible identities and insisting on a single monolithic vision; or by seeking harmony and coherence amid diversity. Only the latter approach derives directly from human rights. The problem to be solved, therefore, is that of educating young children in a plural, diversified and heterogeneous society so as to favour the emergence of a firm and dynamic identity while enabling other identities to be accepted without demure. The solution is not to create identities of a 'stronghold' kind and then attempt to educate them in open-mindedness but to recognize plurality from the outset as an integral part of socialization and acculturation.

Since words and speech cannot come to the assistance of practice, the educator has to rely on an impressionistic approach, on a permeation. It is no use trying to make children aware of the great humanitarian causes by means of spectacular actions that resort to dramatization. For one thing, very young children cannot grasp remote concepts; and, secondly, repeated appeals to their feelings merely blunt their sensitivity. Human rights education for the very young must therefore be based on the humility inherent in the daily round. Instead of a hard-hitting approach, encouragement should be given to the learning of diversity through experience and observation rather than through the acquisition of broad principles of respect presented outside the context of contemporary life.

Then why not, for example, substitute a heterocultural educational environment for a resolutely monocultural one? Miscellaneous objects, games and bilingual and/or foreign-language books, photographs, pictures and so on all offer opportunities for introducing diversity without embarking on a specific project or lecturing on respect for 'differences'. How would a child dare to display her cultural characteristics in a monolithic world? If all differences are respected, then her own differences will be respected implicitly and naturally. Morality in action is the best proof of respect. Teaching centred on the child as a particular object, along the lines of 'Show me what makes you different' or 'Tell us how you live at home', leads to a form of marginalization through excessive differentiation, as the child is treated as the object rather than subject of her singularity. It is wrong to impose a cultural identity in the name of respect for diversity; instead, everyone must be given a chance to express his or her identity. The right to 'non-differentiation' also exists! This desire is sometimes very strong in children and should not be neglected.

And since words are not the best way of communicating with very small children, teachers and educators should be familiarized with the different forms of non-verbal communication: postures, facial expressions, looks, proximity and touch are all ways of saying things or transmitting messages and hence potential sources of misunderstanding and disharmony. Games, attitudes, and ways of eating and sleeping can all convey conceptions and therefore misconceptions.

Accordingly, all activities designed to develop self-expression contribute in some way to this education in diversity. Aesthetic activities, in particular, lead directly to individualization, provided of course that they are not reduced to the inculcation of prevailing cultural tastes and values and thus to an abitrary definition of beauty based on set models. Work appealing to the imagination is an especially effective device as it is enhanced by diversity without singling out this or that form of difference. Reality, on the other hand, is more likely to engender attitudes of rejection, for putting things in perspective is a difficult 'art', particularly at such an age, whereas aesthetic creation thrives on a maximum of variety.

Another form of alertness to others is solidarity. This cannot be achieved simply by overcoming children's egocentricism. From the earliest age children should be confronted with tasks which require a number of complementary skills. This means not only developing group work but also organizing activities according to each child's potential contribution so as to promote a truly joint effort. If each child possesses only part of the solution, the result will depend on the group's ability to pool scattered elements.

These few thoughts do not exhaust the subject but, at the most, define its scope and indicate the spirit in which it should be approached. The wealth of experience of teachers and educators will advantageously compensate for the absence of specific examples. It would seem that the real challenge in human rights education for very young children lies not so much in the practical implementation of human rights as in the comprehension of objectives and of the general conditions for achieving them.

Although ubiquitous in child education, human rights do not constitute a subject requiring special teaching at particular times and by specific methods. And yet their requirements are no less great for all that. Being more diffuse, they call for even more rigour in the definition of objectives. As they form the basis of the educational contract, they are an integral part of the concept of an educational project and accordingly pose the true problems of education.

REFERENCES

Abdallah-Pretceille, M. (1989) Report on the 40th Council of Europe Teachers' Seminar *Human Rights Education in Pre-primary Schools*, 20–25 June 1988.

Ricoeur, P. (1985) 'Avant la loi morale: l'éthique', in *Encyclopaedia Universalis*, Symposium volume, Paris.

Schauder, C. (1989) 'A few points to stimulate thought on the birth of hatred of others', in *Human Rights Education in Pre-primary Schools*, op. cit.

Woodhead, M. (1979) *Pre-school Education in Western Europe: Issues, Policies and Trends*, Longman, London and New York, for the Council of Europe.

CHAPTER 5

Human Rights in Primary Education

Pauline Lyseight-Jones

THE ROLE AND NATURE OF PRIMARY EDUCATION

Primary education fulfils a pivotal role, together with the child's parents, in helping to form an individual to play a significant, compassionate role in society. The implicit sanctions on behaviour towards other people and to the self which are exemplified in the authority figure of the teacher are powerful influences for the young child.

In many countries innovation in teaching practice remains most vibrant in the primary sector. This is possibly due to the more family-orientated structure of the primary school or, less charitably, because the primary-age pupil's prospects are not constantly overshadowed by crucial state examinations which will affect the pupil's life-chances. A view which paradoxically helps this innovatory climate is a suspicion that primary education is not real education – real education happens in the secondary sector in the examination groups.

In the primary sector in Britain one finds vertical grouping, family grouping, and corporate decision-making of staff members and also of pupils and teachers. The climate of the school usually welcomes and nurtures the pastoral. Generally, the links with parents and community are strong. Parents are welcomed into the school to talk about their own child's education. They help in many constructive and essential ways in the classroom. Many primary schools have parents' rooms, and the schools encourage home visiting by staff and have close links with the social services so that school staff may play their part in helping parents and children who are in need.

In the primary sector there is always an understanding of the need for all adults involved with pupils to be carers, supporters, nurturers and developers. For all these reasons, the primary school is a fertile base for the building of human rights in education and human rights education.

There is anxiety, however, about the range of changes which are inevitable following the many recent Education Acts. The national curriculum and its assessment, the possibility of schools opting out of the state sector and becoming grant-maintained schools and the local management of schools, to name a few fundamental changes to the English and Welsh school systems, may mean a change in what is understood as good practice in primary education. As the balance of accountability changes, so parents and teachers may view their tasks in relation to pupils differently. This will present a challenge to human rights education in the primary school.

THE PAST COLOURING THE PRESENT AND THE FUTURE

During my teaching career I have never taught in a school where human rights education was explicitly featured in the curriculum. This is common. I can, however, in reviewing my career, identify specific points where I feel I operated in a way which upheld the principles of human rights education.

I remember having to make a case for the buying of texts which were not racially or gender biased; thinking of ways of ending the teaching day in an orderly fashion which did not involve saying, 'Girls first, now the boys'; arguing in the staffroom for the folklore of the institution not to be visited on individual children. I would hear 'All the children from that road are difficult', 'I taught his mother – hadn't got any sense – the child hasn't either', 'Her sister was trouble all of the time – I suppose she'll be the same'. I would try to give children space to talk to me and each other. We used to book in time at the end of each day – the whole class would get together for 30–45 minutes and the person or group who had booked the session would lead us in whatever they wanted to do. There was the questioning of implications in set texts, and a moving away from didactic modes of teaching so that the individual child could have a greater possibility of being happy in school through achieving an amount of success. There were other struggles, though we were not campaigning classes – I would not have been sufficiently confident to have supported the children in that. But we did have our own class group values. Name-calling, denigration and exclusivity were not supported. Independence, interdependence, responsibility and respect for the individuals' ability were supported.

In schools where I taught, the statements of the schools' aims could broadly be called human rights based. Yet, the statements had been devised by the headteacher with minor adjustments made to them by staff. They described what the school wanted from pupils: cleanliness, compassion and good conduct. Within the statements of the school aims there was no indication of a reciprocity apart from the opening, anodyne phrase, typically 'we aim to provide every pupil with an education appropriate to their needs and ability'.

My next career step found me teaching in an institution of higher education while having a brief related to race equality across the county. Here I had to impress upon student teachers, graduate teachers, and headteachers and their staff the underlying factors which inform the implementation of race equality in practice in educational institutions. That exposition had to involve examination of 'other equalities'. At this point I used to teach explicitly about human rights education within the context of modules on the curriculum.

Now, as a primary phase inspector, in London, I seem to have fewer opportunities to promote human rights education. After all, the delivery of a human rights curriculum is not primarily in my hands but in the hands of school staffs and headteachers. I can try to ensure that the school does not break the laws which we have – for example, the Race Relations Act of 1976 or the Sex Discrimination Act – yet the growing autonomy of schools following the Education Reform Act 1988 leaves local education authorities and local inspectorates with lessening power (if they ever had any) and only the leverage of influence and advice. Local inspectorates now have largely a monitoring and evaluation role in relation to the degree to which a school is delivering the national curriculum and providing appropriate resources and levels of staffing.

Clearly, advice given to schools on the curriculum and other matters will affect the life-chances of the pupils in the school if the advice is taken. Yet inspectors also know that, in the primary school, the teaching staff have a great need for support, for an eye to be kept on their rights, and for recognition to be given to their integrity and ability, perhaps even more than in the past. For our children to be successfully educated in the primary phase they have to be happy and well-motivated. I believe that our pupils have a right to expect that happiness and appropriate motivation should occur in school because it is unlawful for pupils of compulsory school age not to receive an education. For the vast majority of children that education takes place in the state education system. Pupils have no choice as to whether or not they attend school. Teachers do have a choice. They need not choose teaching. They need not stay in teaching once it becomes arduous or disheartening. Teachers have no right to take out their discontents on their pupils.

My concern is how we can ensure that pupils are happy and well-motivated when the morale of many good teachers is being diminished. Without high esteem, happiness and self-motivation amongst teachers, pupils will suffer educationally and emotionally. A primary phase inspector has to recognize the ways in which teachers are becoming de-skilled and seek to redress the balance. I heard someone say some time ago that the oppressed and the degraded are not necessarily going to be attractive. The more demoralized our teaching force becomes, the less likely it is to realize the legitimacy of human rights education.

Given the problems of low morale, the implementation of human rights education in the primary school seems an enormous challenge. But stress is not only negative. A recent report (Rees, 1989) cites Selye.

> It has been maintained that stress is a necessary condition of life, since without stimulus an organism will die, and the distinction has therefore been drawn between 'eustress' and 'distress'. At one extreme (eustress) this is the situation which can be described as stimulating, challenging and exhilarating; at the other a situation which is threatening, disturbing, distressing.

An important argument in favour of human rights education is that human rights educators can expect to experience much 'eustress' and the minimum of distress.

Inspectors are acutely aware of constraints of time. Human rights educators need time, as I described earlier. At the moment, teachers do not have enough time to cope with their present workloads and therefore do not do tasks as well as they ought. Rees (1989) writes

> Many teachers attempt to deal with their excessive workload by arriving at work early or by working for several hours in the evening and at weekends: as a consequence they become progressively more tired, and are eventually unable to continue to use this as a coping strategy. Not only does this deprive them of the feeling of satisfaction that comes from satisfactory completion of a task, but it also makes them feel guilty for not putting in the extra time and effort which might enable them to feel 'on top of things'

This context of lack of time and feelings of failure underlines the necessity for human rights education in the primary school to be part of a teacher's day-to-day operation – not a cumbersome and non-relevant addition. This may mean that for the primary school to become a human rights school regard has to be given to the processes and practices in the school which contribute towards the lack of worthwhile time which a teacher has at their disposal. Without this a new initiative will shrivel or be perpetuated as merely a tokenistic gesture (Lyseight-Jones, 1990).

A further problem is that teachers are transmitters of social norms. To act against such norms can sometimes be anti-professional, anarchistic, inhumane, amoral or crucial. For instance, the educator can be tied within a very strong state establishment which may dictate both curriculum and syllabus content. Furthermore, the individual's school may be a model of dictatorial, hierarchical, non-participative repression. The human rights educator may, therefore, be working for change which is not readily acceptable to other teachers or to parents. In such a situation, conflict inevitably arises because of the mismatch of interests and ideals between protagonists.

On the other hand, as a parent of school-age children I have seen the effect of their being at the receiving end of inequities visited upon them by particular teaching staff. I have seen the catastrophic effect on a child's self-confidence and stability of a teacher's low expectation and lack of respect for that child's ability. I have been at the receiving end of stereotyped responses from teachers who suppose that because 'some children in this school have language difficulties' that all of the children do, of a teacher whose religious beliefs resulted in her class group having a narrow and unstimulating year and of a teacher who gave his pupils a topic entitled 'Cavemen' and looked genuinely perplexed when we asked about cavewomen and cave girls and boys. I have experience, as a parent, of a school where the children were allowed to use only pencils for writing. They changed to pens when they were in year 7 (11–12 years old). These may seem like tiny examples of dis-ease but the effect, cumulatively, that these episodes had and are having on the life-chances of the primary-age pupils in the school are too serious to be considered deeply without shuddering.

The children in the school to which I am referring are of primary age. The school contains some good and a range of less good staff members – most seem to be operating at less than par. The parents of pupils at the school are unlikely to be able to compare the education and ethos of the school with any other as the school takes children from 3 years to 12 years. The children in the school come from a wide range of backgrounds – middle class and prosperous, working class and prosperous or not so prosperous, immigrant families from Pakistan and India, whose children are operating in two or three languages from about the age of five, and itinerant families. The great majority of the pupils are from South Asian backgrounds. There are many Sikh and Muslim pupils. The school is not extraordinary – except that it triumphs rather less than I should wish. How can human rights education come to that primary school?

THE SCHOOL AS AN INSTITUTION

For a primary school to operate successfully in a way which upholds human rights principles requires staff, pupils and parents to recognize the values which the school upholds, to agree with them and to promote them. This is also a prerequisite in a school which chooses to be academic or sports orientated. The Inner London Education Authority Junior School Survey in 1987 listed factors which had emerged as being determinants in 'the development of a good school'. Firm leadership from the headteacher was one of the 12 values. Intriguingly, so was 'Being a church school'. I tried to think why this should be so. I concluded that, whatever else a church school is, it is a place of shared values and compacts. There is a contract about the way in which the institution operates which involves staff, parents and pupils. This contract is understood before pupils enter the school and before staff members are employed. Frequently, staff, pupils and parents are required to be part of a faith community and are required to have evidence of recent practice in that faith community. In a country like England where there is an Established Church and where religious studies and collective worship are a legal requirement, surprisingly our state schools are largely void of a definite set or range of spiritual and moral values. Let me pause for a while lest I be charged with advocating a revival of the church school in its most fundamentalist of forms. My point is that for many pupils, teachers and parents the state school (for I know little of the independent sector) has no apparent shared value system. Where there are shared values they focus on what should not occur.

If there is a value system it confers neither rights nor responsibilities. The criteria by which decisions are made are secret and probably flexible, giving the decision-maker much scope for manipulation, whether benign or not.

A focal role for the human rights educator is thus to help a school to define the values which it shares, the unbreakable tenets of that value system, the negotiable elements of it, the operationalizing of it and the publicity which should surround its development, implementation and revision. This process may be helped when there is a statement of policy to refer to.

As I have seen no local education authority policy statements on human rights education, my examples come from the area of race equality. Berkshire's policy on education for racial equality (Director of Education, 1983) was radical, so much so that it caused scepticism and ridicule – among other more favourable reactions. Its value was in its modification. Let me explain. Teachers in schools had been trying to make changes regarding education for racial equality. Their efforts had been missing high-level legitimization. The new policy gave them legitimacy, theory, principle and directions for practice. Teachers operating in their own institutions moderated (not diminished) the policy. In doing so they were able to make progress on education for racial equality in excess of what may have occurred in the absence of a policy.[1]

Hampshire Local Education Authority has produced a fulsome statement on education for a multicultural society. Its idealism is demonstrated in brief statements like 'commitment to the need for action – Positive response based upon value position, educational philosophy etc. . . . .' 'Policy dissemination – Promotion to parents and the community' (Education Department, 1988). Policies such as these provide a necessary element of idealism. As schools use them and implement them, this idealism confronts the problematic reality. But human rights education needs both idealism and realism.

Policies may refer to specific features of schools. The hidden or the informal curriculum is an important area which has to be addressed in the primary school. A statement from one outer London local education authority states:

> On the physical side, school buildings, their arrangement of furniture, and the provision of learning materials, equipment and their use by different [sic] sexes all make a great impact. As profound an effect on the personal and academic development of children is made by emotive elements. These include school rules and procedures, the values that are promoted, teaching practices, role models and methods of assessment. All important are the attitudes of children, staff and parents to each other and to the work of the school.
>
> We take the greatest pains to see that the Informal Curriculum is as free as possible of those traditional practices and attitudes which, perhaps unintentionally, discriminate against one group or another (London Borough of Ealing Inspection and Advisory Service, 1989).

In 1985, following a Council of Europe seminar on human rights education in the primary school, I wrote (Lyseight-Jones, 1985):

The teacher should try to examine what the children may be learning from the hidden curriculum

People are able to pick up non-verbal messages from each other in a very efficient way. The two-way traffic of such messages does not end outside the classroom door.

Teachers wishing to have human rights issues as the basis and bedrock for their work may be found unconvincing if:

1. talking is only permitted when sanctioned by the teacher;
2. children have to seek public and specific permission to use the bathroom;
3. sanctions are irrelevant, unjust and unfair;
4. grading systems are used whose main purpose is the identification of an elite and which promote the few at the expense of many;
5. children's family patterns are not respected by the teacher;
6. the teacher makes little effort to have in the classroom items and information which are familiar to the children and their background;
7. decisions are made by the teacher alone;
8. the teacher does not see that there is a place for humour and levity in the classroom, among and across the class group, as well as residing in the teacher.

All of the above indicate just a few facets of the hidden curriculum which may serve to expose fine words as being just a ruse to cover up a lack of commitment to the principles of human rights teaching.

I had not read that last sentence for some time, two or three years. It comes over to me now as angry. Yet it still seems valid. Hypocrisy will always be an enemy of human rights education – especially with young children where loss of faith can have such far-reaching effects. My hope is that I do not too often confuse hypocrisy with humanity and fallibility.

RELATIONSHIPS OF PARENTS AND SCHOOLS: CONFLICTING RIGHTS

We have noted earlier that shared values are a factor for success in primary schools. Parents have not always been considered as partners in the formulation of shared values. However, in order to be a member of staff in a human rights school one has to acknowledge, respect and nurture the compact and partnership with parents, regardless of whether the parent is personally liked or not liked. Schools which I have visited have shown various responses to the reality of partnership with parents. These include:

- curriculum evenings;
- social events;
- the provision of a parents' room;
- language classes with a creche provided;
- parents being taught how to teach a facet of a curriculum and then working with small groups once weekly;
- management of the library;
- assistance in home economics, reading, computer study;
- parent–teacher associations;
- speaking at school assemblies;

- groups of children visiting parents' workplaces;
- open visiting system;
- translation of relevant materials into necessary languages;
- seating and shelter made available when parents come to collect their children;
- home visiting;
- liaising with social services agencies.

These developments present the teacher with a problem, for teachers have a right to enjoy domestic life and leisure as well as obligations to fulfil professional commitments. They face directly and personally an issue of conflicting rights. Rees (1989) paints a succinct picture of this phenomenon, while commenting on the 'work/home interface', 'that is, the way in which work fits in (or does not fit in) with private life'.

> This appears to be a source of pressure among teachers. While there was an acceptance that a certain amount of preparation, marking and routine administrative work need to be done outside the teaching day, many felt that their evenings were so taken up with work that it was an unacceptable encroachment on their private lives. This meant that they were unable to relax and enjoy a period of recreation in the evenings, and so were not able to go into the classroom the next day feeling alert and able to cope with the demands of a lively or difficult class. In addition, the amount of work done in the evenings meant that they grew progressively more exhausted as the week, and then the term, wore on.
>
> For some teachers, the obligation to attend a number of after school meetings (in directed time) posed a further problem in relation to their home life. Those with very young children might have to make special arrangements with a childminder, and even those with children of school age might have to make special arrangements for them to be collected from school.

The partnership with parents at primary phase requires accessibility of parent to teacher and vice versa. Teachers are not usually able to leave their pupils during the teaching day. In consequence they have to meet parents before school begins, in the lunchtime or, more usually, after school or in the evening. The teacher with young children who are at a school other than the one in which the teacher is employed has to play their part as parent partner to their child's teacher. The conflicts in time and energy are apparent and inevitable. What can be done – the burden of guilt is as much on the teacher-parent who has missed a meeting as on the worker-parent whose work shift militated against getting to a school meeting? I believe that partnership does not mean abdication of responsibility. As much as a school needs to work with parents, the greatest achievement of a school is that it shows constant capability through its staff to support each individual child. While that capability is informed by parental involvement in education, it should not (and in reality, cannot) be predicated upon it.

While continuing with the theme of conflicting rights, it is idealistic to say that there is no hierarchy of rights. Reality requires us to make such discriminatory decisions daily. If a child is being ill-treated, what is the teacher to do? If a teacher suspects that a child is being abused, what is he or she to do? If a child comes to school tired because of having to work late each night, what is to be done? If a child acts in a racist or sexist or violent way at school and such actions are condoned by the home, what action should be taken? Conflicts between the rights of the parents and the rights of the child are frequent. What judgement should teachers make? A possibility is that the rights of the weaker or less powerful or less protected party should have precedence when action is being considered.

CHANGING ATTITUDES

The possibility of changing the views of people, as distinct from the processes and practices which they follow, seems to recede as people get older. This is not a function of increasing age but of evidence of people's views being shown to be appropriate in practice. The self-fulfilling prophecy begins to be confused with notions of truth. The notions of truth become fact. These facts of experience are then the framework for the individual's own notions of justice and equality.

Three examples of this process might be:

1. Black people are shown in books to be exotic and different from me – I meet few black people – when I meet black people we seem not to have anything in common – we can't speak to each other – black people's concepts of white society are not in accord with white society – black people could be judged to be anarchistic and therefore have to be treated harshly by the judicial (and social) systems of white society – police brutality to black people is tacitly condoned.
2. Disabled people are not in my school – disabled people are taught separately from me and live separately from me – disabled people are different from me, are less than me – disabled people are not whole people, and therefore other people have to speak for them – disability is not part of a vision of the 'normal' world – disabled people should not reproduce in case the disability is reproduced – the progeny would be a burden on the working people of the society – it is right to compulsorily sterilize mentally or physically disabled people and to condemn all sexual relations of disabled people.
3. Immigrant people are in my school – they have to go to special classes away from the rest of the class – this happens because they are not as bright as us – they don't play with us in the playground and they don't speak English properly – they don't want to be with us – they didn't have to come here – we don't owe them anything – their rights to social security benefits should be questioned very closely.

In these and other similar scenarios, the individuals holding these constructs cannot be held to be prejudiced. Their views have been formed and confirmed by their own experience. Yet such views cannot further the greater vision of equity and justice for all people, corporately and individually. The task of the primary educator is to widen the knowledge and experience base of the individual. Paths to this widening involve analysis, review and hypothesizing.

Even teachers may have such a narrow base of knowledge and experience. A teacher may hold a stereotype in a child's name – what do Patel, Hofstedt, de Freitas, Papritz or O'Sullivan mean to you? At a course which I attended[2] we were given an outline of a problem involving either a teacher or a child. Unbeknown to course members, other groups at the course had been given the same problem with either the name of the focal actor or the name *and* sex changed. For instance, a 15-year-old girl who wanted to leave school to get married with her parents' blessing would have been, say, Neelam Dhardvar in one account or Patricia Davies in another. Consideration of the home background with presumptions of arranged marriages under duress were considered as part of the discussion on Neelam. Patricia Davies was adjudged as sufficiently sensible to be making the decision on good grounds and on her own judgement. This exercise is a salutary one for all liberal-minded people who believe that they have generally got their principles and prejudices in order.

Children *as a group* have less experience vicariously or theoretically of the possibilities of humankind. The teacher at primary phase is expected to broaden the experience base for pupils. The human rights educator would expect that ethnic minority people, women, disabled people and itinerant people (among the largely disadvantaged groups) are not looked down upon by their pupils. In the case of gender equality there is usually no difficulty in using the children's and the teacher's own experience, as most of our schools are coeducational and our streets, shops and televisions are also able to display a range of versions of men and women constantly. To denigrate women as a class denigrates our own mothers, aunts, grandmothers and childminders. To diminish girls diminishes our own sisters, nieces, aunts, and so on. But who is affected when someone passes comment on the shortcomings of the disabled? Who will notice the omission of the values of the itinerant in a project on houses?

While not advocating a hierarchy of 'equalities' it is clear that in England now the probability is that the only equality which one can expect pupils to have in their own experience is that of gender equality or inequality. The toddler in Barnstaple who called out 'Look, there's a black girl', the young men in Kirbymoorside who shouted 'Yeah, man' from a speeding car to a black stranger, and the judge who said that 'Chink' was not a derogatory term for Chinese people are victims of first-hand ignorance and second-hand gullibility. Their experience of black people comes via the media and is not moderated by educators, given that the educators are in the same position. Today, or maybe tomorrow, look through the journals which you have in your home and look for two things – firstly, disabled people in active leadership roles which are not newsworthy because the person is disabled, and secondly, black people in colour pictures who are happy and not illustrating a charity programme, athletics or tourism. This lack of other images Gillian Klein characterizes as 'residue'. The primary phase educator has to guard against this residue of images and preconceptions being laid down and impacted. To do this they must look to their own conceptions of people and their knowledge of peoples who are not like them.

The primary-phase human rights educator needs to take action to promote positive views of others. It is not enough that there does not seem to be in the class base evidence of negative views.

MATERIALS AND RESOURCES

Human rights education is informed by lots of other 'educations' (peace, political, development etc.). To realize human rights education it is not sufficient to collect enough project packs from each of the other disciplines and put them into the school resources base. Nor is it sufficient to take the project packs from the base and use them with the pupils. The process is the important factor and the child is the beginning. However, materials are, of course, essential. Here are a few, brief thoughts:

- It is necessary to use authentic voices and in using authentic voices to use a range of voices. It may be commendable to have some books in the school library on Jamaica. It is better if they are books which have been produced in Jamaica by Jamaican people. It is better still if they depict a range of versions of Jamaica. It is clear that one author is not a nation nor is one book in a primary school library on a city in India a definitive voice. For those of you who know London personally, does its daily life accord with the encapsulated vision of it in children's reference books – a world of rampant pageantry, costermongers' cries, Carnaby Street and pearly kings and queens? Why should the depictions of places or situations that we do not know well be any more accurate or truthful?
- It is also worth remembering that until oral history projects developed, writing was almost totally an occupation of the middle classes. Accounts and views as evidence in books in our classrooms are largely as mediated by the middle class. This does not make them accurate. I condemn myself here. Yet I know that some (most?) of the battles which I fight are an irrelevance to people who have to fight daily for survival – in Britain and elsewhere. A little thing, like being called Ms, is just that – a very small item. In the context of my life it meant a little step towards being my own person; to a woman on family credit there would be no thought of refusing to accept an order book because it did not say 'Ms'. The honesty is in accepting that we write from our own contexts and in not being reticent about explaining what that context is.
- It is necessary to know of reference works which will help when accessing resources so that the presence of sexism, racism and other offences are minimized or eliminated (e.g. Michel, 1986).

- It is necessary to look for compilations of papers or accounts from other histories and other standpoints in those histories – 'others' meaning not your own (e.g. Black, 1983).
- It is necessary to remember that there is the development of thought over time. The view held of William Wilberforce nowadays is not necessarily of his being a jolly nice man who freed the slaves but as someone with a close eye on his own pecuniary interests. It may be worth considering what is a riot, what is a rebellion and what is an uprising? What is a guerrilla, what is a freedom fighter and what is a terrorist? What is a democracy, what is a dictatorship, what is a right-wing democracy, what is a left-wing dictatorship? We do not necessarily have to know where we stand on these issues but we should be able to acknowledge the bias in texts and to be personally equipped with the skills and confidence to assist our pupils to take account of that bias when using texts provided in school and from elsewhere.
- It is necessary to remember that people need their histories – as individuals, as families, as nations. An interdependent world requires the realism in our resources to acknowledge that there were Victorians in the Caribbean and they were not white. There were Victorians in India and they were also not white.
- I am reminded of a David Lodge novel where he explains that one decoding is another encoding. For you to agree that I have received what you have said, reiteration unchanged is not sufficient. You must reinterpret it and see if I agree that that was what I had meant. This underlines the use of primary sources or compilations of them and the use of authentic voices. A friend from Ghana said, 'You call it the extended family, we call it the family.'

TEACHING AND LEARNING STYLES

Human rights education begins with the individual. In this it accords with good primary practice. There are many versions of the factors which have to be taken into account when considering the individual child. They are all as good as each other; they all seek to define the whole through the parts. I tend to consider the whole child as being contributed to by academic, social, moral/spiritual and physical/creative factors. A human rights approach to primary education has to take cognizance of all of these. What tends to happen is that one or two of these factors predominates as a constituent of the school's ethos. This may lead to the life-chances of many children being altered or diminished through the lack of an opportunity, in the primary phase, to reach the widest bounds of their ability and personality.

Could this be just a counsel of perfection born of being out of the classroom for far too long? I know that these were my concerns as a teacher and how I attempt to live now. I regularly fail miserably, of course. It is hard to make just decisions when they go against my own preferences; I am not sweetness and light in business meetings; my family would not characterize my nature as placid, joyous and predictable. Yet I do know where I stand when it comes to justice amongst people. I know that I am culpable if an injustice is done and I do not speak out or take action at the time. I know that there is a time when I have to stop holding my parents responsible for who I am, and to take responsibility myself. There is no room for adults to use a defence of 'I was only obeying orders'.

'The spirit of the principles [of the Universal Declaration of Human Rights] is needed in every school from the first day', wrote Hans Fuglsang (Lyseight-Jones, 1985). What kind of teacher and what style of teaching will uphold such a statement? The teacher needs to work to:

- build trust within the class group;
- establish a mode of working together;
- promote free discussion;
- advocate conflict resolution without aggression;
- develop in class members responsibilities to those outside of the class group;
- devise problem-solving techniques which need not be teacher-orientated;
- be prepared to take action for change.

The teacher should:

1. *Try to avoid corporate monologues* – that is, believing that a change of views is happening just because more than one person contributes to the discussion. Discussion involves listening and analytical skills.

2. *Try to develop the group process within the classroom* – this would involve working on projects within and without the classroom which involve group responsibility and which provide areas for the peaceful resolution of conflict.

3. *Try to relinquish authorization elements of the teacher's role while remaining a responsible adult.* A teacher cannot relinquish responsibilities which are legally or morally binding in respect of pupils, but some elements of teaching style are matters of custom and will certainly not promote an ethos in which human rights education can flourish.

4. *Try to ensure that time is given within the school day for problems to be talked over.* There can be no free exchange of ideas if the school day is organized in such a way that the young child has to think only of particular subjects or tasks and has no time to discuss matters which are personally important to the child or important to the development of the class group.

5. *Try to encourage enquiry by the use of open-ended questions.* The area of human rights is full of contradictions and complications. The human rights teacher should not insist on each question having an answer and each answer being regarded as 'right' or 'wrong'. It would be impossible to discuss marriage, war, employment etc. with a class if that was the case.

6. *Try to develop teamwork with other teachers.* This should help them to understand the group process with the class group and could lead to

work across the age ranges as well as the development of corporate projects.

7. *Try to make time to watch children at play and to make time for social activities in class.* It is at play that the influence of leaders of the group and opinion are visible. It is at play where it can be seen whether children are isolated willingly or unwillingly. It is at play where one sees conflicts arise which will inevitably be brought into the classroom. It is at play where one can assess whether problem-solving or conflict resolution techniques are actually working.

8. *Try to make time to talk to children privately.* If circumstances within the class promote wide discussion and trust in the group, then children will feel able to confide. Sometimes, those confidences are most appropriately told in private. The aims of human rights education are not fulfilled by one family's secrets being reported to the class and then relayed to adults at home.

9. *Try to make time to return to important topics.* Sometimes a teacher has to take a risk when expanding upon an important issue. It is possible that just a few children in the class will be on the brink of understanding it. This means that other times must be found to reiterate points made and issues raised to try to ensure that as many children as possible are being reached.

The statements made above are certainly conducive to child–centred learning. One outer London Borough puts it in this way (London Borough of Ealing Inspection and Advisory Service, 1989) child-centred learning 'promotes learning by discovery and questioning'. It means creating a flexible timetable. It involves pupils in active research not just within the school but at home and in the community as well. We all learn best through experience. Traditional techniques also have their place but child-centred learning recognizes this crucial fact, and provides effective means by which we honour the rights of every child who passes through our schools.

Clearly if children are accorded such an education which allows them self-respect, respect for others and the possibility of personal growth then spectres of prejudice may conceivably fade or be disarmed.

In interviewing for primary teachers we ask a question which is concerned with sensitive pastoral support for a child and with the creation of a working environment which is fruitful for all who work within it. We sometimes ask two related questions:

'How do you help children to feel good about themselves?'
'How do you help children to feel good about other people?'

We need to praise, and to encourage assertiveness, sensitivity and reflectiveness. We need to help our pupils to understand structures and processes – their variety, constraints and advantages. In some primary schools this is done through the mechanism of the school council. Typically each class group elects one or two councillors. Matters which are of importance to pupils, whether raised by students or staff, are debated in it. This exercise is meant to demonstrate democracy in action. For this to have any deeper reality the nature of delegate or representative councillors needs to be discussed. The staff also have to demonstrate that the council has an integral and decision-making role in the school and that the staff decision-making processes are themselves exemplars of democracy in action.

TEACHING ON HUMAN RIGHTS

Much has been written on this topic. Materials are readily available to support the class teacher in some depth and detail.

It is necessary to consider the balance of human rights education delivered through permeation of a system (school) and that which is explicitly taught. It is clearly a nonsense if class teachers focus on human rights yet pupils see examples of injustice in abundance in every other facet of school life. Within a teacher's own class base a session on campaigning for the building of sheltered housing for the mentally handicapped cannot be followed by that teacher calling a lower-ability child or a child with learning difficulties 'stupid'. Let that be left to be considered.

'The greater the understanding of justice, and the application of its principles, the more likely a reduction in prejudice and discrimination will occur.' With younger children it is not appropriate to have a human rights lesson. The issues have to be presented through many different activities. The broad nature of human rights education predisposes teachers towards choosing the best elements of many different disciplines. Participants at the Donaueschingen Seminar 1985 gave examples of ways in to human rights teaching in the primary school. Some examples are noted here.

Concepts

Winning, Losing, Fairness

- Help children to handle both winning and losing.
- Use sports and games activities as examples.

Justice and Equality

- Use fairy tales, myths and legends to try to help children to manage these issues and to deal with some emotions.
- Use the drama method for conflict resolution and for acting out situations which are different for children to relate to in another way.

Trust and Co-operation

Encourage individual responsibility and abide by decisions which have been corporately made:

- Use a class council as a forum to discuss class matters openly.
- Use exercises from the drama method to promote trust; for instance,

blindfolding class members and having a partner lead them around the class or school.

Project Possibilities

Comics

Use comics which are read by the class as a jumping off point for a series of activities:

1. Looking at depictions of war. Comics tend not to show war scenes from post-World War II conflicts. This means that children may not be aware of modern weaponry, may hold stereotypical views of the Germans or Japanese people and may only read about scenes leading up to battle and possibly the battles themselves but not the consequences.
2. A visit to a war memorial or cemetery may be relevant for older children. The purpose would be to show that there are irreversible consequences to violent conflict.

Daily Life across the Generations

Looking back to the time of the children's grandparents may be a way of showing what children have achieved as rights which were not seen to be applicable 40 or 50 years ago. Free speech and freedom from certain types of punishment are possibilities.

How Little I Am

Develop further an idea which defines peace more widely than just an absence of war:

- paint peace;
- paint war;
- compare the processes.

My Rights

Children are asked to list what they feel are their rights as children:

- They compare their findings, and, as a class or in groups, try to pick out the rights which occur most frequently on the lists.
- Compare these with the United Nations Declaration on the Rights of the Child (1959) or the Convention of the Rights of the Child (1989) and discuss the similarities and the anomalies.

Mass Media

Consider the messages which are transmitted to many schools via radio and television:

- Have children consider how far the events depicted are recognizable from their own experience.
- Discuss how children may decide on the accuracy of representation of what they do not know from first-hand experience.

- Discuss or rescreen television programmes which children have been talking about or generally watch.
- Discuss the kinds of view which are taken as usual, the style of dress, standard of housing and cognizance of outside events which occurs in the programmes.
- Take action by writing to the programme writer or producer if the class believes that the programme is unjust, unfair, biased (by omission or commission) or xenophobic.

NOTES

1 In working with Berkshire teachers in implementing the policy on education for racial equality I found that some teachers were glad of the authority of the policy because it gave legitimacy to what they had been trying to achieve in their schools but with little success. Equality issues suffered from status and priority problems when compared to mathematics.

2 This was a gender equality course, run by the Gender Equality Team, London Borough of Ealing, in 1987 for the Ealing Education Inspectorate.

REFERENCES

Black, C. V. (1983) *History of Jamaica*, Longman, Harlow. The history is told by the government archivist.

Director of Education (1983) *Education for Racial Equality: policy papers 1, 2 and 3*, Royal County of Berkshire.

Education Department (1988) *Education for a Multicultural Society*, Hampshire County Council.

London Borough of Ealing Inspection and Advisory Service (1989) *In Ealing Every Child Is Given Space to Grow: Towards a Charter for All Children at School*, London Borough of Ealing.

Lyseight-Jones, P. E. (1985) *Council of Europe Teachers' Seminar on Human Rights in Primary Schools*, Council of Europe DECS/EGT (85) 46–E.

Lyseight-Jones, P. E. (1990) 'A management of change perspective – turning the whole school around', in Coles, M. (ed.) *Education for Equality*, Routledge Education, London.

Michel, A. (1986) *Down with Stereotypes! Eliminating Sexism from Children's Literature and School Textbooks*, UNESCO.

Rees, F. (1989) *Teacher Stress: An Exploratory Study*, NFER, Slough.

CHAPTER 6

The Human Rights Secondary School

Jeremy Cunningham

Schools are communities which can, and should be, an example of respect for the dignity of the individual and for difference, for tolerance, and for equality of opportunity, *Council of Europe Recommendation No. R (85) 7.*

States Parties agree that the education of the child shall be directed to . . . (b) the development of respect for human rights and fundamental freedoms, and for the principles enshrined in the Charter of the United Nations.

States Parties shall take all appropriate measures to ensure that school discipline is administered in a manner consistent with the child's human dignity and in conformity with the present Convention. *UN Convention on the Rights of the Child, 1989.*

FRAMEWORK

The great human rights documents of our time make it quite clear that education is to be directed towards the fulfilment of individual potential and the support of justice and peace. They implicitly reject the assumption that children are the slaves of their parents or of the state. States should not be organizing educational policy along totalitarian lines for the greater power of the state itself. Parents should not be exploiting children for immediate economic gain at the expense of their long-term intellectual and emotional growth.

Schools are intermediate institutions between parents and the state. They can be used for political socialization where states have strong centralized education systems. In return for the right to universal education, parents accept the state's compulsion and in many countries its tight control of curriculum. On the other hand the teachers are given the responsibilities of parents for the hours that the children are in school. They are assumed to be caring for children rather than exploiting them and as well as teaching information they have a moral duty to provide a fair structure of rules which create the ordered community of learning. In Britain, where the common law has had to decide on the limits to teachers' authority, the Latin term *in loco parentis* (in the parent's position) has been the basic principle. The contract between school and parents was of the type 'Hand her over to us and we'll manage everything just as you would.'

This approach is relatively problem-free where home values and school values are identical. For example, parents who use corporal punishment on their children are unlikely to complain about a schoolteacher doing the same. However, it causes difficulties where values are different. In a state school system, many parents have no option but to send their children to the nearest school, and the systems or values of that school may be abhorrent to the parents. If the parents' values are those of a small minority their chances of changing school policy are slight, but society's values are changing all the time, and human rights texts may start as statements of principle to be aspired to and later become legal conventions with legal force and direct effect on policies. The decision of a Scottish family to fight their neighbourhood school's use of corporal punishment led eventually, via the European Court, to the abolition of caning in all British state schools.

The idea of the child itself being a passive party in the contract between state/school and parent is changing too. As more becomes known about the exploitation, and physical and sexual abuse suffered by many children, absolute parental power seems less and less acceptable. The UN Convention on the Rights of the Child provides a clearer and firmer foundation for children as individual legal entities than anything that has existed before. The working group tackled the difficult issue of the growth from absolute dependence to autonomy. For example, Article 14 has 'States Parties shall respect the right of the child to freedom of thought, conscience and religion', and 'States Parties shall respect the rights and duties of the parents and, when applicable, legal guardians, to provide direction to the child in the exercise of his or her right in a manner consistent with the evolving capacities of the child'. Schools acting as 'reasonable parents' should recognize that parents' powers lie in the framework of international legislation as well as the mores of their particular society. Should it be thought that documents like the UN Convention are far removed from reality, it is worth recalling that child abuse legislation has removed the assumption that a child's testimony is automatically less trustworthy than an adult's. The acceptance that evidence can be given on videotape suggests that children are being afforded legal rights to counterbalance their relative powerlessness against adults. At the same time there are great difficulties in industrialized countries where young people have increasing spending power without commensurate opportunities for stable employment and the exercise of responsibility.

The balance between rights and responsibilities is of great importance in schools, where the developments outlined above are affecting the climate in which teachers have to apply their authority. The increased emphasis on the care of the individual, awareness of special needs and equal opportunities is coupled with a greater insistence by parents that they have rights too. In some countries legislation has given parents more chances to become involved in school policies. The teacher's task is to reconcile what may be conflicting demands of state, parents and children. The main international declarations and conventions on human rights provide an essential foundation for this task.

ETHOS

School atmosphere or ethos is the result of the combined actions of all members of the school community. Although this is not necessarily the result of conscious policies, where a school is working to a baseline of shared, openly expressed principles the ethos is easily perceived by anyone who spends even a short time there. Because it is the intangible 'soul' of the school it is difficult at first to think about how it can be developed, but the clue lies in the team nature of the school. Staff, students, parents and the wider community are partners in the enterprise, and there are ways of encouraging a particular ethos by carefully planned actions which lie inside a framework of principles. That framework should be human rights and responsibilities.

That is not to say that everything that happens in school can be measured against major international human rights conventions, but that in multi-ethnic, highly mobile and information-overloaded societies schools which have not thought about the moral aspects of their work are in danger of acting in mechanical fashion. 'The rules are the rules because they are rules' means playing for short-term order at the expense of long-term moral development. Strongly religious schools have no difficulty with this approach to ethos because they are working to commonly understood and accepted principles. Schools caring for communities with mixed social and religious backgrounds must base their work on more all-embracing principles than those found in any one religion, and indeed must allow for variety of religions and political beliefs.

The headteacher has the main responsibility for ensuring that all the partners develop a shared understanding of the essential principles. Whatever the style of leadership, there has to be open communication, consultation and debate. Unless people have the opportunity to engage in discussion, statements of values are likely to be followed more in theory than in practice. The notion of an authoritarian leader setting down human rights principles and then telling everyone to get on with the task of applying them is a ridiculous one.

All members of the school community are entitled to dignity and respect. That means students, teachers, non-teaching assistants, caretakers, cleaners, and parents. It also means fair treatment irrespective of race, gender, age, capability, social class, or religion. The head has particular responsibility for ensuring that the staff has a good programme of staff development with regular opportunities for guidance, counselling and training. Recruitment and promotion policy should be explicitly based on equal opportunity principles, and consideration should be given to affirmative action in favour of women, people with disabilities or people from ethnic minority groups. Non-teaching staff should be treated as full partners. For example, care should be taken to ensure that teaching staff know the names of cleaners, that students appreciate the work of caretakers and that on important public school occasions the work of all staff is duly celebrated.

Mutual respect between adults and students is vital. The style of communication and the standards of courtesy are good indicators of this respect. The treatment of students as partners can be shown by the noticeboards, social facilities, cloakrooms and storage. These details matter for they create a climate of care and consideration. More important still are the opportunities for students to take responsibility. In the form group the foundation values of discussion and fair debate are essential. We should ask ourselves whether all members of the group are given equal respect in class discussion. Are there some people who are never listened to? The skills of chairing a discussion or debate are the cornerstone of the development of democratic decision-making, and the school must ensure that staff are adequately trained for this. From a healthy culture of class debate it is easier to develop social responsibility and leadership. School councils, social committees, common room committees, and fund-raising and charity groups can give a large number of young people the experience of combining to achieve targets or solve problems.

The issue of political participation is a sensitive one because of the dangers of manipulation and indoctrination. Controversial issues should be dealt with in an even-handed way, and yet the experience of political commitment is an essential part of education for democracy. Few schools are likely to be nervous about 'mirror' election campaigns to coincide with national elections, but there may be extremist political groups which are legal in society at large but unacceptable in school. Racist groups bent on inciting hatred should not have the opportunity to gain platforms in schools. On the other hand, local political issues can provide fertile ground for political education; for example, controversial proposals for local development can be examined in, say, an English lesson, and then 'for' and 'against' letters sent to the local press, and representatives from various viewpoints be invited in to make their case.

Relationships with parents and the wider community must reflect the commitment to dignity and fairness. There must be clear and consistent efforts to ensure that people's social, religious and cultural backgrounds are understood and respected. There are sure to be differences of opinion about aspects of school policy, but they will be resolved in a principled manner.

For example, a group of parents is dissatisfied with the organization of mathematics teaching. First an informal meeting is held with the head of mathematics and the Head to make sure that the parents understand the school's reasons for the policy and that the school understands the parent's concerns. If the group is not satisfied, there may be a more formal hearing, in which case the chairperson of the governors may act as a neutral chair. This is not the same as a judge for there are further difficult questions, such as 'Should parents try to directly influence academic policy?' and 'In what sense does this group represent the views of all or a majority of parents?'

Complaints about an individual teacher or a specific matter are particularly difficult to deal with fairly. Is this an isolated allegation or part of a pattern? Is a child giving a distorted picture of an incident to the parent? The Head will have meetings with teacher, parent, and child to establish the facts, any common ground and clearly opposing interpretations. To bluntly support parents, student or teacher in any dispute is both unfair and destructive of morale and principle.

The school environment will be welcoming and cared for. Signs and waiting areas should make it clear that the community has a part to play in school life. It could be said that everyone has a right to a healthy environment, and students are entitled to learn about the importance of caring for it. There are opportunities for students related to nature areas, gardens, displays and murals.

Expressions of collective identity such as assemblies, meetings, award-giving and presentations allow for public reinforcement of the school's fundamental values. Where daily worship is part of the school programme, there must be allowances made for those who wish to withdraw. One difficulty is that collective worship often merges with other features of school collective life, such as bulletins, public praise and celebration. Is a religious service at the end of a school term simply a matter of individual conscience or is it part of the group life of the school? The answer will depend on the circumstances, but teachers should be sensitive in their dealings with individuals who wish to opt out. Many schools will have followers of a variety of religions. According to the numbers represented there will be a need to consider organizing a variety of visitors from different religions. In any case specific reference should be frequently made to religious tolerance, and the acceptance of diversity.

There are many opportunities for the leaders of assemblies to make specific reference to issues of human rights. Not least of these is Human Rights Day, 10 December, which commemorates the signing of the Universal Declaration of Human Rights in 1948. Key figures in the struggle for human rights like Martin Luther King and Andrei Sakharov can be celebrated on appropriate anniversaries. In a more down to earth way, in-school disputes or problems often provide examples of common human rights issues; for example, the right to freedom of speech is curtailed by the responsibility of not damaging someone's reputation (the dividing line between fairly expressed opinion and name-calling). Some matters like racism must be approached on a public, whole school platform as well as gradually and persistently through the curriculum. It has to be made absolutely clear what the school stands for, and, for many school members, assemblies and meetings are the main channel for reinforcement of fundamental principles.

Awards and presentation ceremonies must convey the message that all types of student can achieve recognition and success, not only the high academic achievers. People are very sensitive to status and care must be taken over the order of awards. Are all the academic awards at the beginning and those for other achievements left to the end? This will convey that the school values some more than others. An alphabetical system can help create a 'status spread'. Awards may be given for service, for charity fund-raising, for care of disabled students, and for the overcoming of obstacles.

Finally, it is necessary for the human rights school to have its own statements of principle. These will not be referred to daily, and they may lie in brochures or staff handbooks or be pinned to walls for weeks at a time, but they represent the bedrock of values on which the school rests. They may be in the nature of statements of intent which act as a spur to better practice, and which particular actions may be judged against. As an example, 'This school is committed to equality of opportunity irrespective of age, gender, race, capability or social class', provides the backdrop for an investigation of the proportion of absentees from different groups. Should the school find a significant trend related to one group, it would need to examine the reasons and to set about rectifying the pattern. Another example could be checking a proposed new departmental policy against school principles to ensure that it is in harmony with them. It is in the nature of debate that any set of principles will be open to interpretation but the ensuing discussions are themselves part of the process of becoming a human rights school.

I have devoted considerable space to the question of ethos because it is the product of a variety of policies and actions unified by fundamental values. The idea of every member of the school community subscribing to every last point is, of course, impossible and undesirable. It is not unrealistic, however, to make coherent policies which are based on human rights and responsibilities which are themselves the distillation of those values common to the vast majority of humankind. In many respects, any good school is almost certainly doing this without making it explicit.

In England and Wales, all schools are required to have a curriculum policy statement, accepted by the governing body. This is a good platform for essential school principles. An example is given from a small 11–16 Community College. This statement is based on the Oxfordshire Local Education Authority draft curriculum statement and is intended to be broadly in line with it. The full document is available from the Head or any governor.

SAMPLE DRAFT CURRICULUM STATEMENT

Introduction

1. We believe that education should continue throughout life. We encourage parents, employers and the community to play an active part in helping the college provide effective learning.
2. The curriculum is everything that is learnt under the community college organization, not only subjects but also personal development, preparation for careers and adult life. Classroom work, homework, assembly, games, theatrical and musical productions, displays,

residential courses, field studies, community and work experience are all part of the curriculum.

3. Education encourages individuality and co-operation. We are determined that students should appreciate this country's past and culture and also the variety of cultures in Britain today. We stand for equality of opportunity and a respect for rights, responsibilities and justice. We care about those in need.

General Aims

1. To promote the self-development of children so that they are able on leaving formal education to be active, responsible, confident, independent and contributing members of society.
2. To build up children's skills, knowledge, experience, imagination, appreciation and moral awareness.
3. To keep under regular review and refine through self-appraisal the school's own practices.

To achieve these aims we will encourage:

1. Parents to consider themselves as the first educators of the child with a powerful influence on learning.
2. A stimulating and attractive environment, within and outside the classroom.
3. Recognition of and provision for individual needs.
4. Learning methods which lead to motivation, initiative, success and fair play.
5. Continuity and progression at 11+ and 16+ by having close links with neighbouring schools and colleges.

We are determined:

1. To give pupils experience of the wider world in which people live and work.
2. To support positive teacher attitudes, and a firm approach to equal opportunities – of gender, race, age, and capability.

DISPUTES PROCEDURE

How the school sets about resolving disputes is a good test of its commitment to justice, equality and peace. A large community is certain to generate interpersonal problems, between students, between staff, between staff and students, between staff and parents and so on. There will also be some serious incidents, conflicts, fights and even crimes. Most schools have a variety of formal and informal systems for handling them.

The essential principle is that disputes are not to be seen simply as irritating interruptions to the essential business of the school which are to be dealt with and 'buried' as quickly as possible in no matter what way. Disputes are, in fact, a means by which the school can express its moral values and nurture effective moral development. Students learn about justice, equality and peace from the experiences they have, and the examples they live through, not simply from the words they hear spoken. 'Do as I do as well as do as I say', is the watchword of the successful role model just as 'Don't do as I do, do as I say', is a bankrupt maxim.

Lawrence Kohlberg (Kohlberg, 1971) suggests that people pass through stages of moral understanding and that their passing on to a 'higher' stage is accelerated by having to resolve dilemmas through discussion and the use of reason.

The stage at which many adults stop is termed the 'law and order orientation' – a rigid respect for fixed rules and the social order. This can be observed in those people who are very concerned with the letter of the law, who want a detailed list of rules so they can know exactly where they stand on every issue (and what they can get away with without technically breaking the rules). Progression to the next stage ('social contract orientation'), where individual rights are understood to be balanced with social standards, and where essential principles and conscience may have primacy over a legalistic interpretation, can take place more easily where the individual has to confront real-life dilemmas.

One cannot assume that all adults have reached this stage, and therefore it is not automatic that any adult dealing with a dispute is going to resolve it better than any student, and so the school has to develop its own 'due process' for the resolution of problems and disputes, a process which rests firmly on human rights principles and which in its application can provide a constant example of justice, equality and peace.

One of the major problems with 'due process' in school is that an essential condition of justice – the separation of powers – does not apply. Consider the case of a state where the police, judges and prison authorities are the same people. Its human rights record is unlikely to be a good one. In schools, teachers are often investigators, interrogators, adjudicators, counsellors, and sentencers rolled into one, and often in their own cause.

The traditional discipline model of 'investigation–punishment' is easy to operate without reference to essential principles, and has a relatively high potential for miscarriage of justice, especially where time is perceived to be more important than fairness. The classic school solution to some minor offences is to apprehend and punish anyone nearby on the principle that 'if they had not actually done it they probably wanted to anyway'. Other classic school principles are 'no child is to be trusted to tell the truth', 'an adult's word is worth two children's words', 'better ten innocent people be punished than one guilty one escape'. Of course, these have been phrased for stylistic effect, but all the same there are many schools where adults feel under siege from a generation of amoral outsiders. In this 'state of siege' normal procedures are suspended and maintaining power is the most important factor. As with political systems, the movement from a 'state of siege' school to a 'human rights' school has to be gradual and based on secure principles. An alternative to 'investigation–punishment' is 'investigation–resolution––restitution–sanction–communication'. It looks more complex because it is designed to cover a variety of disputes, disagreements and offences.

Investigation

The essential principles here are 'everyone shall be presumed innocent until proved guilty' and 'distinguish between facts and suppositions'. The first step is to carefully assemble the facts. In interpersonal disputes, it is useful to take written notes of statements to clarify essential points of difference. Students can be asked to name someone they would trust to be a fair witness – not a close personal friend. In a dispute where a teacher has a serious complaint against a student, the teacher should be heard first in deference to professional responsibilities. The student must be able to put their side of the case. A device for avoiding an argument or a recurrence of the original problem is for a senior staff member to act as a chairperson allowing each party to make an uninterrupted statement. It is unlikely that she will find it easy to be a *neutral* chair, because of the tendency to side with one's own staff; nevertheless, efforts should always be made to hear both sides of the case. Some teachers will find it unacceptable to go even this far, feeling that even listening to the student is evidence of taking the student's side and so it is important to explain the role of due process in moral education.

When investigating the causes of a fight between students, tempers must be allowed to cool down first. A physically injured party is not necessarily guiltless. Although the one justifiable blow is in self-defence, provocation may have to be considered. Fights can sometimes happen almost accidentally. 'Are you normally friendly?' is a useful question to begin such an investigation. More difficult to pin down is the fight which has been caused by a manipulator who is aiming for some emotional 'payoff'. A manipulator is in a way more to blame than the participants, for exploiting other people. The 'manners' of an investigation are vital too. Anger or hostility should not be shown towards someone who is a suspect, and extreme care should be taken over the use of moral pressure to obtain a confession. It is in any case well known that people under stress can make false confessions. The school's knowledge of the individual's past history will be of great value – how trustworthy is this person? Does he or she have a record of honesty? How has he or she responded to previous problems?

Resolution

Resolution means that the dispute or incident is accepted by all parties as finished. A compromise, or an apology, may lead to parties being asked if they are satisfied that the matter is resolved, and, if they are, a symbolic gesture like a handshake or a written statement about intentions in future sets the seal on the agreement. In the case of a dispute between students, the adult who spent time sorting matters out would become an injured party in the event of anyone breaking the agreement. In the case of a serious offence against the school code, other people's rights will have been violated, for example the right to property, or the right to peacefully pursue one's studies, for the code is designed to protect the rights of all and to encourage responsibilities. It is essential then to explain the relationship between fairness to others and the offence itself. Sincere remorse may be perceived by the way in which the offender speaks about the offence and their stated commitment not to reoffend. In some cases there may be no need for restitution or sanction – a kind of suspended sentence may be the most effective course of action.

Resolution can be connected to a contract. To be worthy of the name, a contract has to be freely entered into, and its terms explained very clearly, and written down. One advantage of a contract is the provision of short-term concrete goals with a directly connected payoff. For example, a student who has been disruptive can 'earn' points on a report card for every successful lesson. At the end of a defined period a certain number of points may earn a particular privilege. Contracts can work well if the essential goal is positive, clear and accepted by all parties, and if the payoff is worth while to the contractor. Because schools may have a limited number of worthwhile rewards, it is best to involve parents, and if they do not understand or if they disapprove, a contract will be flawed.

Restitution

Restitution means paying back or making reparation for injury. On the individual level this may mean that an injured party is not ignored while the wheels of justice grind away, but it is not always possible to make direct reparation for physical or mental suffering. It can be done with theft or property damage, but how does one tally up a hurtful remark or conscious vocal bullying? The school has to act as an intermediary and receive restitution on an injured party's behalf. Also, an offence against a school human rights code is a blow to the self-respect and morale of the community. It will have cost precious energy, time and goodwill. It is perfectly fair to expect an offender to pay something back through some activity useful to the school. The perpetrator also has the opportunity to gain self-respect, the lack of which is so frequently a root cause of misdemeanours.

Community service may include contributions to the school environment, tidying, gardening, repairing, help for non-teaching staff such as filing, organizing or collating, and responsibility for visitors or younger students.

Barry, who had been daubing the school with technically skilled graffiti, was encouraged to make some larger murals which involved considerable mathematical skills and which were assessed for external examination.

Samantha had lost her temper in a playground incident. She spent several afternoons caring for the ducks in the small rural studies unit, and was so successful that she continued in a voluntary capacity.

Angela's community service consisted of helping the audiovisual aids technician. She learnt how educational programmes are recorded and did valuable service filing.

Michael helped the glazier replace a window he had broken and then spent several hours repairing shelves in the art department.

The school's aims must always place long-term moral growth above the desire for simple revenge, but traditional disciplinarians are not happy if community service appears to be a privilege or a reward instead of a punishment. It is in the nature of us all to notice the failures, rather than the successes, and this impression can be countered by keeping careful records of decisions about restitution and of the individuals involved. Service to the community should, of course, be undertaken in the student's own time, and there are always difficult decisions about the degree of supervision needed.

Sanctions

'No-one should be subjected to . . . degrading treatment or punishment' (Article 3, European Convention). Anyone reading this far will know that physical punishment has no place in a school aiming to foster personal moral growth. The word 'degrading' means humiliating or creating a sense of ridicule or shame. The following could be interpreted as degrading punishments: sarcastic remarks, forced apologies, personal indignity, meaningless tasks. Exactly what is degrading may depend on the context, and is certainly open to interpretation.

Sanctions are the symbol of the community's determination not to tolerate particular infringements of its code. They are designed to give clear warning to potential offenders and to deter them from offending. They may be identical to restitution, but some sanctions cannot be regarded as creative or positive, even where they are necessary. The ultimate sanction is exclusion, temporary or permanent, from the community. English education law has complex and definite procedures designed to protect the interests of student, parent, staff, governors and education authorities. Exclusion is seen as a last resort, for it effectively denies the student of his or her right to education until alternative arrangements can be made.

The school's aim should be to create an ethos where 'objectively' mild sanctions, such as withdrawal of privileges, are treated with the utmost seriousness of purpose and used seldom. The law of diminishing returns applies to any sanctions which are over-used, however severe they seem at first. In the ideal position the parent's ethos is exactly the same as the school's, but this is seldom the case and this provides a host of difficulties. According to families' own codes, some offences are more serious than others, and parents often wish to impose their own punishments, which may or may not be more severe than the school's. It is just reiterating normal good practice, and nothing particular to the human rights school, to note that open and easy relationships with parents will at least allow matters to be thoroughly discussed. The double-jeopardy rule says one should not be punished twice for the same offence. It is often possible to negotiate with parents about the most appropriate joint course of action.

Lastly, it should be quite clear that in a community where individuals are well known to each other there can be no system of fixed penalties – such is the offence, and therefore such is the punishment. Previous records are always available, and any offence is in the context of a person's overall development – including, of course, his or her successes, contributions and assets. To treat each individual as a cipher or a blank page is the antithesis of equal treatment.

Communication

One of the weaknesses of a large centralized system of state justice is that the machine seems to operate without reference to the individuals for whose benefit it is supposedly working. It is quite common for a victim of crime not to be informed when suspects are apprehended, when the court case is called, or when a sentence is given. In a school community, we should take advantage of the relative smallness of scale to ensure that good communication maintains the ethos and respect for the school code. First and most important, any injured party must not be forgotten in the effort to put the offender on the right track. Those who have suffered need reassurance that the school is working for them, not just demonstrating some abstract system of rights and responsibilities. We must ensure that where possible they play their full part in the resolution of the matter and receive any reparation due to them. Attention to detail here is repaid by the respect they will give the institution. On the other hand, people who have been abandoned are likely to say 'When I had a problem, nobody cared for me, why should I care for anyone else?'

As noted above, parents are key partners in any major matter concerning their child. Their ideas and advice should be listened to, and there will be times when much work has to be done to convince them of the correctness of a course of action. It is sometimes tempting to deal with a matter by promising immunity from parental involvement in return for information or a confession. This is a dangerous path to follow, as it violates parental rights. Only in extreme cases, such as suspected child abuse, can it be justifiable to maintain secrets from parents. It is particularly important only to maintain files that can be opened to parents. In some countries, like the United States and Canada, parents have the legal right to see all files kept on their children. In Britain, the Data Protection Act of 1984 does not apply to normal files. Nevertheless, there are good grounds for supporting the principle of open files. School files often play a crucial role in juvenile court proceedings, and it is quite possible for general statements of opinion based on scanty factual knowledge to find their way on to school files. Furthermore, some schools maintain unsubstantiated statements about parents. Denise Annett (Annett, 1984) from the Children's Legal Centre points out 'If information about parents is included in school reports this should be on the basis that it is relevant to educational decisions being taken about the young person, in which case that young person should also have a right of access.' She goes on to argue for a statutory right of access to all reports and records, a right to challenge or correct records, and individual rights to privacy. This is a complex area, but it is clear that, where communication is open and trusting, the school will be more effective in fostering good education in human rights.

CURRICULUM

'The understanding and experience of human rights is an important element of the preparation of all young people for life in a democratic and pluralistic society. It is part of social and political education and it involves intercultural and international understanding.' This is the opening paragraph from the appendix to the key European document on human rights education, the Council of Europe Recommendation No. R (85) 7 of the Committee of Ministers to member states on teaching and learning about human rights in schools. In succinct form, the document lays out the skills and knowledge to be acquired from the effective study of human rights in the curriculum.

The context or subject in which the study can take place will vary from school to school – history, geography, social studies, moral and religious education, language and literature, current affairs and economics. As with many other cross-curricular themes, such as environmental awareness, it is difficult to be assured that effective work is being done if every department claims to be 'doing some'. Schools have to vary such themes across a number of departments and it is always important to have a specialized 'core' course at some stage taken by all students, to guarantee a minimum level of understanding. Human rights studies will generally be under pressure, because of their association with political education. There is wide misunderstanding of the nature of real political education – that it is education about political process and skills. Many parents associate the term with indoctrination, and teachers sensitive to this potential source of criticism prefer to leave out this 'high-risk/low-status' subject. Of course, the result is that ill-educated young people are more prey to indoctrination or extremist ideologies once they have left school, never having had the opportunity to develop their own critical faculties (McGurk, 1987). To take international agreements and covenants as foundation reference points is to base the work on impartial standards. There are now simplified versions of the universal declaration available (Pike and Selby, 1988; Richardson, 1978). Human rights educators now distinguish between 'teaching/learning *about* human rights', e.g. key documents, and 'teaching/learning *for* human rights', e.g. having the opportunity to develop and practise skills necessary for their own and other people's rights. The skills include those of oral and written expression, judgement and the identification of bias, and social skills of recognizing and accepting differences, taking responsibility and resolving differences. The classroom must be in harmony with the climate of the school in promoting such skills through a varied learning methodology. Group discussion, role play, experiential activities and simulations are the appropriate vehicles for the development of human rights skills, and effective courses must create a balance between teacher-led knowledge input and student-centred activities.

A third phrase 'teaching *in* human rights' is another version of 'the human rights school'; the work on knowledge and skills in the classroom would be undermined if the whole institution were not committed to the meaning of human rights in its daily life. A single teacher could set up a human rights course but what is the hidden curriculum conveying for the rest of the time?

The freedom of schools in Britain to decide on their own curriculum has been severely curtailed by the Education Act of 1988. The national curriculum, which will demand up to 80–90 per cent of the teaching time in school, is a very traditional model in which geography and history have the status of foundation subjects and social education, personal education and citizenship appear only as desirable cross-curricular themes. A determined school may be able to map out effective human rights education across different subjects but will still have great difficulty in finding curriculum time and space for any coherent courses, for there are many other cross-curricular themes with good claims. The task of human rights educators in Britain is to work through the powerful new centralized structures and the National Curriculum Council to ensure that the Recommendation is effectively implemented.

Reuven Feuerstein[1] developed successful learning programmes for young Jewish immigrants from Morocco who were so culturally deprived that they were actually mentally disabled. Their deprivation had been the result of the destruction of their community values under the pressure of itinerant work. The parents were away from home for long periods of time, and while there were grandparents still alive, the group and family values were transmitted across the generations. When the grandparents died, there was no one left to hold the community together. Feuerstein's observation was that value-free learning is an impossibility, as it is part of our progress to rationality that we work in a value-laden context. Extreme relativism is a threat to reason. This suggestion reveals the danger facing modern cultures outside a religious value system. If everyone else's values are as good as my own, is there any *central* meaning? What can I have to test out my moral position?

The philosophy of human rights provides a value system which is tolerant and yet firm. There is a recognition that, because of the indivisibility of human rights, reason and discussion will always be needed to resolve particular disputes and dilemmas. Human rights themselves must not become another doctrine to be learnt by heart and applied by rule in every case. The human rights secondary school stands on this philosophy and its value system is the essential basis for learning and individual moral growth.

NOTE

1   For an introduction to Feuerstein's work see Sharron (1987). This has a comprehensive bibliography.

REFERENCES

Annett, D. (1984), 'Who sees your file?' *World Studies Journal*, Vol. 6, No. 2.

Kohlberg, L. (1971) 'Stages of moral development as a basis for moral education', in Beck, C., Crittenden, B. and Sullivan E. (eds.) *Moral Education*, University of Toronto.

McGurk, H. (1987) *What Next?*, London, ESRC, p. 50.

Pike, G. and Selby, D. (1988) *Human Rights Activity File*, Mary Glasgow Publication, London.

Richardson, R. (1978) *Fighting for Freedom*, Nelson, London.

Sharron, H. (1987) *Changing Children's Minds*, Souvenir Press, London.

CHAPTER 7

Active Learning for Human Rights in Intermediate and High Schools

Patricia Dye

Enter any American secondary classroom today to introduce the topic of human rights by asking students for a definition: 'The right to free speech!' . . . 'the right to assemble' . . . 'the right to protest' . . . 'the right to a free press' . . . 'the right to a trial' . . . sometimes, even, 'the right to own a gun'. Indeed, recent assessment results of high school students in citizenship items clearly indicate that one particular area of strength is student understanding of 'rights'. Unfortunately there is concomitant recognition that the topics of 'citizen responsibilities' are much less understood by students. In one recent state-wide test, almost half the twelfth graders believed that citizenship responsibility included voting with the majority. A New Jersey survey of high school students revealed that most teenagers favour requiring a teacher loyalty oath upholding the Constitution; most favour the right of the police to administer the 'third degree'; and only half the students opposed the right of school boards to remove books from school libraries (Tanner, 1985). Almost every teacher has had the experience of being shocked by ethnocentric and prejudiced viewpoints expressed by students.

Students tend to personalize the concept of human rights, i.e. 'my' rights or 'our' rights – they have great difficulty in grappling with the concept of universal rights for all peoples in all places. The fact that Americans have certain political rights unknown to most of the world's people is taken for granted by our students. Their general acceptance of 'my rights' combined with their very narrow definition of human rights demonstrates the need for educators to treat the topic in every classroom at each grade level in a sequenced and meaningful way.

Luckily, the instructional materials available for teaching about human rights are plentiful, designed to provoke thoughtful discussion, and certain to engage student interest. In this chapter, I will describe some such materials but would first list some guidelines that might assist in choosing lessons or activities for your particular curriculum, a few *do's* and *don't's*.

1. *Do* provide a classroom climate that serves as a model for human rights learning. Be receptive to open discussion, avoid judgemental responses, be willing to listen, and probe with patience until you are able to elicit from students answers to 'why do you think that?' In short, human rights instruction must never be a vehicle for indoctrination, but should always serve as a forum for students to question their teachers and themselves, to think critically about issues, to understand that there are a myriad historical reasons for the present status of the human predicament.

2. *Do* carefully outline what student outcomes you expect as a result of teaching about human rights. Concentrate on hoped-for changes in behaviours or attitudes, but be sure to consider how you will determine when and how these are achieved. When your cognitive and affective objectives for students have been listed, use them as a yardstick to measure the value of various instructional materials. If possible, design a short before and after survey for students – they, and you, will enjoy seeing actual changes in perceptions and attitudes.

3. *Do* infuse human rights instruction into the content and context of your present curriculum. If human rights is taught as an isolated topic, students will think the subject is isolated from the reality of the history or government course they are studying, or, more importantly, they will see it as a topic unrelated to their own lives. Once introduced, human rights learning needs to be reinforced with continual application to all relevant content that follows. Establishing and using a common vocabulary with broad definitions that are clear to all is an additional aid to the transfer of learning.

4. *Do* plan for experiential learning wherever and whenever possible. Classrooms organized for a day with different rules for 'different people', role plays, simulations based on actual events involving real people and case studies, are all strategies to enhance learning. Classroom experiences that force students to empathize, to feel, and to examine their own values in an introspective way will be much more successful in helping attain those student outcomes you have delineated.

5. *Do* provide for some plan of positive action, some way to help avoid the student syndrome of 'It's all hopeless, there's nothing *I* can do to change the world.' Some suggestions for action are found in this chapter and throughout this book, but it is essential for your students to understand that their future choices and actions 'can make a difference'.

6. *Don't* expect teaching about human rights to be without difficulties and stumbling blocks. The topic cannot be separated from individual value systems, there are sometimes cloudy areas, and certainly there are no easy right answers. Be upfront with your students when they ask you for help. Assure them that they are wrestling with many of the same dilemmas that have troubled philosophers and scholars throughout the

ages. The fact that they have come up with unanswerable questions proves they are learning and that they care.

MATERIALS FOR INTRODUCING THE TOPIC

The activities and materials described in this chapter represent only a sample of the many that are available from a variety of sources. Each of them in this particular section has an emphasis on definitions of prejudice and/or human rights, and thus could be used to introduce the topic of human rights into any secondary classroom.

1. Give students a grid containing 100 squares, 10 by 10. On the vertical axis, list numbers 1 to 10, bottom up; on the horizontal axis list letters A to J from left to right. The letters represent 10 groups of people, different races, ethnicities, handicaps, religions, from the most to the least familiar to your students. The numbers represent 10 questions indicating a descending range of tolerance, i.e. No. 1 asks 'Would you marry a _____?', No. 5 asks, 'Would you dance with a _____?', and No. 10 asks 'Should _____ be admitted as immigrants into this country?' Students are told that this exercise is *only* for their own use and the grid will not be collected, but used as a basis for discussion. During the debriefing of this exercise, students should identify their reasons for feeling differently about various groups of people. Who are the 'in groups' and who are the 'out groups'? Why are we prejudiced and what are the roots of our prejudices? (Frelick, 1985).

Table 1 Self-test: in-group–out-group relations.

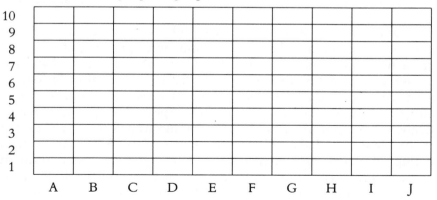

On the grid chart answer Y for yes and N for no. Consider how you would respond to each question (1–10) for each of the following groups (A–J). Assume that you have a real choice, and that it is not dictated by another authority. This test is for your personal benefit and will not be collected.

1. Would you marry a _____?

2. Would you kiss a _____?
3. Would you have as a close friend a _____?
4. Would you accept a _____ as a roommate?
5. Would you dance with a _____?
6. Would you sit next to a _____ in your classroom?
7. Would you accept a _____ as a next door neighbour?
8. Would you admit _____s into your school?
9. Would you admit_____s into your neighbourhood?
10. Would you admit _____s into your country?

Assume each of the following is a resident of the United States belonging to one of the following ethnic, social, religious or handicapped groups (except for question No. 10).

A. Puerto Rican
B. Arab
C. Japanese
D. Blind person
E. Black
F. WASP (White Anglo-Saxon Protestant)
G. Catholic
H. Jew
I. Italian
J. _____ (choose another group)

Used by permission of National Council for the Social Studies.

2. Draw a scale on the board with five indices moving from left to right – antilocution, avoidance, discrimination, physical attack, and extermination. Ask students to describe or identify behaviour that illustrates each phase of this scale. Pass out a list of events from history or from current events that describe a range of negative actions against a specific group. In American history, for example, a listing might include the Chinese Exclusion Act, the hanging of an escaped slave, a sign that states 'No Irish Need Apply', the Indian Removal Act, literacy tests for voting, the Battle of Wounded Knee, burning crosses on a Southern lawn, and others. Tell students to place each event on the scale based on the intensity of prejudice exhibited. In discussion, be sure students

| Antilocution | Avoidance | Discrimination | Physical Attack | Extermination |

Used by permission of National Council for the Social Studies.

Table 2

understand that although those who 'speak against' another group rarely move to genocide, the latter could not occur without progression in stages (Frelick, 1985, p. 513).

3. Have students brainstorm to list all those human rights that they consider important. When they have completed the list, ask them to rank each in a descending order of importance. Next ask them to list as a class all those factors which they consider to be vital in having a 'good quality of life'. Again, all the factors should be ranked as to their importance. Students should begin to realize that no other item on the second list is of any value if they do not have good health. How do the two lists compare? What on the human rights list relates to the list of items required for a good quality of life? Are the right to live, the right to eat, the right to have health care, the right to work, the right to have an education on that first list? Which of these should be considered basic human rights? Are the right to vote or to speak freely on the second list? From the two lists, students should then compile a third one ranking the most important human rights that should be considered universal for all peoples. They should then compare their list with a copy of the Universal Declaration of Human Rights.

4. Another activity designed to help students understand a broader definition of human rights is a survey which may also be used as a pre-test. Five situations involving issues about rights are described from different parts of the world. Students are asked to identify the conflicts implied and thus are introduced to the fact that human rights are perceived differently based on different human needs. (King and Flitter-man-King, 1982).

Activity 2

Students need to become aware of the differences in the ways in which human rights sometimes are perceived in various parts of the world. Here is a very simple pre-test which could be given to generate discussion. This pre-test also could be used as a means of evaluating changes in awareness and attitudes, if used again at the end of a unit of study.

Pre-Test. Direction to students: This test will NOT be graded. It will be used only as a basis for discussion. Read each situation, then choose the answer that you consider to be the best. If none of the answers supplied seems correct to you, write your own answer in the space provided. Be prepared to tell *why* you answered as you did in the discussion which will follow this pre-test.

[1] The leader of the country was very proud of what he had done for his people over the last twenty years. The standard of living had been improved, children were being educated, and no one was hungry.

'But,' said the visitor, 'there is no freedom of the press here. You only have one newspaper, and it only gives one view.'

The leader replied, 'Some freedoms are more important than others.'

Which freedom do you think he had in mind?
a. Freedom of speech
b. Freedom of worship
c. Freedom from want
d. Freedom of choice
e. Freedom from ignorance
f. _____

[2] Maria got along well with her visitor. But they did argue about differences between his country and the United States.
   'But you have no freedom in your country,' Maria said. 'There is only one party in elections. Your newspapers are run by the government.'
   'We do have freedom,' he insisted. 'No one goes hungry. Any person can find work. Medical care is free. Can there be greater freedom than that?'

What is the best conclusion to draw from that debate?
a. The visitor does not really understand the meaning of freedom.
b. The two countries differ in their ideas about freedom.
c. There is freedom in the United States but not in the other country.
d. People have greater freedom in the other country than in the United States.
e. _____

[3] A journalist from the Philippines who made a ten-day visit to the United States wrote: 'The country is very rich, but the workers are badly exploited. It is clear that America could only have achieved such wealth and power by making certain sacrifices. The workers recognize that they must suffer so that industry can prosper.'

What would be a good way for an American to respond?
a. It is always necessary for certain people to suffer in order for a country to advance economically.
b. The rich are generous in their support of charities, so their profits really help the poor.
c. The American political system gives workers important freedoms. They can elect representatives to protect their rights.
d. A visitor can only catch a glimpse of things, so he or she has no right to make a statement about how a country operates.
e. _____

[4] India's Prime Minister, Indira Gandhi, once said: 'How can you expect people to care about the environment when their lives are polluted at the source?' In terms of human rights, what do you think her first priority would be?
a. Basic political freedoms, including the right to vote.
b. Environmental protection laws to stop pollution.
c. An end to environmental restriction in order to encourage economic growth.
d. Basic food and health care programmes.
e. _____

[5]   In 1958 the people of French Guinea declared their independence. General
Charles de Gaulle, then head of the French government, warned them that they
would suffer serious economic consequences. He urged them to remain a part
of what he called 'the community of France'.

Sékou Touré, who later became President of the New African nation of Guinea,
replied, 'We have a great and pressing need. Our dignity! But there can be no
dignity without freedom. When you are ruled by others, you are dishonoured
and turned into inferior human beings. We prefer poverty in freedom to riches
in slavery.' Which of the following human rights do you think Touré had in
mind?
a. The right to own property.
b. The right to recognition as a person before the law.
c. The right of self-determination.
d. The right to a standard of living adequate for health and well-being.
e. _____

5.   Distribute to students abbreviated copies of the Universal Declaration
of Human Rights and the first 10 amendments to the United States
Constitution. How are these two documents similar? How are they
different? Give each student a recent copy of a city newspaper and ask
them to identify all news articles which relate to one of the rights in
these documents. Poll the class results and identify those rights with
the highest exposure in the press.

Used by permission of National Council for the Social Studies

HUMAN RIGHTS AND THE SECONDARY SCHOOL CURRICULUM

One widely used programme used effectively at both middle school and high
school levels is the *Facing History and Ourselves* programme developed by
two Brookline, Massachusetts teachers.[5] Margot Strom and Bill Parsons,
while teaching about World War II and the Holocaust, found that they were
unable to answer student questions about how and why a civilized world in
the twentieth century could witness the planned genocide of millions of
innocent people. Together they began to develop the format and gather
instructional materials which now comprise a model curriculum, one which
is used in over 350 schools throughout the United States. The basis for the
FHO programme is to look at historical events as the result of a series of
decisions made by individuals rather than as inevitable happenings. By helping students examine their own perceptions and prejudices about people
and by introducing such concepts as 'victim', 'victimizing,' 'stereotyping',
'scapegoating', 'bystander', and 'obedience', the FHO curriculum engages
students by having them address the moral dilemmas faced by people like

themselves during this period of human history. A bibliography of primary source documents, films, biographies, and fiction is supplied by the FHO Foundation, along with teacher-training and support programmes. Although school districts have implemented this programme at different grade levels and within a variety of subject disciplines, the FHO Foundation finds that most frequently it is used by social studies or English classes in the eighth or ninth grade.

We introduced the programme into our eighth-grade curriculum in the Plymouth–Carver regional schools as an interdisciplinary unit for all social studies and English classes during the last nine weeks of the school year. Our focus is decision-making – how individuals make decisions, how they learn to live with those decisions, and how individual decision-making may affect society as a whole.

Teachers begin by having youngsters examine the concepts of human rights and human prejudice as they apply to the American history which students have been learning. The treatment of Native Americans, the slave trade and practices, the rise of the Ku Klux Klan, the 'immigrant' experiences, Japanese internment camps, and the civil rights movement all are reviewed in the context of defining human rights. Films are used to help define prejudice and the dilemmas of choice – *Prejudice* by Bill Cosby, *After the First*, the *Milgram Experiment, You Have to Be Taught to Hate*, and *The Eye of the Storm*. Literature is chosen for the same themes, i.e. *The Bear That Wasn't, The Boy from Old Prague, Chernowitz!, The Wave*, and *Friedrich*. Teachers work together to help students make connections between the readings and the films, to clarify and encourage use of the same vocabulary, and to encourage students to question, and to discuss their feelings. Students keep a daily journal to help them express such feelings and to record their questions and reflections. These become a wonderful way for teachers and students alike to evaluate what is being learned, and to show evidence of changed attitudes and introspection about personal choices.

The use of these materials avoids students' believing that the Holocaust was an anomaly in history, that the genocide of World War II was an isolated event 'that could never happen again'. By looking at their own prejudices in their own lives, students realize that the potential for discriminatory behaviour lies within each of us, and that we are able to make choices about our actions. As the unit progresses into the Holocaust, additional concepts are introduced, i.e. power and charismatic leadership, authoritarianism, the human need for group acceptance, propaganda, and dehumanization. The role of the bystander in Nazi Germany is discussed with the use of diaries and written materials – at what point, and at what level of motivation, do people rise up to fight against inequity?

At the same time that they are learning about the vulnerability of any society to the abuse of power, students also make discoveries about 'people who make a difference' – people such as the Danes who helped Jews escape, Raul Wallenberg, and the many citizens who risked their own lives to hide Jewish refugees. The culminating assignment of the unit asks students to research and write a 'compare and contrast' report about a bystander and a person who made a difference – real people in real situations. We evaluate our FHO unit in several ways – through the reading of student journals, changes in a pre- and post-attitudinal survey, observations of classroom discussions. However, the following comments from students' letters and journals say it best:

> I think that you should show this movie again because it opens eyes, hearts, and the very feelings of a person . . .
> I was upset because it's very scary to think that the whole world just stood by and watched . . .
> I didn't believe that people could be so cruel to other people . . . another thing that really got me was how they said they were just following orders . . .
> . . . now I look at things differently. I don't judge people before I get to know them. I don't try and make them into something they are not . . .
> . . . one thing I will always remember from this unit is never to be a passive bystander, but to stick up for what I believe is right . . .
> I understand why this unit is called 'Facing History'. If we cannot face the crimes of other human beings, we are closing our eyes to understanding ourselves . . .

(student journals, collected by Evelyn Dewar, 1988)

USING A COMPUTER TO COMPARE HUMAN RIGHTS

In this day of data collection and analysis, a computer database offers another excellent opportunity for secondary students to examine human rights issues. There are several world and country databases available which might be useful as a springboard: *NewsWorks'* 'World Community' file by *Newsweek*, *World Geograph* by MECC, *The Power of Nation States* by ICCE. However, it is also possible to give students a chance to design their own database geared specifically to human rights issues.

Step 1

Hold a class brainstorming session to list all possible statistical measures which might have an impact on human rights: per capita income, literacy rate, life expectancy, infant mortality rate, and comparative percentages of government expenditures on health, education, and the military are a few of these. Percentages of the citizenry with access to safe water, the number of doctors per 1000 people, the percentages of eligible school-age children who attend school, and distribution of wealth are other statistics which might be used. Each of these categories contains objective data, and most of these figures are available for a majority of countries today, through the United Nations or the World Bank.

Step 2

Assign each student two or three countries for which he or she must obtain the data necessary to complete a database. When the information has been collected and input, print out an alphabetical list of the countries with all the statistical information. Ask students to compare the data, and to form hypotheses about the relationships of one category to another. For example, in what ways is the per capita income related to literacy rates? How do statistics on life expectancy relate to government expenditures on health, or the number of doctors per 1000? Can students determine countries where human rights are being denied? Is it possible for a country to have a relatively good standard of living, but to deny its citizens basic human rights? What other information would they like to have to examine national human rights policies?

Step 3

Students will soon determine that they need to qualify the type of government found in a country within some type of index indicating political freedoms. Although it is fairly easy to obtain a description of various national governments, it is impossible to determine how much freedom exists by examining the types, i.e. republic, parliamentary, socialist, etc. In fact, the word democratic frequently appears in the names of countries which are anything but. Some indices of political freedom are available, but warn students that these may be biased at the source. What criteria were used to formulate the index? What types of subjective decisions were made in determining the index scale?

Step 4

Therefore, the only way really to determine how human rights are valued by specific governments is to create an index designed and scaled by the students themselves. This stage in creating a database thus becomes a very real opportunity for students to examine and weigh their own values about what constitutes human rights, and to apply these without prejudice or preconceived ideas on a numeric scale. Begin with a perfect index score of 100. Does the country hold regularly scheduled elections? Who can vote? How many candidates are there? Who chooses the nominated candidates? How many political parties are represented? Are all political parties legal? Are write-in candidates allowed? Is there a secret ballot?

What other information can become part of the index? Is there a free press operating in this country? Is information publicly and regularly broadcast? Are news broadcasts from other countries available without restrictions? Is government censorship used? Are people arrested for political crimes? What form of trials exist? How are judges selected? What form of court appeals are permitted? What are the laws about marriage and divorce? Are there restrictions on inheritances? Who has the opportunity for higher education?

Are people allowed to travel freely? Is equitable health care available for all? These are but a few of the questions your students may wish to investigate. Although such information is not as easily obtainable, answers to most may be found through careful research.

Step 5

Now comes the difficult part in the formulation of the freedom index, and the part that will allow students to experience consensus-building. Students must decide what segment of the 100 'perfect' score should be assigned to each category they have researched. Are free and open elections worth 20 per cent or 30 per cent? Does a free press count 15 points or 50 points? What needs to be done is a prioritization of all the categories and a percentage weight assigned to each. When these decisions are made, facts about each country's human rights are able to be transferred to a numeric scale and input into the database. Students should be encouraged to compare their results with other political freedom indices and with other classes who have gone through a similar process.

Students who will research, synthesize, and evaluate data are not only learning and applying life-long skills, but also gaining a deeper understanding of the many facets of global human rights.

HUMAN RIGHTS CLASSROOM SIMULATIONS

No better way to help students grapple with human rights exists than to use (or create) a simulation which forces a degree of empathy from students. Employing a 'learning-by-doing' methodology is not easy, frequently involving risks of criticism and/or unexpected results, but for those who have used simulations, the long-range results are well worth such risks. The famous 'blue eyes–brown eyes' lesson on the dangers of prejudice, created by Jane Elliot in an effort to eliminate such attitudes among her students, has enjoyed national attention and praise (Peters, 1986). The television documentary about Ms Elliot's 'Discrimination Days' simulation is called *Eye of the Storm* and should be mandatory viewing for all those entering the teaching profession. Another simulation, *The Wave*, has also been relived in film – this is the story of a high school teacher who decided to have his students participate in a new elite group in order to learn about the allure of belonging without regard to the values of the organization.

Using the simulation *Bafa Bafa* to teach youngsters the difficulty of empathizing with very different values from another culture can be a wonderfully exciting experience for students and teachers alike. This game also serves as an excellent ice-breaker at the start of a new school year – those walls with which our students surround themselves for new situations come tumbling down really quickly after the two days spent in role-playing. An added twist to the end of the game can easily be focused on the subject of human rights by asking students to describe who were the in-groups and the out-groups in each of the two cultures. Another successful simulation is *Summit: A Game of International Compromise* where students are divided into seven fictitious countries and charged to negotiate a treaty that will be acceptable to all. Students are warned that if more than one country ends up in the minus column for points, none of the treaty will be valid for any of the countries. For each section of the treaty, points are awarded on the basis of national priorities – at the beginning of this three-day game, students representing the wealthy and powerful nations easily lead the others by being able to make promises or influence their weaker neighbours on the less important issues. Towards the end of the simulation, it becomes apparent that in order to make the treaty valid, the strong nations are going to have to make sacrifices or the treaty will never be ratified. Although I have had different results every time I have used *Summit* in a classroom, the lesson to be learned is clear: some type of equitable distribution of resources is essential to international and national security.

A teacher in one of our high schools this year used another simulation with great success in a sociology class. The game, *Star Power*, clearly illustrates the dangers of abusive human rights policies.

> This is a game in which a low-mobility, three-tiered society is built through the distribution of wealth in the form of chips. Participants have a chance to progress from one level of society to another by acquiring wealth through trading with other participants. Once the society is established, the group with the most wealth is given the right to make the rules for the game. They generally make rules that the other groups consider to be unfair, fascistic, and racist. A revolt against the rules and the rule makers generally ensues. When this occurs, the game is ended. The game is useful for raising questions about the uses of power in a competitive society.

Teacher Scott Froman spent two days with his classroom noisily filled with students competing for a chance to improve their social and economic status in ten-minute trading sessions until, as predicted, one student rebelled against the system and the game ended. The next day was critical to the lasting impact of the simulation. How did students feel about their roles? What could have made differences in the way they felt? What did they learn about the use of power? Are there any parallels between this and our society? What happened when two groups worked together against the one in power? Are there any similarities between the game and international politics? Did the squares (the top power group) have the right to change the rules? Why or why not? Who are the circles and the triangles in American society? Who are the circles and triangles in our world today? Mr Froman recorded some of the student responses as follows:

> Now I know what it's like to be treated unfairly . . .
> It was so frustrating when a square refused to trade . . .
> I couldn't believe that [our friends] could treat us this way . . .

I don't know why they got so upset . . . they should have realized that
we had to make rules like that to stay in power . . .
The only part that was fun was when we ganged up on the squares . . .

Certainly this activity provoked thoughtful, as well as emotional, discussion.
None of these 'circles' or 'triangles' will ever forget the injustice of a society
where rules are made by the powerful in order to increase the stability of
their power base. Their understanding of the plight of those less fortunate
in our society will hopefully remain caring and empathic.

PROJECTS/PLANS FOR STUDENT ACTIVISM

This final section contains several suggestions to help students overcome that
previously mentioned syndrome, 'Well, it's all terribly unfair . . . and I feel
really badly about things . . . but *I* can't *do* anything about it.' It is almost
better for teachers never to address the inequities of our world than to have
students believe that they can do nothing to change those inequities. A few
ideas follow, but these merely scratch the surface – the very best suggestion
that I would make is to have students themselves come up with ideas and
action plans for improving human rights within their communities, their
societies, and their world.

1. Ask your school librarian to help you in collecting a vertical file with
    information about agencies and organizations that attempt to help
    resolve abuses of human rights. This might include everything from
    Foster Parents and the Heifer Project to Oxfam and UNESCO. Ask
    students to read and collect advertisements from newspapers, maga-
    zines, and television about such agencies. Find out if there are local
    connections to such organizations – have speakers come in and talk to
    students about what they can do to help.
2. Assign students to investigate the goals and the work accomplished by
    five different national and international human rights organizations.
    They should find out what membership entails, who makes decisions
    about proposals for action, and what kind of actions are possible. Ask
    them to use their findings to choose one organization they would most
    like to join, explaining why.
3. Frequently, international problems may be transferred to smaller locales
    where individual specific action may serve as a change agent. For
    instance, an international controversy over the plight of the Brazilian
    rainforest could be applied to the need for public park land or open
    space in a local community. Students are always welcomed as active
    helpers in local campaigns – they will have the opportunity to see the
    effectiveness of action locally and to recognize that this same action can
    be used on an international scale.
4. As described in the *Facing History* programme, students need to have
    an avenue for becoming a person 'who makes a difference' instead of
    a bystander. Ask them to record incidents in the school for a week

which they consider to be in violation of human rights. This could be as simple as noticing that there is no way for a wheelchair student to access a specific room in the school. It could be as complicated as an issue involving a student suspended for violating a school rule. It could be as awkward as hearing a friend use a discriminatory label about a fellow student. Use a class period to discuss the collected inequities – help students to weigh the issues, look at every side of the problem from every point of view, and then have them vote on three or four issues that they would like to act upon collectively. Have them brainstorm for solutions, then help them to prioritize what actions might really be effective – finally send them forth to 'do battle'. And, in the long run, it does not matter whether the battle is lost or won, but the fact that they take a pro-active position is critically important.

5. Teachers frequently assign their students to write a letter about an issue which is controversial and has been discussed in class. These letters are collected, graded, sometimes mailed and sometimes not. What can often make a real difference, however, is planning a mail blitz to a specific person about a specific issue. Because politicians today have to weigh what priorities they may be able to act upon in light of public opinion, an occasional letter will rarely make an impact on the political scene. However, a flood of letters from people in the representative's district will make a difference, will frequently impact an action position, and will certainly ensure some attention. Planning a mail blitz for the chief executive officer of a company selling infant formulae to a developing country where people have no access to sterile water, or to a prime minister, expressing concern that the government is taking no action against a trade partner which consistently ignores human rights, has a far greater chance of provoking response. For added effectiveness, ask students to send copies of their letters to other involved persons such as the chairman of the board of that same company (by name) or the minister of foreign affairs. Do not give up the letter-writing assignment, just plan these to become more effective.

6. Finally, one of the best vehicles to encourage student action is to use a nucleus of interested youngsters to organize an action club, as an after-school activity. Another one of our teachers, John Robinson, has done just that. Mr Robinson writes

. . . the most active way I can think of to teach human rights in high school is to start a chapter of Amnesty International on campus. Amnesty has a wealth of materials (literature, video and a guest speaker referral service) especially geared to the high school level. The most valuable tool that Amnesty International uses, however, is its Urgent Action letter, a published-as-needed white paper that details one specific human rights violation, recommends an appropriate student response and provides names and addresses for students to write. Geographic learning can be incorporated with human rights education if the group plots human rights abuses on a world map such as I have done. Current events can also be combined with research skills in learning when students are assigned to do some background research into events surrounding the specific human rights violation.

Although curriculum content may vary widely among our secondary schools, there is definite consensus among teachers at this level that the adolescent age groups offer an opportunity and a need for value education, for broadening horizons, and for exploring human themes that hold a personal interest. Any of the typical content areas in social studies and the humanities can be used as a vehicle for human rights education. However, any curriculum for these students is only effective in so far as it can show relevance to their own experiences, and as it is handled with delicacy by teachers sensitive to the demands of peer pressures and volatile teenage emotions. The hope of our planet's future is in the hands and minds of our young people – let us give them the tools for inquiry, decision-making, and critical thinking!

RESOURCES

Bafa Bafa, cross-cultural simulation, available from Social Studies School Services, 10200 Jefferson Boulevard, Room 161, PO Box 802, Culver City, CA 90232.

Facing History and Ourselves, National Foundation Inc., 25 Kennard Road, Brookline, MA 02146.

NewsWorks, computer databases and activities, Newsweek Magazine, 444 Madison Avenue, New York 10022.

Shirts, R. G. *Star Power*, a simulation.

Summit: A Game of International Compromise, Edu-Game, Creative Classroom Activities, PO Box 1144, Sun Valley, CA 91352.

The Power of Nation States, computer software and databases, International Council for Computers in Education, 1787 Agate Street, Eugene, OR 97403.

The Wave, a film by Prime Time School Television, 40 E. Huron Street, Chicago, IL 60611.

World Geograph, computer software and database, MECC, 3490 Lexington Avenue North, St Paul, MN 55126.

REFERENCES

Frelick, B. (1985) 'Teaching about genocide as a contemporary problem', *Social Education*, September, p. 512.

King, D. and Flitterman-King, S. (1982) 'Teaching human rights in secondary schools', in Branson, M. and Torney-Purta, J. (eds) *International Human Rights, Society, and the Schools*, NCSS Bulletin No. 68, Washington, pp. 64–66.

Peters, W. (1986) *A Class Divided: Then and Now*, New Haven, Conn.: Yale University Press.

Tanner, D. (1985) 'The student is also a citizen', *Social Education*, September.

CHAPTER 8

Human Rights Education and Teacher Training

Francine Best

Defending and promoting human rights is largely a matter of education, including education at school; and education in human rights at primary and secondary schools depends on the attitudes and efforts of teachers.

In other words, education in human rights will not develop unless teachers are first of all convinced of the need to teach human rights, then given special training in the methods of such teaching. The problem of extending education to include human rights is now becoming crucial; the current situation is highly unsatisfactory, human rights teaching often being limited to the odd project in a few particularly innovative and dynamic schools and never anywhere else.

It is true that, although recommended in official texts, human rights education is difficult to put into practice. It calls for a multidisciplinary approach (hence for understanding and co-operation between several teachers), a democratic school system (hence educational attitudes on the part of all adults), and a knowledge of legal principles and of the fundamental texts proclaiming the universal nature of human rights.

In spite of these difficulties, teams of teachers are drawing up and implementing sound and lasting human rights projects. For the most part they are teachers who have either attended specific human rights education courses or done some educational research into the subject. This shows that in-service training courses, sessions or seminars on human rights education serve some purpose: those who attend them are motivated by them and, on their return to their schools, they embark on action projects aimed at generating awareness of human rights or else teach human rights as part of their own subjects or as an aspect of civic education. At least in Europe, therefore, the teaching of human rights on a general scale depends on the provision of initial or in-service training in the subject for teachers.

The first question to be considered is whether priority should be given to initial or to in-service training. Initial teacher-training courses, whether conducted in training colleges or at universities, are still geared to a particular discipline, at least in the case of secondary education. Furthermore, one or two years of vocational training is often too short a period for a complete course unit to be devoted to the history of human rights and the relevant legal concepts. And even if it is desirable to include such units in basic teacher training, such is the urgency that training in human rights cannot be confined to this initial phase. The plain fact is that all teachers must be trained in the subject as quickly as possible. Consequently, it is further or in-service training that offers the most appropriate framework for this specific form of instruction, especially as one-week courses, sessions or units have many of the features of human rights education itself. Grouping together several disciplines (history, law, teaching methodology and so on) in a single place at the same time provides the multidisciplinary context necessary for the treatment of human rights questions. Better still, if the approach to human rights education is directed along the lines described below, three or four well co-ordinated sessions lasting four days each should suffice to cover the whole area which human rights education can and should fill.

Thus, the training that seems appropriate to human rights education consists of a continuous five-day course or of four well co-ordinated three-day units alternating with classroom practice.

The next step is to consider the themes which such training should treat. There seem to be four essential ones:

1. Legal concepts and approaches concerning human rights.
2. The history of human rights and the philosophy underlying them.
3. An intercultural approach to education with the aim of implementing human rights.
4. School life, educational attitudes and human rights.

These four themes are all equally important and are all necessary in order to ensure teachers training of a sufficiently comprehensive and dynamic kind. But for the sake of coherence it is a good idea to distinguish between them or even deal with them separately in four different course units spread over a school year, for example.

A study of the basic texts seems essential. In each unit the major declarations, covenants and conventions, and in particular the 1948 Universal Declaration of Human Rights, should be presented, analysed and discussed by the participants. This declaratory legal material constitutes the main basis for teacher training, and for training provided in the French language all the texts are available in a single publication entitled *Conquête des Droits de l'Homme*. Such material should be used even for the themes of 'inter-cultural approach' and 'school life'. The distribution of these texts to the participants, an analysis thereof and group discussions aimed at devising methods suited to pupils' ages are three steps that should form part of all vocational training courses concerned with human rights education. Otherwise, the study of human rights is liable to remain a shallow exercise, however well-meaning. Enquiries have shown that teachers are still largely, not to say totally, ignorant of these fundamental texts.

Alternatively, the above four themes can be tackled simultaneously during a course lasting eight or ten days, although the approach should still be of a multidisciplinary and comprehensive kind.

As for teacher trainers, they undoubtedly need to be provided with detailed instruction in one or another of these four themes, together with introductory lectures on the other three. An examination of the documents produced by the Council of Europe after the many symposia on the subject shows that by far the greatest emphasis is being given to themes 3 and 4, i.e. intercultural teaching on the one hand and school life and the encouragement of democratic attitudes on the other.

This is not to be regretted, however. The presence of so many children from different cultural backgrounds in Europe made such training necessary; and with the disappearance of some of Western society's traditional values at the approach of the twenty-first century, it was quite legitimate for teachers and education policy-makers to wish to reinculcate a sense of liberty, equality, democracy and solidarity in the younger generation.

It is time now, however, to take teacher training on the subject of human rights education a step further. Children and young people, and hence, their teachers in the first instance, should all be familiarized with the corpus of concepts and texts relating to human rights.

Let us look, for example, at the programme of a summer school held at the Council of Europe jointly by the French Institut National de Recherche Pédagogique and the International Institute of Human Rights. The juridical aspects of the subject (legal concepts, international guarantees) figure prominently in the programme, as do references to the fundamental texts. The programme was designed, it should be remembered, from a teaching point of view, with an eye to the subsequent transmission of knowledge and the creation of learning situations. In accordance with this aim, training courses intended to enhance the professional skills of teachers may include workshops on 'cases' contributed by the trainees or on 'action plans' devised by them for the purpose of promoting and teaching human rights.

In connection with the intercultural approach, there are simulation and role-playing games which can be organized to add a personal dimension to the learning process: the teachers become deeply involved in such games, often discovering in themselves reflexes and feelings the existence of which they had not previously suspected. However effective they may be, these recreational activities should not preclude rational philosophical and legal thinking. A teacher's action needs to be based on sound ethical and educational principles.

These principles, the very ones proclaimed in 1948 in the Universal Declaration of Human Rights, form the content of teacher training for human rights education. This is a content of a positive kind. Of course, the purpose of human rights education is to uphold the human rights that are being flouted in many parts of the world (as shown by the reports of Amnesty International) and are never sufficiently supplied or implemented under national legislation, even in the most democratic countries. But this is a negative approach which, even though indicative of the need for worldwide concern for human rights, is far from adequate: it might result in concern for human rights being confined to remote areas and hence to the main objective being missed, namely realization by every child or young person of his or her own responsibility for the advancement of human rights as well as the acknowledgement of those rights by all individuals and groups.

Teachers who have taken as their basis the reports of Amnesty International or the apartheid situation in South Africa have encountered this obstacle. They have found it very difficult to go on to a study of the fundamental texts and international legal instruments so as to create individual awareness of human rights.

There is also another negative approach that should be guarded against. It is, of course, desirable to inform teachers that an intercultural view of human rights education does not mean the cultivation of differences for their own sake, nor the mere juxtaposition of folk traditions. Interculturalism signifies respect for otherness, for others, for *all* other human beings; but this respect is itself universal. Liberty and the equality of human beings before the law are the right of each and every individual. This tug-of-war between diversity and universality is difficult to comprehend and even more difficult to incorporate in a teaching methodology. However, this difficulty should not lead to an accumulation of insurmountable obstacles: stating what an intercultural approach does *not* mean should not result in the approach being abandoned.

Teachers should be provided with keys to the various problems arising. Geography, the plastic arts, dance, music and school twinning form part of those keys and of a positive approach to interculturalism.

To relate intercultural practices to human rights is to give them a meaning. This positive aspect should be highlighted in teacher-training courses, otherwise teachers will become discouraged and stop behaving in a manner consonant with human rights, equality and cultural diversity.

In other words, to give training too negative or too cautious a tone is to miss the purpose of all vocational training for human rights education, which is to make human rights tangible and real in teaching and learning situations.

Accordingly, the positive content of human rights education, as constituted by the basic international legal texts and by educational methods that have succeeded in winning the active support of pupils, should occupy a prominent place in teacher-training courses.

If this positive content is to be realistic rather than idealistic or utopian, it must be the result of educational research clearly concerned with human rights education or at any rate with one of its three dimensions, i.e.

- the cognitive and didactic aspect;
- attitudes and school life;
- the intercultural approach.

It is a striking and regrettable fact that although there is a great deal of legal research on the subject of human rights, there is hardly any actual educational research or research on human rights education. And what little there is consists merely of accounts of experiments carried out by the odd enthusiastic teacher and more or less confined to the teacher's own school.

This is one of the shortcomings of present-day educational research: it remains too descriptive and is not forward-looking enough. Yet research and training can go hand in hand: the participation of teachers in a well-organized research programme network comprising, say, a hundred teachers and a dozen or so schools, is in itself a form of training for those involved. Any seminars held in the course of the research are also a form of training, to which exchanges of views, discussions and criticisms all contribute.

The INRP's research report on human rights education (*Education aux Droits de l'Homme*, No. 13 in the series of research reports) was the fruit of a research project of this type, and the teachers themselves agreed that it had been a highly instructive experience for them. Another reason for mentioning this particular report is that it could serve as a basis for teacher-training courses on human rights education. Each chapter heading could form the title for a lecture or the theme of an activity at a training session. Research, then, plays a training role while it is actually in progress; but it can also have after-effects by being instrumental in the design and organization of subsequent training programmes.

Research into human rights education should therefore become the basis for teacher training of a specific and relevant kind covering the three dimensions mentioned above.

This mention of specific training leads on to the third question to be considered, which is: Should human rights be made part of general teacher-training programmes, or should separate courses in human rights education be provided?

This question may be raised particularly in connection with training courses on school life and the atmosphere of classrooms and schools. In France, for example, there are initial and further training courses on this subject for school heads and educational advisers, but they include no explicit reference to human rights education or to the concept of democracy.

Is this satisfactory? Surely not. If no such reference is made, school life will go on and the pupils will elect their representatives without any guarantee that they understand the fundamental relationship between human rights and the orderly, democratic running of an institution.

In order to make pupils as well as teachers aware of their duty to respect human rights in their everyday lives and in their attitudes and behaviour towards one another, that duty should be explicitly related to the transmission of knowledge (historical, legal and civic) on human rights. This means organizing specific courses on 'school life and human rights education' for the benefit of school principals, educational advisers and guidance counsellors with, of course, the participation of teachers.

During such courses it can be demonstrated that the credibility of human rights education depends on the degree of internal democracy resulting from the school's regulations. It has repeatedly been proved that young people are sceptical about ethical principles and values which are not applied in everyday life at school. Human rights education thus becomes the concern of all the adults in the school and hence part of the school's policy.

The board of governors of a primary lower secondary or upper secondary school can then make provision for a whole range of activities designed to promote awareness of and respect for human rights, such as:

1. Human rights action projects (exhibitions, special events, performance of plays with a human rights message, etc.).
2. Systematic transmission of knowledge connected with human rights, with a concerted sharing of effort by the different teachers concerned.
3. Democratic drawing up of the school's regulations and the provision of machinery for the peaceful settlement of conflicts.
4. Organization of lectures and debates on developments concerning human rights.

There is thus every reason to hold specific courses on 'Human Rights and School Life' in order to develop a realistic perspective based on human rights in a democratic context.

Even more specific are training courses on the teaching of human rights, where legal, historical, sociological and philosophical strands of knowledge converge and overlap. These are multidisciplinary courses in which a single approach (an historical one, for example) would be insufficient. Law is one of several subjects which are not part of the general training provided for teachers. Yet it is essential that teachers learn about the mechanisms by which human rights are enshrined in laws and international covenants, by which they are guaranteed in individual states and internationally. It is essential, for example, that European teachers should be aware of the existence of the European Court of Human Rights and of the way it functions, as well as, of course, the text by which it was instituted: the 1950 European Convention on Human Rights together with its protocols.

It should be clearly understood that I am referring to courses where the transmission of legal information is essential but where such information is always accompanied by guidance on educational methodology. For each new piece of information, the following questions should be addressed:

*   When or at what age should such and such a concept or fact be taught?
*   How should such concepts and facts be taught?
*   What form of evaluation should be adopted?

Teachers who have attended such courses should be capable of setting up with their colleagues some real multidisciplinary human rights projects designed to serve as a basis for the teaching of human rights throughout an educational cycle (lower secondary education, for example, where the pupils are the right age for this type of learning).

Reference was made earlier to school policies reflecting a constant concern for human rights, and mention has just been made of multidisciplinary teaching projects on human rights.

All these training courses are in fact different stages in the process of preparation for teaching by projects, an educational method admirably suited to the subject of human rights. Does this signify that human rights is but a means of training teachers in teaching by projects? Not at all. Even if human rights is a highly suitable subject for such teaching, it still requires specific training. We have seen this in respect of the cognitive aspects (the first two themes mentioned at the outset, with their legal, historical and philosophical connotations) as well as in respect of social life at school (theme 3).

We could repeat the same analysis in connection with the intercultural approach to education. Here, too, it is the teacher's educational project that gives a precise meaning to the intercultural dimension, preventing the teacher from making mistakes and digressing from the subject of human rights.

All these forums of teacher training on the four themes mentioned should be internationalized or, to begin with, at least Europeanized. Europe is being built. Indeed, it already exists. But an education for Europe or an educational Europe cannot exist without reference to, or, indeed, being based on, human rights. And so how can we continue to let each European state go its own way and act independently when it comes to training teachers in human rights?

Either human rights are universal and apply to all human beings, or they are meaningless. To create unequal groups, even if they are 'national' rather than ethnic ones, is to fail to show respect for human rights. As well as corresponding with the universal essence of human rights, international training courses provide an opportunity to compare the experience of different countries, benefit from differences in teaching practices and promote cultural and personal exchanges amongst teachers.

The Council of Europe and UNESCO already organize numerous seminars and symposia for teachers and educationists on the subject of education in human rights. However useful these encounters may be, though, they merely serve as stimuli or incentives and are no substitute for systematic training in human rights education on an international scale. This training is the responsibility of member states. What, then, can be done to give teacher training the international dimension it is lacking?

The Council of Europe could persuade its various member states' education ministers to undertake jointly to organize a given number of training courses on which so many places would be reserved for teachers from the other states. This would be done on a reciprocal basis, of course, with travel and accommodation costs, but not other course expenses, being borne by the teachers' countries of origin. I am convinced – the success of the summer school and training courses organized by the International Institute of Human Rights in Strasbourg, as well as those organized by the Geneva Training Institute in conjunction with the EIP (École Instrument de Paix) gives me every reason to believe this – that large numbers of teachers would be willing to travel abroad to attend these international training courses of a multidisciplinary kind, yet specifically geared to human rights education.

During these courses, the non-governmental organizations recognized by UNESCO or the Council of Europe would have an opportunity not only to describe their activities but also to demonstrate clearly the international solidarity existing among their members and the assistance (in the form of teaching aids, for example) they are able to offer teachers and pupils.

Experience in France has shown that NGO participation in teacher-training courses is much more effective than direct intervention in schools. Teachers are better informed of each NGO's possibilities and aims, and they can thus choose whichever NGO is most in tune with the action they have in mind and plan their educational projects in co-operation with its representatives. Their school will benefit in the process by being offered a window on the outside world. Experience has also shown us that language is not a barrier but merely a difficulty to be overcome. Indeed, it is a difficulty that can be a source of linguistic enrichment and advancement.

There is nothing utopian about such proposals for international but specific training courses. Once again, the Council of Europe and UNESCO have demonstrated that they can be put into practice. The problem, as stated earlier, is one of dissemination. If the various governments can be convinced by these international organizations of the need for genuine teacher-training programmes leading to sound and coherent human rights education in their countries, then the expansion of such education is a realistic prospect.

Without education, human rights will stagnate and remain a superficial concept. As Federico Mayor rightly stated: 'Studying human rights and transmitting them to others is one way of contributing to their recognition.'

But a knowledge of human rights cannot be achieved without sound and coherent teaching and education aimed at human rights themselves, and there can be no teaching and education designed to promote a knowledge of and respect for human rights unless teachers receive specific training in the matter. The fact is that for teachers, as for other human beings, including their students, 'a knowledge of the law and of rights is not natural . . . As with every idea created in and by history, education is needed to transmit the principles and values that give human rights themselves their legal basis. Defending human rights and condemning violence are necessary yet negative actions that cannot be understood or desired rationally unless a knowledge and awareness of those rights is developed through education.'

APPENDIX

Strasbourg Summer School, 1988

Organized jointly by the INRP (National Institute of Educational Research), the R. Cassin International Institute of Human Rights and the Council of Europe, this summer school was designed to inform and train teacher trainers; the course directors were François Audigier, research officer at the INRP, and Guy Lagelée, a secondary school teacher.

Programme

Day 1

The different dimensions of human rights education.
The foundations of human rights.
   Two approaches:
   – *philosophical approach*: human rights and natural law.

– *economic approach*: rights; freedoms and rights; claims.

Day 2

Historical approach:
The 1789 Declaration of the Rights of Man and the Citizen.
The 1948 Universal Declaration of Human Rights.
– How to co-ordinate education in human rights and peace with education in development and international understanding.
– Human rights education and teaching by projects.

Day 3

– An example of the study of the 1789 Declaration by fifth-formers.
– Round-table discussion: the definition of equality by an historian, a lawyer and a philosopher.
– Group work designed to devise methods of studying the 1948 Universal Declaration.

- in primary schools
- in lower secondary schools
- in upper secondary schools
- in teacher training

Day 4

– Outline of the international protection of human rights.
– The state based on the rule of law.
– The Council of Europe.
– Presentation and critical analysis of audiovisual material.
– NGOs and schools.

Day 5

– The principles of law and human rights in French law.
– The young and their rights.
– Incorporating an introduction to law in teaching.
– Analysis of civic education syllabuses.

Day 6

– Group work: human rights education and school life.
– Discussion of the book *La démocratie dans l'école* with the author, F. Rueff Escoubès.

Conclusions

The organization of teacher-training courses.

REFERENCES

Abdallah-Pretceille, M. (1989) *Human Rights Education in Pre-primary Schools*, Donauechingen Seminar, Council of Europe, DECS/EGT (88) 31.

Audigier, F. (1987) *Éducation aux droits de l'homme*, Research Report No. 13, Institut National de Recherche Pédagogique, France.

Best, F., Kahn, J, and Stobart, M. (1989), 'Mediathèque' of the French Community of Belgium, in *Droits de l'homme, droits des peuples*, first chapter, MCFB, asbl, Brussels.

De Raymond, J.-F. (1988) *Les enjeux des droits de l'homme*, Larousse, France.

Heater, D. (1985) *Human Rights Education in Schools: Concepts, Attitudes and Skills*, Council of Europe, DECS/EGT (84) 26.

Lagelée, G. and Vergnaud, J.-L. (1988) *La conquête des droits de l'homme: textes fondamentaux*, Le Cherche Midi, Paris.

Perotti, A. (1985) *Action to Combat Intolerance and Xenophobia and Action to Promote an Intercultural Society*, Council of Europe.

Rey, M. (1986) *Training Teachers in Intercultural Education?* Studies by the Council for Cultural Cooperation, 1977–83. Council of Europe.

Starkey, H. (1987) *Teachers' Course on 'Teaching and Learning about Human Rights in the Compulsory School'*, Birkerod Seminar, Council of Europe, DECS/EGT (86) 91.

Zweyacker, A., Lagelee, G. *et al.*, (1988) *Éducation civique* (3rd-year textbook), Paris, Hatier.

PART 3

MEETING THE CHALLENGE OF CONTEMPORARY SOCIAL AND EDUCATIONAL POLICIES

Preface

Human rights education is one aspect of education being experienced by young people whose adult and working lives will be in the twenty-first century. It is one movement among many movements in education and in society. One feature of human rights education is that it brings together a number of concerns, particularly those which intend to promote justice and peace in society and in the world. In this sense human rights education may be swimming with the current where there are social and educational policies designed to bring about great justice. On the other hand, economic policy, in many parts of the world, receives precedence over social and educational policy. Where this is the case the effects are often, in the short term at least, to widen the gap between rich and not rich. This is true globally, where the debt crisis sees the world's poorest countries paying tribute to the world's richest banks to the detriment of social and educational policy. It is also true locally, where the drive to economic liberalization and renewal has been accompanied in many countries by cuts in education and welfare provision.

The concern for justice and peace implicit in human rights education may thus be a challenge to political and economic priorities. Conversely the fact of liberal economic policies and the political movements and parties associated with them may, in the end, be a challenge to human rights education itself. Can education for justice and peace in the world have any sense in a fundamentally unjust and unpeaceful world?

Educators are optimists. Faced with unjust systems we prepare people to play their part in changing them. One way we do this is to offer alternative visions of the world. Micheline Rey, for instance, points out that intercultural education demands new norms and new reference points. Where frequently educational policy has been of assimilation of minorities, that is, of adjustment of the minorities to the system, a human rights approach demands that the system also adjust. It should take account of the background and experiences of all individuals involved. In any case there may well be greater and more significant differences between members within majority groups than between them and people from minorities. Caroline Roaf asks us to consider whether differences between people are relevant to the educational process. She concludes that, as things stand, membership of a minority group is certainly a relevant difference. However, just as access ramps for people in wheelchairs make their difference less relevant, so other provision, such as language support, may make linguistic background a less relevant difference.

Caroline Roaf also points to the importance of advocacy and the assertion of rights for those not receiving their entitlement to equality of respect and concern. This group may well include women and girls, as Margherita Rendel argues. Women's history, for example, is barely represented yet in schools, but it is 'a different record and a record with different values'. Such a view of history must surely, she maintains: 'contribute to greater respect for women and hence to a willingness to accord women a more equal place'. Human rights education, here too, is concerned to change perceptions of the world. That this is a challenge to education structures is confirmed by Keith McLeod, who notes that, in spite of legislation couched in human rights language and much official backing for multiculturalism, as it is termed in Canada, there still remains resistance to changing the cultural content of secondary education. Much has, however, been achieved in the Canadian system as multiculturalism has shifted from simply celebrating cultures to a concern for equity and a regard for outcomes.

David Shiman also stresses the importance of offering students the opportunity to create new world-views. Human rights charters are in themselves, he points out, lenses through which to view the world. One activity he proposes involves studying different charters and human rights documents to try to ascertain the world perspective adopted by their drafters. He stresses the need for a global framework and the interrelatedness of human rights issues and environmental concerns. As with the other contributors to Part 2 he is anxious to stress action skills. Students should be alert to possibilities for intervention.

In democratic societies it is often non-governmental organizations that lead the way in intervening to combat injustice and promote human rights. Pippa Bobbett's account of the activities of a number of such organizations working in the UK demonstrates the interaction between schools and groups in society. Students wishing to act to change an unjust situation may well work through or on behalf of a charity. Many schools have groups supporting the work of UNESCO, Amnesty International or Oxfam. At the same time the organizations and charities have an interest in producing educational materials, often of very high quality. The Council of Europe has always included NGOs, as such groups are called, in its discussions on educational matters. They are important and legitimate partners in education. Chapter 14 gives an indication of the range of groups and their concerns. Such groups represent also a sizeable constituency in society through their supporters and members. They are part of the international system of solidarity and advocacy on behalf of others that is a global challenge to injustice.

CHAPTER 9

Human Rights and Intercultural Education

Micheline Rey

EXPERIENCING HUMAN RIGHTS IN AN INTERCULTURAL CONTEXT

Human rights are not just those stodgy texts gathering dust under a pile of other documents waiting to be read on your desk. They are also references in the field of individual and collective rights that are as relevant to our own social behaviour as they are to the behaviour of others in far-away places of little concern to us. They are also projects which bear the stamp of the periods when they were formulated and which demand to be critically assessed by us as well as updated, implemented and further developed.

Teachers can teach human rights, but they can also experience human rights with their pupils, in their own environment: they can experience diversity and thwart the mechanisms of domination, inequality, rejection, intolerance and denial; they can overcome the misunderstandings which differences tend to generate; and they can promote the same awareness in others.

Some feel that such concepts as 'interculturalism' and 'human rights' are irrelevant and superfluous in education. What purpose is served by interculturalism and human rights education, they ask, when all education is 'obviously' aimed at the development of all children? They forget that saying is not the same as doing and that our references are not universal. Education is threatened by individual and collective egocentrism as well as by socio- and ethnocentrism. Particular vigilance is necessary.

Accordingly, human rights education is a matter of experience and awareness (which undoubtedly stimulates thinking and knowledge) rather than a question of teaching a 'subject'. And, to my mind, an intercultural approach is essential if human rights education is to transcend ethnocentrism. It should be envisaged in terms of strategies and relationships. The strategies should be aimed at:

- challenging our egocentric certainties;

- modifying the weight attached to different skills, values and cultures, whether or not they are represented in our communities;
- transforming and diversifying balances of power and offering a position of equality to those who have been devalued as well as to their skills and modes of expression;
- fostering desegregation and the recognition of the complexity of relations existing not only between human beings but also between cultures, social classes, institutions, education systems, academic subjects, scientific objects and so on;
- and, finally, developing communication between individuals, groups and communities and ensuring that it is positive and enriching for all concerned.

That was how interculturalism was construed when, upon completing its work, the group of experts set up by the Council of Europe's Council for Cultural Cooperation to study the training of teachers responsible for educating migrants' children stated in its conclusions that the intercultural approach encapsulated the Council of Europe's whole action:

> The intercultural approach is recognized not only as worthy of inclusion in the Council of Europe's cultural priorities, but also as a means of recapitulating its whole activity, in the double sense which can be given to this term. On the one hand, the intercultural approach defines and sums up the nature of the efforts made by the Council of Europe since its creation in developing human rights, promoting international understanding and establishing the European Cultural Convention. On the other hand, it constitutes a point of reference, a method and a stimulating theoretical framework for carrying out all its programmes and activities. (Rey, 1986, pp.7, 8)

Since then the term 'interculturalism' has become more widespread and been the subject of much controversy. I should, however, like to demonstrate that, when all is said and done, an intercultural approach, which covers the social field in its entirety, is essential if human rights education is to go beyond the latent egocentrism, sociocentrism and ethnocentrism which distort our view of the world.

I shall attempt to do this in three different ways: first, by presenting an historical outline of the context in which the intercultural concept developed in the Council of Europe and of the Council's activities in the matter, then by making some terminological remarks, and, finally, by giving some examples of the methods that can be used in human rights education.

THE MIGRATION PHENOMENON AND THE DEVELOPMENT OF THE INTERCULTURAL APPROACH IN THE COUNCIL OF EUROPE
From Education of Migrants to Human Rights Education

I shall use the term 'migrants' in a generic sense, even though other terms might be more accurate in certain cases, such as 'emigrants', 'immigrants' and 'cultural, linguistic, ethnic or religious groups or minorities', for the choice of words depends on the historical context and the scientific references used.

The intercultural approach in the Council of Europe was first developed in connection with the migration problem, as part of the Council's work on the integration of migrant workers into the industrialized countries of Western Europe. Although it cannot be limited to such a context, the context is nonetheless significant. For one thing, it underlines the attention paid to *relationships of domination* and to those who are left out of the process of development in the industrialized countries and, secondly, it points the way towards the *recognition of others regardless of national, economic, social, ethnic and religious barriers*.

What is more, the attitudes of industrialized countries towards migrants, asylum-seekers and refugees is illustrative of their relations with 'others' and of the place they reserve for those who are different. And the attitudes of schools are indicative of the attitudes and choices of the community both in its present circumstances and in its projects for the future. The fluctuations and changes which have occurred over the last 20 years thus reflect how our schools and communities viewed and continue to view human relations and human rights in terms of realities, hopes and disillusions.

Of course, this outline of developments in perceptions of migratory movements and the education of migrant groups and the indigenous population in a migration context will not be an exhaustive one. The choice of aspects covered will be subjective, and particular attention will be paid to the educational field, which is what concerns us here, and to activities in which I myself have taken part, partly because they are what I know best and I am therefore better placed to identify their effects, and partly because this participation illustrates a genuine form of interaction which is common in the Council of Europe and essential in the promotion of social action at international level, namely the network of collaboration between local and national field-workers and the staff of the institutions concerned. But what I am most concerned with and would urge the reader to observe are the changes of outlook brought about by the intercultural approach, in terms of the recognition of others as partners, the joint study of our society's problems, and the sharing of its assets.

These changes of outlook are also to be found in the sphere of human rights. First of all: marginalization of the problem, Manichaeism, attitude of superiority, egocentricity and ethnocentrism ('Violations of human rights occur elsewhere, not in our countries'), and shifting of responsibility on to others. Then: thanks to human rights education, a gradual awakening to cultural interactions and to the need to learn intercultural communication, a common questioning which postulates the existence of universal, worldwide responsibility and considers humanity in its diversity and human rights in their spacial and temporal framework ('There is room for improvement in human relations and human rights both here and elsewhere. However, such improvement is not a matter of course; it requires time, a particular form of social behaviour and education in solidarity.').

Some Salient Aspects of the Activities of the Council of Europe and the Council for Cultural Co-operation With Regard to the Education of Migrants and Intercultural Relations

As early as 1965 the Council of Europe concerned itself with the situation of migrant workers. At that time of economic expansion, the industrialized countries of Western Europe were importing manpower on an ostensibly temporary basis to make up for the shortage of local workers. They were little inclined to consider the problems of social integration, family reunification and training. The work of the CAHRS (Special Representative's Advisory Committee for National Refugees and Overpopulation) led to several resolutions being adopted.

1970: Adoption of Resolution (70) 35 (of the Committee of Ministers of the Council of Europe) school education for the children of migrant workers, recommending that member states guarantee the exercise of the right to school education for children of migrant workers and take all necessary steps for their integration (information, assistance with enrolment, academic and medical reports, special classes or lessons whenever appropriate but only for as long as is strictly necessary, supervised study periods, access to pre-school education and leisure activities, participation by parents in the life of the school, teaching of the language and culture of origin, training of teachers, co-operation between immigration and emigration countries, recognition of qualifications and diplomas, courses in the host country for teachers from the country of origin and vice versa, educational reintegration in the event of a return to the country of origin, etc.).

1972: Running of experimental special classes to encourage the implementation of Resolution (70) 35.

Having personally been responsible, in 1974–75 and 1975–76, for some of the Council of Europe's experimental classes in Geneva, where reception classes had existed in secondary education since 1968, I was asked in 1978 to assess the methods used to organize and implement the programme of experimental classes (Rey, 1979). Following the proposals put forward in my own report and in subsequent reports (Perotti, 1982; Karagiorges, 1984), the programme was extended and transformed in 1986 into a programme of experiments in intercultural education, conducted both in countries of origin and in host countries under the supervision of a joint group of experts of the CDCC (Council for Cultural Cooperation) and the CDMG (European Committee on Migration, which had replaced the CAHRS).

1973 and 1974: The CDCC took over responsibility for the matter and organized meetings of experts to examine the problems of specialized training for teachers responsible for teaching the children of migrant workers. I took this opportunity to stress the importance of training for *all* teachers and all educational staff (advisers, etc.) in primary and secondary schooling, not only for those teaching in 'special' classes of migrant children.

1974: *Ad hoc* conference on the education of migrants.

1977–1983: The CDCC set up a working group to develop its action concerning the *training of teachers* responsible for teaching the children of migrants. After being appointed to chair the group, I invited its members to adopt an *intercultural* approach (an expression borrowed from a report on an experiment conducted by the IRFED in Fontenay-sous-Bois in 1975, where exchanges had taken place between migrants and local people on a *reciprocal* footing). It was on the basis of this programme that the intercultural approach was developed and conceptualized in the Council of Europe (Porcher, 1979; Rey, 1986), while numerous consciousness-raising measures were carried out: reports on the sociocultural situation of migrants and minority groups such as gypsies and nomads, survey of intercultural education schemes, bilateral and multilateral teacher-training seminars and detailed investigation of certain fields (the situation of Muslim children, the education of gypsy children, collaboration with the media, etc.).

Looking back over the ground covered so far, we can see that for a long time in Europe the integration of families of migrant workers into their host countries or upon their return home was not considered a priority concern and that their rights as human beings were not always recognized. Those who did show concern for them (individuals or institutions) were themselves in danger of being ostracized. In view of the magnitude of the educational problems facing not just migrant children but also the children of workers belonging to the disadvantaged social strata, the term *handicap* was used to describe the difficulties experienced by them (either linguistic or social handicaps). On that basis, various compensatory educational measures were introduced. This approach went hand in hand with a policy of assimilation or integration (for those able to stay on in the host country) requiring one-way adaptation of the migrants to the local community and its standards. These measures came in for considerable criticism: not only did the compensatory education prove inappropriate, increasing the workload without solving the problem, but also the very notion of handicap was misleading, for it implied that responsibility for the difficulties lay with the victims, whereas the causes were in fact external.

Then there was talk of *denial*, in the form of non-recognition of the skills, references, values, modes of expression needs and sociocultural rights of the populations concerned. Awareness of this denial led to a reverse trend: the host community and schools were asked to adapt to the migrants. It was important to recognize their needs, languages and cultures. But this reaction was also criticized. The highlighting of cultural differences entailed a risk of caricatural folklorization as well as stigmatization and ostracizing of the individuals or groups concerned. It was also pointed out that schools, having long been instruments of conservation and unification, could not suddenly become factors for openness and diversity. And finally it was considered misleading to talk about culture when the causes of the difficulties were social ones. Wherever schools were still grappling with the problem of educating for newly arrived immigrant children with numerous adaptational difficulties (as in Switzerland, for example), this approach was felt to be a luxury rather than an urgent necessity.

The truth of the matter is more complex than is suggested by these two trends in favour of one-way adaptation on the part of the migrants or the host community. It was therefore important not to reject either but to attempt to perceive the links between the different factors involved and combine them in a *dialectical* approach. The *intercultural* approach stressed the fundamental importance of interactions and the need to appraise them more fully and act accordingly. Let us not forget (Bordieu, 1977) that people's behaviour with regard to society, education, learning, etc. is influenced by the practical benefit they hope to derive from their linguistic, social or cultural activity. That is the basis on which their personality is forged (confident, hesitant, shy, passive, aggressive, etc.). The recognition – and schools have an important part to play in this respect – of migrants' status as human beings and social beings in the first instance, then of their languages, values, cultural references and forms of expression, not forgetting their right to choose their own means of identification, was seen to be an essential condition for breaking out of the vicious circle generating the real difficulties which are perceived as internal ones (handicaps), but whose causes actually lie mainly in social balances of power and in the hierarchization of values. The accent should therefore be placed on mutual respect and interrelations at all levels and between all individuals and groups making up the educational, local and international community.

> 1984: Recommendation (84) 18 of the Committee of Ministers to member states on the training of teachers in education for intercultural understanding, notably in a context of migration.
>
> 1985: Recommendation (84) 9 of the Committee of Ministers to member states on second-generation migrants.
>
> 1980–1984: In view of the interest expressed by many member states in the continuation of work on the education of migrants, the Council of Europe set up a broader project with the help of experts from many member states, under the chairmanship of L. Porcher, encompassing the whole educational and cultural field in countries of origin and host countries. The project was known as CDCC Project 7 on the education and cultural development of migrants. It was concerned first and foremost with the integration of second-generation migrants. In order to relate theory to practice, the group of experts made analyses of significant educational and/or cultural experiments in the form of case studies or visits, and prompted various activities in host countries and countries of origin. To elucidate the more difficult aspects, the group conducted studies and held hearings of experts (for example, on the concept of immigrant culture, the effects of migration on the role of women, the

economic and political dimensions of migration, sociocultural innovation and the role of associations in member states).

From the conceptual viewpoint, Project 7 confirmed the fundamentally dialectical and dynamic intercultural approach and laid stress on the relations underpinning our societies. Migratory phenomena are made up of the functional interlocking of differences and similarities (Porcher, 1984). Both amongst migrants and between migrants and local citizens the differences are numerous (diversity of ethnic, national or cultural groups, social classes, ages, languages, lifestyles, statuses, needs, etc.), but so are the similarities (living in the same place at the same time, being dependent on the same socioeconomic structures, belonging to the same human species having the same rights, aspiring to the same right of expression, etc.). To understand the reality of the situation is to understand the interactions between these two dimensions.

The reality of the situation is that immigrants have become an integral part of the community. In other words, European societies have become multicultural. They can no longer be defined as consisting of local citizens on the one hand and immigrants on the other. The question of identity arises to the same degree for all. The fact is that values are diverse, identities are multidimensional, affiliations plural and differences shared. Networks of communication and participation need to be developed which both preserve plurality and ensure social cohesion and justice (Porcher et al. 1986; Rey, 1987).

At the end of Project 7 the CDCC handed over the baton to individual member states, leaving it to them to continue on a larger scale what it itself initiated by way of pilot schemes. It did, however, co-operate by co-financing many activities: conferences, workshops, magazines and competitions designed to develop intercultural education and communication.

The concept of responsibility towards migrants and the intercultural approach were also included in other CDCC projects (modern languages, primary education, etc.), or taken up, as appropriate, by other sectors of the Council of Europe. The following examples are just three of many:

1983: a symposium on the human rights of foreigners in Europe;
1987: the Parliamentary Assembly's European Days on the theme 'Enjoying our diversity';
The CDMG's current project on intercommunity relations.

Other international organizations, both governmental and non-governmental, also took up the intercultural approach and continued the investigation, not only in the educational field, e.g. UNESCO, the Commission of the European Communities, the World Organization for Early Childhood Education, the Association for Teacher Education in Europe and the International Association for Intercultural Education, but also in the social field in general, at local, national and international level.

While the predominant trend at the end of Project 7 was towards the integration of second-generation migrants and of ethnic and cultural minorities of migrant origin, other responsibilities were emerging and new challenges looming up (Widgren, 1987) in connection, for example, with:

- clandestine migration, which is basically due to the economic imbalance between emigration and immigration countries and which calls for a worldwide effort of North–South co-operation;
- the civic rights of foreigners;
- the combating of xenophobic and racist tendencies;
- the reception of asylum-seekers.

Migratory movements may be changing in nature, but they are still continuing and indeed increasing. The interactions and responsibilities involved have taken on worldwide proportions. Respect for human rights, equality of educational opportunity, social recognition and intercultural communication in the local and international community are all interdependent.

A WORD ABOUT TERMINOLOGY

Regardless of the context in which it is used, the word 'intercultural', precisely because it contains the prefix 'inter', necessarily implies: interaction, exchange, desegregation, reciprocity, interdependence and solidarity. As it also contains the term 'culture', it further denotes in its fullest sense: recognition of the values, lifestyles and symbolic conceptions to which human beings, both as individuals and in groups, refer in their dealings with others and in their vision of the world, as well as recognition of the interactions occurring both between the multiple registers of one and the same culture and between the various cultures, in space and in time.

The intercultural approach has two dimensions:

- Firstly, in terms of facts (objective, descriptive and scientific dimension), the approach means recognizing the dynamics which were set in motion by migratory movements and all forms of contact between individuals, social groups and peoples; as well as recognizing the *reality of the interactions* which shape and transform our communities and trying to describe how they operate, for dialectics, interaction and intercultural dynamics appear to give a better picture of reality than mere juxtaposition.
- Secondly, in terms of a *project* (political and educational dimension), the approach means making sure that these interactions contribute to mutual respect and the formation of cohesive communities rather than accentuating relations of domination and attitudes of exclusion and rejection.

English-speaking countries have often preferred other terms, such as 'multicultural' or 'antiracist', to describe their approach. The intercultural approach does not preclude this, but it goes an important step further by challenging segregation, exclusion and egocentrism. Its strength lies in the fact that, even in the choice of terms, it explicitly affirms the essential role of interactions and of our responsibility towards them in everything concerning human beings and their rights.

And how does intercultural education fit in? It fits in fairly easily, for it is neither more nor less than an acknowledgement of this multiple reality and its interactions applied to a particular environment (schools and educational establishments in general) which uses its own resources (those of intercultural teaching) in a context of mutual comprehension, respect and enrichment.

INTERCULTURAL EDUCATION AND HUMAN RIGHTS EDUCATION: METHODOLOGICAL APPROACHES AND LINES OF ACTION

A Word about Methodology

It should be made clear first of all that intercultural education is not only aimed at migrants, minority groups or 'others' in general. It is aimed to the same extent and at the same time at 'ourselves', whoever we may be. This is a fundamental principle which, for all of us, underlines any educational activity – from infant schooling to vocational training, university studies and adult education. But it is not an end in itself. It is but a means of better achieving the more general objectives of democratization of education, equality of opportunity, promotion of human rights and learning of solidarity.

It should also be clearly understood that intercultural education does not mean substituting new concerns for the tasks which schools and educational institutions already perform, or adding an extra subject to the curriculum.

But there can be no respect for or promotion of human rights without a reappraisal of the egocentric relations and socio- and ethnocentric standards prevalent in schools, i.e. without a re-examination of schools' criteria.

Of course, nobody perceives the world, life, reality or nature itself in a completely objective, universal manner. We view life through the prisms and systems formed by our culture and social background and inculcated in us by our education. Reality may be said to be a sort of chaos which human beings view through the lenses of their cultures and social experiences, organize by passing it through their filters and manage according to their systems of *codes* (all these metaphors being suitable for use by educators to help their students to understand diversity). In our multicultural communities it is important to be aware of this. We also know that it is beneficial for the cognitive and relational development of the child to bring him or her into contact with several languages (the 'stereolinguistic' approach). Similarly, he or she can benefit from coming into contact with various cultures and social environments which differ from his or her own. In this way schools can help children to discover and accept diversity, thus enabling them to overcome cultural barriers and misunderstandings and acquire a communication basis which is not distorted by a lack of suitable references for interpreting the behaviour of others.

Every aspect of school life and its relationship with families and the community lends itself to an intercultural approach and an enquiry into respect for human rights, whether it be the cost of education, the way in which children are selected and classified, the design of school premises, the teaching methods advocated, the training of staff (and of which categories of staff? – either teachers alone or everybody involved in the educational process, such as psychologists and social workers, librarians, secretaries, caretakers, teacher trainers and health personnel?) or the organization of curricula and timetables. In the same way, all school subjects may provide vehicles and opportunities for (intra- or interdisciplinary) intercultural activities.

However, just as the intercultural dimension is not an end in itself but a means to an end, so intercultural activities are merely tools – necessary ones, it is true, but not sufficient in themselves. As instruments of intercultural teaching, they raise a twofold problem: how to put the guidelines into practice ('What can we *do*?') and how to assess the results ('What purpose does it serve?').

In other words, teaching materials and intercultural activities considered as objects are merely residual factors. What really counts is the quality of the relationships they help to develop. They should therefore be designed in terms of strategies and dynamics. What should be assessed, then, is not the intrinsic quality of these media (when the wise man points at the moon, the fool looks at his finger), but rather the efficacy of these strategies – their positive effects, as well as the attendant traps and pitfalls. We must gauge the risks involved and weigh up the probability of failures or adverse side-effects in relation to possible alternative courses of action, so that the risks can be controlled. But this is no easy matter, for such an assessment can only be made in context and over a period of time, taking all the groups concerned into consideration (students, parents, teachers, social community, migrants, indigenous population, etc.), and bearing in mind the multiple nature of these effects (on learning, identities and relationships in schools and in the community).

Suggestions for Intercultural Activities

How can intercultural activities be discussed out of context when their very purpose is to materialize the intercultural dimension and bring it to life in everyday communication and encourage a committed process of thinking?

The interests and professional activities of readers of this volume will cover various sectors of the educational field; their teaching responsibilities will apply to students of all ages in a variety of institutional structures and in countries whose political systems, laws and terminologies differ, where the range of cultures in contact as well as the history and forms of such contacts differ . . . How can everybody's expectations be fulfilled in practice? It is impossible to allow for every possible situation or give an account of all the many projects carried out in Europe, particularly with the help of the Council of Europe. I shall therefore merely suggest one or two lines of action that can be followed with students or partners of different ages and statuses, illustrating them with examples from the professional, social, political and linguistic context in which I work. The reader is requested to forgive this ethnocentrism and make the necessary transpositions – and intercultural exercise in itself!

Line I: Education Experienced 'in Stereo'

From early infancy a stereocultural approach to education is beneficial. Sensory and motor development, expression and communication and relations with the environment are amongst the primary aims of infant education. They can give children an opportunity to discover the diversity of tastes, forms of expression, languages, social organization, lifestyles, rules of behaviour and relationships to life, time, animals and objects, the real and the imaginary, as well as learn to respect the freedom of others. Here are a few ideas:

- Filters, lenses and codes can form the basis of many practical activities designed to stress diversity: drawing what one sees through one's spectacles, inventing communication codes.

See, for example, Munter (1973) and UNICEF–UNESCO (1986).

- Rhythms, music, musical instruments and dances of various origins and their transition from one culture to another.
- Nursery rhymes and children's songs in several languages.

See, for example, Husler (1987).

- Observing how names vary from one region to another and from one environment to another and how great is the emotional charge they carry.
- Drawing the tree of life, or other subjects calculated to arouse intercultural awareness.

See, for example, Berefels et al. (1978).

- Kamishibai theatre.
- Fairy tales and short stories.
- Books, selected and used in accordance with the educational approach adopted.

See, for example, Spier (1981) and Ducamp (1983).

- Inviting teachers and children from other local kindergartens or schools (where a different language is spoken or a different religion practised, for example).
- Inviting parents and preparing for the occasion.
- Meals with dishes from different cultural traditions (educating the senses of smell, colour and taste; the importance of meals and their preparation in family and social life).
- Festivities, including family celebrations of different geographical or religious origins; if Christmas is celebrated, for example, the act of giving presents and the customs and rituals connected therewith can be studied.

- Pen-friend correspondence, which is possible even for young children through the use of cassettes, photographs, drawings, etc.
- Visits to places of culture (markets, museums, churches, mosques, pagodas, etc.) and participation, according to age, in local events (exhibitions, puppet theatres, films, artistic activities) which offer varying views of the world.

Line II: Intercultural Books, Libraries and Workshops

The space which school and public libraries allocate to books and audiovisual documents in the languages of the different cultural groups represented in the community, and their selection of documents relating to different cultures and regions of the world, are indicative of the way in which our schools and institutions view community relations. The arguments put forward in defence of egocentric attitudes are often dubious from the human rights point of view: 'Immigrants don't read anyway', 'They ought to become integrated and learn the local language', 'There is not enough room on the shelves', 'Only the local prison ever asks us for books in that language', 'How can we possibly classify books written in alphabets we do not understand?', and so on. What is to be inferred from such answers?

The provision of libraries with a wealth of documentary material representing different cultures and the organization of intercultural activities based on books can prove highly fruitful, particularly in primary education, as well as initiate a change in public opinion.

In the canton of Geneva, 140 nationalities are represented in the schools and more than one-third of all pupils have a mother tongue other than French. All the children from one of the canton's schools take part once a week during school hours in activities run at the intercultural workshop. The activities are based on the reading of a children's book (documentary, short story or fairy tale). The activity inspired by a particular book may take the form of the staging of a play, the making of an object or the learning of a dance, song or some words in a foreign language, often with the collaboration of language teachers or parents from the countries concerned. Other possible activities are a critical study, a research project, a survey, an exhibition, an exchange of documents with schools in other countries or a comparative investigation into living conditions in different places (e.g. the work children do, the games they play, the languages they speak and the occasions they celebrate). Children from every origin and every social background are encouraged to participate. Those of foreign origin feel recognized and show great enthusiasm; little by little, they pluck up the courage to speak about their countries and borrow books in their mother tongues. They gradually learn to share what they know and be tolerant towards others. On the basis of this experience, the workshop leader recently compiled a set of teaching sheets suggesting various activities: reading, writing, oral activities, vocabulary, geography, drawing, music and games (Zurbriggen, 1989).

During holidays, 'street libraries' visit multicultural working-class districts and organize activities based on books, which can be another means of democratizing reading and a source of fruitful cultural exchanges.

Books are undoubtedly an important element in the educational process, but not all texts lend themselves equally well to intercultural use. It is important in teacher training to consider how books should be selected and used. This was done in Geneva, for example, at an intercultural teaching seminar based on a display of 200 books selected by the Bern Declaration (Abdallah-Pretceille, 1984; 'Dis-moi comment ils vivent', 1983).

Line III: The Intercultural Dimension and Human Rights Education Through School Subjects in Secondary Education

All school subjects, be they modern languages, geography, history, civics, science, religious studies, ethics or whatever, can serve as a basis for intercultural practices and thinking, providing an education in human rights without necessarily requiring a departure from the set curriculum (indeed, teachers often have more room for manoeuvre than they realize).

I shall limit myself here to one or two examples.

Language teaching can open doors to other worlds besides the mother-tongue environment. It can provide an opportunity, for example, to discover how phonological 'filters', relations between written and oral codes, links with spelling and morphological and syntactical systems vary from one language to another, how words migrate in various forms from one language to another, and how the rules governing conversation and social intercourse differ from one language or culture to another. Students can also be encouraged to consider the role of their mother tongue as a vehicle of their identity and take an interest in the choice of languages taught at school as well as in linguistic rights (Rey, 1985).

The teaching of languages, including the mother tongue, gives an opportunity to *study different cultures and literature*. It is often forgotten, for example, that literature in French does not come only from France, Belgium, Switzerland and Canada, but also from the Maghreb countries and the French-speaking countries of Africa.

Supervised reading and literary analysis: although it is stated in curricula that teachers should study texts with their students, the choice of texts is sometimes left to the teachers. So why not choose texts that will make the students think about intercultural communication and human rights? The secondary education orientation cycle in Geneva is in the process of publishing some methodological sheets and packs on intercultural teaching compiled by a number of teachers. Among other things, they contain suggestions concerning Marie Féraud's novel *Anne ici, Sélima là-bas* (ed. Ducolot) and Montesquieu's 30th Persian Letter (Nouveaux Classiques Larousse).

History and geography can provide an opportunity to study migratory movements and the migration of foodstuffs. Gastronomy and exchanges of recipes can be a basis for studying the relationships between climate, agriculture, stock-breeding, fishing, local produce and food (meat, fish, cereals, spices, etc.) in different countries. Preparing meals consisting of traditional dishes from one region or another – an activity often suggested in connection with intercultural education, but which can also be a mere caricature unless it is incorporated into everyday life at school and is not dependent on the unreciprocated goodwill of migrants or minority groups – can be another source of learning and sharing rather than a confirmation of personal prejudices or a mere pandering to a taste for exoticism.

What idea of life in our countries, of international relations and of respect for human rights shall we offer through a study of *history*, and what *civic education* shall we provide?

The age of the 'Great Discoveries' is not, of course, viewed by the Swiss in the same way as by the Portuguese. This could offer a pretext for contacts and joint projects with teachers and pupils in classes studying the Portuguese language and culture. And what do non-Europeans think about this?

When students study the history of democratic Athens in the fifth century BC and learn to their surprise that people of mixed parentage did not vote, are they encouraged to think about voting rights and suffrage in our present-day countries, which also have foreigners and second-class citizens?

The bicentenary of the French Revolution and the Declaration of the Rights of Man and the Citizen was a fine opportunity to stimulate thinking about citizenship and the rights of non-citizens and foreigners. What are the disadvantages of non-citizenship and of being a foreigner? At its sitting on 15 March 1989 the European Parliament approved a proposed directive on the voting rights of member states' nationals in municipal elections in the member state of residence. But what rights do immigrants from non-member states enjoy?

There is no doubt that the non-citizens with the fewest rights of all in their country of residence are the increasingly numerous clandestine immigrants as well as seasonal workers. But they too are human beings, and what rights do they enjoy in each of our countries? The question of a right to schooling for clandestine children who cannot always be enrolled at state schools was, for example, recently raised by teachers in Geneva with the support of schoolchildren and members of the local community. Solutions are in preparation. This example illustrates the dynamic dimension of human rights education and the influence that the educational environment can have on the local community (Perregaux and Togni, 1989).

Line IV: Training of Teachers and Other Categories of Educational Staff

Teacher training should provide:

- conceptual tools (in this case, for the intercultural approach and for human rights and the promotion thereof) that will enable them to cope properly with the situation at local and international level and interpret instances of diversity in an appropriate manner;
- a knowledge of the relevant facts and documents as well as of the interactions between the populations involved, so that teachers may overcome their prejudices and one-sided attitudes;
- a subjective and relational experience that will make teachers aware of the complexity of the feelings and relationships involved in human and

intercultural contacts as well as of the potential for mutual enrichment which can be tapped;
- methodological tools that will equip teachers to apply the intercultural approach to their own teaching;
- suitable teaching aids.

One idea seemed to me particularly useful as a means of combining knowledge (of the migration phenomenon) and *experience* (of the complexity of the resultant relations), i.e. work based on the family trees of the trainees. In Switzerland, as elsewhere, almost every family can show examples of migration and experiences of rejection and curtailment of human rights – but also, when positive relations develop, of mutual enrichment. Realizing that they are personally affected by these matters modifies the trainees' outlook and their attitudes towards others (Rey, unpublished).

Line V: Transverse Strategies and Setting Up of Networks of Intercultural Thinking, Action and Training

One swallow does not make a summer. One intercultural activity does not make an intercultural education; and one discussion on human rights does not make a human rights education. It is important to organize networks of projects that combine various forms of intercultural practice in schools, training of teachers and educators, co-operation between the various levels of the education system, the sensitization of public opinion, the development of a sense of responsibility on the part of education authorities, and so on. The co-ordination of local, national and international activities is also of prime importance, since each of these dimensions can make an invaluable contribution to the others. A knowledge of local problems provides international organizations with the foundation they need, while the wide range of information and research they themselves provide, the recommendations made by them (often as a result of such co-operation) and subsequently disseminated by the media, and the symbolic or financial support they give to various activities constitute an appreciable form of backing for those working in the field, whose efforts are thus lent a certain status and sometimes given a wider impact.

Many things can be done to help to set up such a network. I shall give just one example to illustrate the links we are trying to develop in Switzerland in order to establish a network that will promote the intercultural approach in education. Some of the salient events were as follows:

1. For a year, with the participation of teachers, educational activities were conducted and methodological documents drawn up at local level; training sessions were then held to enable the teachers who had contributed to these activities to report on their work (this deadline was in itself a stimulus) and pursue their thinking further. The results were then published.
2. A nationwide competition was held, involving descriptions of practical intercultural education activities and projects and prompting

    contributions from a large number of teachers (including several of those who took part in the previous activity).

3.   All those who had submitted projects were invited to discuss the matter in greater depth at a Council of Europe seminar whose proceedings were published (Cesari, et al. 1985).

4.   Thanks to the setting up of an intercultural team at national level, the joint committee of the Centro Pedagogico Didattico of the Italian embassy in Bern was able, with the help of education authorities, representatives of emigration countries and the Council of Europe, to publish a magazine entitled: *Inter-Dialogos; Idées expériences, nouvelles pour l'éducation interculturelle en Suisse.*

And so the list goes on. Numerous links have thus been established which are helping to stimulate the thinking of all concerned in their everyday work.

These suggested lines of action are by no means exhaustive. They are just some examples which may be used by others who are working in the same direction, for the march towards education in solidarity and human rights goes on.

REFERENCES

Abdallah-Pretceille, M. (1984) 'Le livre dans une perspective interculturelle, comment le choisir, comment l'utiliser?' in Rey, M. (ed.) *Une pédagogie interculturelle: Actes des journées de formation d'enseignants des 8–10 mai 1984 à Genève*, Swiss National Committee for UNESCO, Bern, pp. 90–94.

Berefels, G., Lindstrom, S. and Wik-Thorsell, A. L. (1978) *L'arbre de vie: Le monde raconté par les enfants*, Radda, Barnen, Sweden.

'Dis-moi comment ils vivent' (1983) *Vers un Développement Solidaire*, no. 69 November.

Ducamp, J.-L. (1983) *Les droits de l'homme racontés aux enfants*, Les éditions ouvrières et le Temps apprivoisé, Paris.

Husler, S. (1987) *Trois tristes tigres . . . Drei traurige Tiger . . . Zaubersprüche, Geschichten, Verse, Lieder und Spiele für die mehrsprachige Kinder-(Garten) Gruppe*, Freiburg im Breisgau, Lambertus.

Karagiorges, A. (1984) *Evaluation of the Educational Aspects of the Council of Europe's Experimental Classes for the Academic Years 1981–82 and 1982–83*, Council of Europe, Strasbourg.

Munter, A. (1973) *Il mondo negli occhiali*, Emme Edizioni.

Perotti, A. (1982) *Pedagogical assessment of the Council of Europe's experimental classes from 1978–79 to 1980–81*, Council of Europe, Strasbourg.

Porcher, L. (1981) *The education of the children of migrant workers in Europe: Interculturalism and teacher training*, Council of Europe, Strasbourg.

Porcher, L. (1984) *Education and cultural development of migrants* interim report of the Project Group to the CDCC, Council of Europe, Strasbourg.

Porcher, L. *et al.* (1986) DECS/EGT (86) 11, Council of Europe, Strasbourg. Contains a list of documents published in connection with the project.

Rey, M. (1979) CAHRS (72) (79) rév.: *Assessment of the method for organizing and running the experimental classes of the Council of Europe*, Council of Europe, Strasbourg.

Rey, M. (1984) DECS/EGT (84) 84 (Brochure) du 21.9.1984: *Education of migrant workers' children* – 'The training of teachers', Final report of the working group, Council of Europe, Strasbourg.

Rey, M. (1985) 'Des cribles phonologiques aux cribles culturels: vers une communication interculturelle', *Bulletin Cila*, University of Neuchâtel, pp. 44–84.

Rey, M. (1986) *Training teachers in intercultural education? The work of the CDCC (1977–1983)*, Council of Europe, Strasbourg. Contains a list of documents published in connection with the programme.

Rey, M. (1987) *The educational and cultural development of migrants*, Abstract of the final report of the Project Group, Brochure DECS/EGT (87) 19, Council of Europe, Strasbourg. Contains a list of documents published in connection with the project.

Spier, P. (1981) *Quatre milliards de visages*, Écoles des Loisirs, Paris.

UNICEF–UNESCO (1986) *L'étranger vu par l'enfant*, Flammarion, Paris.

Widgren, J. (1987) *International Migration: New Challenges to Europe. Migrants in Western Europe: Present Situation and Future Prospects*. Third Conference of European Ministers responsible for Migration Affairs, Council of Europe, Strasbourg.

Zurbriggen, A. (1989) *Arc-en-ciel: Activités interculturelles*, Département de l'Instruction Publique, Geneva.

CHAPTER 10

Challenging Patriarchy and Hierarchy: The Contribution of Human Rights Education to the Achievement of Equality for Women

Margherita Rendel

Modern human rights instruments contain explicit articles specifying that the rights claimed or guaranteed are available without discrimination, and there then follows a list of the grounds on which discrimination is forbidden. These lists (which vary slightly) always include sex; and women (and girls) are entitled to the same civil and political, social, economic and cultural, and third-generation rights – peace, environment and development – as men. Human rights education must therefore include issues of gender and is incomplete and inadequate without them. Girls and boys must therefore be educated in such a way as to enable girls to enjoy, to use and to safeguard their rights.

Unfortunately, much of the official curriculum for girls has been and still is directed to fitting them for specific roles in society, especially as wives and mothers in the home, putting husbands and children first, and undertaking housewifely tasks in the labour market, for example as 'office wives', as carers in nursing and teaching, and as workers in catering, the clothing industry and the retail trade.

We shall see that human rights education challenges the ideologies and practice of patriarchy and hierarchy. First it is necessary to examine the provisions of human rights documents on education and, since employment casts its shadow before, on vocational training and employment. Then I shall review how far educational provision, both the official and the hidden curriculum, complies with the requirements of non-discrimination and what contribution equal opportunity legislation, anti-sexist education and Women's Studies make to promoting human rights. We shall find that anti-sexist education and Women's Studies can have a wide impact not only on equality for girls but also on implementing human rights generally.

In this chapter, I shall not discuss the various meanings of either patriarchy or hierarchy. By patriarchy, in this chapter, I mean male domination of females.[1] By hierarchy, I mean the ranking of groups one above the other, with legitimate authority or actual power in the hands of the superordinate group(s). Human rights instruments require equal rights for all human beings, a requirement which, while not claiming the equality of all human beings, must limit the legitimate authority of superordinates over subordinate individuals and groups. Several forms of hierarchy are expressly forbidden, for example slavery, serfdom, apartheid, racism and to some extent sexism.

It is apparent even from this summary that human rights instruments present a challenge to patriarchy and to hierarchy.

HUMAN RIGHTS INSTRUMENTS

I turn now to what some major human rights instruments say about education.

The Universal Declaration of Human Rights 1948 (UDHR) proclaims that

Everyone shall have the right to education. . . . Education shall be directed to the full development of the human personality and to the strengthening of respect for human rights and fundamental freedoms. (Article 26.)

Article 13 (1) of the International Convention on Economic, Social and Cultural Rights 1966 (ICES) is phrased in almost identical terms. In paragraph 2(b) it goes on

Secondary education in its different forms, including technical and vocational secondary education, shall be made generally available and accessible to all . . .

The Unesco Convention against Discrimination in Education 1960 defines discrimination as any distinction which has the purpose or effect

(a) Of depriving any person or group of persons of access to education of any type or at any level;
(b) of limiting any person or group of persons to education of an inferior standard (Article 1.)

However, the next article permits single-sex schools provided the same *or equivalent* courses are available (my emphasis) and private schools and separate religious or linguistic education, provided the courses conform to standards set by the public authorities and reach the same level. These provisions would permit specifically 'feminine' education for girls on the pretext that such courses were equivalent to mainstream courses and reached the same level.

The European Convention on Human Rights and Fundamental Freedoms has a much narrower provision in Article 2 of the First Protocol 1952:

No person shall be denied the right to education. In the exercise of any functions which it assumes in relation to education and to teaching, the State shall respect the right of parents to ensure such education and teaching in conformity with their own religious and philosophical convictions.

The jurisprudence (case law) on that article has widened its scope considerably. As I have argued elsewhere (Rendel, 1988), it might be possible as a result of the judgments in 1976 in *Kjeldsen, Busk Madsen and Pedersen* v. *Denmark* (1 EHRR 711) on compulsory sex education in schools and in 1982 in *Campbell and Cosans* v. *UK* (3 EHRR 531) on corporal punishment in schools for parents who disapprove of sexist (or racist) education for their daughters and sons to challenge it.

The Convention on the Elimination of All Forms of Discrimination against Women, 1979 (CEDW) provides in Article 10 for the same curricula and opportunities for girls and in addition for:

(c) The elimination of any stereotyped concept of the roles of men and women at all levels and in all forms of education by encouraging co-education and other types of education which will help to achieve this aim and, in particular, by the revision of textbooks and school programmes and the adaptation of teaching methods.

The provisions of this Convention and of the Recommendations on the teaching of human rights which I refer to below show a marked development in the recognition of the nature of discrimination against girls in education and reflect the impact since 1968 of the women's movement and of the work of individual feminists working in strategic positions in official bodies.

The recent Council of Europe Recommendation R (85) 7 specifically includes sexism and racism as forms of injustice which human rights education should be concerned about. As long ago as 1978, UNESCO's International Conference on the Teaching of Human Rights recommended:

13. Women's rights and roles in society should be a specific component of university curricula on human rights and steps should be taken to ensure that present curricula, in particular textbooks, are revised when necessary to include appropriate sections and references to women's rights . . . (20C/121, Annexe, 27 Oct. 1978)

Women's Studies are included in the draft seven-year plan for the development of the teaching of human rights (SS-79/CONF.608/4, 31 Oct. 1979). The European Parliament has invited members of the European Community to act on the UNESCO recommendations and has in its own document stressed that particular attention should be devoted to women's rights and the position of women.[2]

Education is both an end in itself and a prelude to and a preparation for vocational and professional training and employment and work. Many human rights instruments assert the right to such training and the right or opportunity for individuals to work and earn a living in an occupation of their own choosing. Such provisions can be found in UN instruments such as the Universal Declaration, and in instruments of UN specialized agencies, such as those of the ILO and in regional instruments, for example the European Social Charter (ESC). CEDW specifically recognizes the right of women working in the non-monetized section of the economy to vocational training.[3]

Provisions in inter-American and African instruments of human rights are much more limited than those in the instruments referred to in the previous paragraph.

GIRLS' EDUCATION

We might expect from this multiplicity of authoritative declarations and conventions that girls' education in Britain would conform to the requirements of human rights standards. Britain is, after all, a country with a long tradition of concern for rights, and demands for equality in girls' education go back to the seventeenth century.[4] However, the research shows that girls and women are still at the present time disadvantaged at school, in further, higher, vocational and technical education, in the official curriculum and especially in the hidden curriculum.

This inequality reflects the continuance of past orthodoxy. For example, in 1959 the influential Crowther Report (Central Advisory Council for Education 1959) whilst noting the human right of boys and girls to education (paragraph 86) nonetheless accepted the existing sexual division of the labour market and merely regretted the inadequate training received by girls. It attributed these outcomes to early marriage, child-bearing and women's pattern of interrupted employment (paragraphs 496–497). It recommended for all girls, except the ablest, that

> though the general objectives of secondary education remain unchanged, [girls'] direct interest in dress, personal appearance and in problems of human relations should be given a central place in [their] education. (paragraph 52)

The subsequent Newsom Report still recommended the pretend-running of a home as a part of the curriculum for many girls (paragraphs 388–401), and expressed doubts about girls' interest in science (Central Advisory Council for Education, 1963; Wolpe, 1977).

The evidence of the courses followed by A-level students do not entirely support such doubts. The proportion of girls following mathematics and science courses at A-level had risen by some two-fifths to nearly one-third of all students between 1969 and 1987. At the lower level of school-leavers with O-level and higher grade CSE in mathematics, nearly half (45) per cent were girls in 1986 and in science subjects more than two-fifths (42 per cent), increases of 13 per cent and of 8 per cent over 1970.[5] However, the proportion of undergraduate students taking mathematics and physical sciences who were women was about 25 per cent and at postgraduate level only 18 per cent. These figures reflect substantial increases in the proportion of women studying these subjects over the last two decades.[6]

It is clear that girls' right to education was restricted and to a lesser extent still is. The figures I have quoted are illustrative of generalized practices reflecting the attitudes expressed in the two reports I have quoted (and in many other official statements of policy). These practices arise from the assumptions of teachers (many of whom are also parents), from specialization, especially for older students, and the way in which choices in the school timetable are structured as a result.

These factors have important consequences for jobs for school-leavers. Many better-paid jobs are those which require mathematics, science and technical skills. With the exception of medicine and veterinary science, these are the subjects in which it tends to be easier to obtain a university place. Thus the official curriculum still tends to exclude girls from the better opportunities for higher education and further vocational training and from the better-paid jobs in both the short and the long term.

The hidden curriculum of school, further and higher education still more clearly cuts girls out. Proportionally far fewer women than men hold headships (and principalships, university chairs) or other senior posts.[7] The example of women holding positions of power, even in schoolteaching, which has a majority of women, is lacking. The message to boys as well as girls is clear: men are the bosses. This absence of women is a cue for boys to resist the authority of women teachers and to resent the skills of clever or articulate girls. The result, as much research has shown, is that boys dominate the classroom and set the agenda.[8] It has been shown that too often boys occupy the central space in the classroom, forcing girls to the periphery, that they are unwilling to let the girls speak and misbehave when girls do, that they insist on their choice of topics when choice is permitted and deny girls their choice, and that they subject both girls and women staff to various forms of sexual harassment. The difficulties of women staff in dealing with such behaviour is compounded by the tendency of men teachers to collude with the boys.

In these ways boys practise techniques for subordinating women, which will assist them in maintaining the patriarchal gender hierarchy in later life. But such practices are intended also to teach girls and women that they must submit to male domination. So boys control a part of the hidden curriculum to the detriment of the rights of girls and of women teachers.

The enforcement of the rights of girls and women is, however, not straightforward, and can give rise to conflicts of rights. What, for example, are the rights of girls to equal education if their parents, for cultural or religious reasons, desire a traditionally 'feminine' education? And most human rights instruments accord parents rights in relation to the education of their children. Does the state have a right or a duty to override the wishes of parents in the interests of girls? Have girls a right to appeal to public or international bodies against the wishes of their parents for their education? Have public bodies a right to insist that the full development of the human personality and the interests of society require that all girls should learn the skills necessary to earn their own living at a level appropriate to their ability? Some would answer 'yes' to all four questions. They are questions which can apply to girls, and occasionally boys,[9] of all races and classes in British society.

WOMEN TEACHERS

Feminists have developed a variety of policies and techniques for countering patriarchal domination. National legislation, the Sex Discrimination Act (SDA) and the work of the Equal Opportunities Commission (EOC) give legitimacy to the techniques developed. The SDA (and the Race Relations Act (RRA)) are part of Britain's human rights legislation, as are the European Community Directives on equal pay and equal treatment. The EOC's large output of advisory material on equal opportunities for girls in schooling at all levels and in all types of subject are of value to teachers in developing their work, as well as more widely. The Commission has, furthermore, intervened with LEAs to secure, for example, that girls are taught craft, design and technology and boys domestic science (there have been more difficulties about the former than the latter). Such information, advice and pressure from a quango obviously provides useful support for teachers, and for non-sexist parents and children.

Sometimes on their own initiative, sometimes in response to pressure, local authorities, education authorities, schools and institutions of further and higher education have developed equal opportunities and anti-sexist policies. Hazel Taylor[10] describes how, for success, such policies require a political and administrative commitment and an educational component. Specific local policies need to be developed from the bottom up, but for this to be possible those 'at the bottom' need to understand the nature of sexism and to receive managerial support within their institutions. In turn the managers need both to receive support from and to be aware of the political will of the authority to see anti-sexist policies implemented. The political, as opposed to the administrative, problems of setting up and maintaining the effectiveness of women's units in local authorities are dominated, as Julia Edwards shows, by the need to overcome the scepticism and the lack of support from central government (Edwards, 1988).

Within schools, work has often begun with the formation of a women's group which has first of all performed a consciousness-raising function among its members. Such groups usually then work for better treatment of girls in the classroom by finding means of exercising greater control over the boys, by making education 'girl-friendly', that is, encouraging the girls and creating an environment which assists them to be active participants in the classroom rather than passive spectators of the boys' activities. One method for doing this in mixed schools has been to separate boys and girls for some lessons. Such lessons have tended to be of two types. In craft and technology, girls have seldom had the same opportunities as boys to handle tools out of school and are therefore at a disadvantage in class. Separate classes have also been used to confront issues of sexuality and sexism directly, sometimes through drama.[11]

Women's groups in schools have also confronted both male staff and boys over issues of sexual harassment. Women staff have concluded that if they depend on men to control the boys in such issues, first, such support may be transitory or non-existent, and second, the women will be perceived as weak and dependent and therefore always vulnerable to harassment. Experience has shown that a group of women have been able to confront these issues and win improvements in the behaviour of men and boys alike – but substantial change takes time and persistence.[12]

Feminist teachers in relatively junior positions have been able to use such methods. If they held more senior positions, they would be able to achieve more with less effort. The SDA is useful in this connection in two ways. First, it legitimates claims by women for promotion, and therefore makes it easier for women to challenge lack of promotion. As a result, heads, LEAs and school governors are led to consider women more seriously, and criteria are formulated or formulated more precisely so that more rational attitudes are introduced into the process of making promotions. Secondly, women have brought cases against their employers in the industrial tribunals. Here the record is far more mixed. Many women have lost their cases (Kant, 1985). Anecdotal evidence suggests that some academic women who have lost their cases have nevertheless won the promotions they sought shortly afterwards. Alice Leonard's research (Leonard, 1987) shows that women have often been victimized and may even have lost their jobs in spite of winning in the tribunal. There is, however, also anecdotal evidence that a lost case leads some employers to give urgent attention to improving selection and promotion procedures.

WOMEN'S STUDIES

The development of Women's Studies has been another way in which feminist teachers have sought to improve girls' educational rights. The first task of Women's Studies has been to complete and correct the record, to correct distortions in the account given of women and to put women into the syllabus, for example by including women authors in the literature syllabus.[13] Since gender has been shown to be one of the most fundamental characteristics by which individuals identify themselves, the absence of women from the syllabus leads girls to see no one with whom to identify and makes education seem irrelevant to them and their concerns. Feminist teachers have found many ways to introduce women into the full range of the curriculum. It is easy to see how this may be done in history, literature, and geography. In sciences and languages, a common method is to choose examples using women and girls as well as men and boys. Some old-fashioned language, mathematics and science texts lead one to suppose that only males exist.

Putting in what has been omitted and correcting misinterpretations means not merely rewriting the record but a complete reorientation and change of direction. The record becomes a different record and a record with different values. In nearly all cultures, women have been specialized in nurturing and caring for others, and in maintaining the fundamental basis of human life. Women's Studies makes these activities and these values a central part of the record and therefore of Women's Studies education. Such an education would give boys a more realistic notion about the value of women's work and a greater understanding of women's struggles for equality. Such knowledge and understanding must contribute to greater respect for women and hence to a willingness to accord women a more equal place. For girls, the joy of learning about the achievement of those with whom they can identify leads to the development of greater self-respect and self-confidence. For these reasons alone, Women's Studies must form an essential part of human rights education.

Women's Studies scholars have long recognized the *political* importance of the omission of women from the scholarly record.[14] Women's Studies research is important for its specific analysis of interpersonal violence and the role that violence plays in the subjection of women. All the evidence shows that more males use more violence than women (I am not claiming that no women are violent or that women are never violent). The violence used by men is often in effect condoned, as feminists have shown in their work on rape, battering and the sexual abuse of children.[15] A similar point could be made about white violence against ethnic minorities. The conclusion must be that we live in a society dedicated to violence. However, female violence is not so easily condoned, nor violence by blacks against whites, nor male violence against males. A further conclusion must be that violence plays a crucial and unacknowledged role in maintaining the gender hierarchy and other hierarchies in society.

The condoning of violence in society also has the effect of inuring individuals to the use of violence and to being forced to submit to violence. For men the condoning of violence against women provides particular advantages. It provides them with a partner against whom they can practise domination – a useful service in a violent and competitive society – and a psychological training in the use of violence in a society in which one of the most esteemed activities is warfare. Furthermore, since most men are themselves subject to domination by other men, the availability of women to be dominated provides some compensation. The gender hierarchy is essential to hierarchical society. It is clear that our planet and contemporary society need far less violence and far more nurturing. In this respect also, Women's Studies is essential to human rights education.

Women's Studies is also concerned with epistemology and research methodology. Like others (e.g. Wright Mills, 1959) feminist scholars have challenged crude positivistic methods and assumptions. They have been concerned with breaking down the distance between interviewer and interviewee and have treated interviewees as participants rather than as 'objects' for research. In other words, they have been concerned for the human dignity of their interviewees. As a result, they have secured much better data. (Oakley (1981) is particularly useful on this.) There is also a class dimension to these research methods. Highly placed interviewees have not been treated and would not allow themselves to be treated as mere objects for research.[16] Feminist values and practices are essential both for getting good data, for humanizing the research process and for discovering the reality of people's lives.

CONCLUSION

Human rights are not merely to have and to understand, but to use. However, the results of a lot of study suggest that many school-leavers may have a very inadequate understanding of the connections between political ideas, institutions and rights and their expression in political life (Fischer and Rendel, 1988). Human rights education therefore must be directed to providing an education which will enable children (and adults) to use their human rights. Such education, in turn, depends on the knowledge and expertise of teachers and through them on the population as a whole. While many teacher-training courses include greater or lesser amounts of material on equal opportunities in relation to race and gender, it is rare indeed for these issues to be set in the conceptual and institutional context of human rights.[17] As a result, issues of equality are fragmented and related to individual groups. The meanings of democracy, freedom and the processes which protect them are not related to issues of equal opportunity. The damaging consequence is that even these isolated expressions of equal opportunity are not related to and embedded in the structural and conceptual concepts of democracy and freedom in which they belong.

NOTES

1 A useful discussion of the various meanings of patriarchy appears in Waters (1989), Walby (1989) and Acker (1989).

2 Resolution, 29 October 1982, OJ, 22 November 1982, No. C304/255; Explanatory Statement to the Motion for a Resolution, PE 76.883/fin./rev.

3 UDHR: Articles 23 and 26; ICES: Articles 6 and 7. ESC: Principles and Articles 1, 9 and 10. CEDW: Articles 10, 11 and 14; numerous ILO Conventions, e.g. Discrimination (Employment and Occupation) Convention 1958, Articles 2 and 3, Employment Policy Convention 1964, Article 1.

4 Stenton (1957) gives information about women writers in the late seventeenth century arguing for equal education for girls. Kamm (1965) discusses girls' education in the seventeenth century in Chapters IV and V.

5 Sources for A-level courses: *Statistics of Education 1979* (1981a) and *Statistics of Schools 1987* (1988). Sources for O-level and CSE school-leavers: *Statistics of*

Education 1979 (1981b) and *Statistics of School Leavers CSE and GCE 1986* (1987).

6   *University Statistics 1987–88* (1988d). The figures for 1972 and subsequent years were compiled in somewhat different form in *Statistics of Education 1972* (1975) but the trend is clear.

7   Excluding nursery and infant schools. Women hold headships in fewer than one-third of junior schools and one-sixth of secondary schools. Only 6.5 per cent of principals of colleges, polytechnics and further education establishments are women and 2.8 per cent of university professors. See *Statistics of Education 1986: Teachers in Service, England & Wales* (1989) and *University Statistics 1987–88* (1988b).

8   There is a voluminous literature on this subject, much of which is cited or reviewed in Weiner and Arnot (1987) and Arnot and Weiner (1987).

9   For example, parents might wish sons to leave school to join a family business or to earn to contribute to the family income.

10   Taylor (1985) gives an illuminating account of developing equal opportunities policies in an outer London Borough.

11   Askew and Ross (1988) discuss the ways of using single-sex classes in mixed schools for anti-sexist teaching, as well as anti-sexist teaching in boys' schools. Smith (1984) reports on a small, careful experiment in single-sex and mixed teaching in mathematics.

12   Jones (1985) discusses both sexual harassment and the ways in which feminist teachers can fight it. Stanworth (1981), Mahoney (1985), Hackshaw (1985) and Askew and Ross (1988) are among the many who have researched and documented sexual and other harassment of girls and women staff by boys.

13   Whyld (1983) analyses sexism in 16 different schools and classrooms.

14   Tobias (1978) made this argument most effectively.

15   There is a large literature on this subject. Among the classic texts are Brownmiller (1975) and Emerson and Dobash (1979). Mitra (1987) makes analogous points about child sexual abuse.

16   Heclo and Wildavsky (1974) give a witty account of how they set about interviewing senior Treasury officials. Zweig (1952) also used open-ended methods in interviewing women factory workers.

17   Courses which do this are the MA in Rights in Education (which can be taken as a Women's Studies MA) and the Diploma in Human Rights and Education at the Institute of Education, University of London.

REFERENCES

Acker, J. (1989) 'The problem of patriarchy', *Sociology*, Vol. 23(2), pp. 235–240.

Arnot, M. and Weiner, G. (1987) *Gender and the Politics of Schooling*, Hutchinson and Open University, London.

Askew, S. and Ross, C. (1988) *Boys Don't Cry: Boys and Sexism in Education*, Open University Press.

Brownmiller, S. (1975) *Against Her Will*, Secker & Warburg, London.

Central Advisory Council for Education (England) (1959) *15 to 18*, Chairman Sir Geoffrey Crowther, Ministry of Education, HMSO, London.

Central Advisory Council for Education (England) (1963) *Half Our Future*, Chairman John Newsom, Ministry of Education, HMSO, London.

Edwards, J. (1988) 'Local government women's committees', *Local Government Studies*, July/August, pp. 39–52.

Emerson, R. and Dobash, R. (1979) *Violence against Wives: A Case against Patriarchy*, The Free Press, New York; Open Books, London.

Fischer, S. A. and Rendel, M. (1988), 'Reflections of Human Rights and Related Issues in Examination Scripts', Report to UNESCO.

Hackshaw, B. (1985) 'The Lessons They Learn: Observing and Monitoring Classroom Interaction with Regard to the Gender of Pupils', unpublished MA dissertation in rights of education, Institute of Education, University of London.

Heclo, H. and Wildavsky, A. (1981) *The Private Government of Public Money*, 2nd edn, Macmillan, London.

Jones, C. (1985) 'Sexual tyranny: male violence in a mixed secondary school', in Weiner, G. (ed.) *Just a Bunch of Girls: Feminist Approaches to Schooling*, Open University Press.

Kamm, J. (1965) *Hope Deferred*, Methuen, London.

Kant, L. (1985) 'A question of judgement', in Whyte, J., Deem, R., Kant, L. and Cruickshank, M. (eds) *Girl Friendly Schooling*, Methuen, pp. 166–190, especially p. 174 and p. 183.

Leonard, A. (1987) *Pyrrhic Victories*, Equal Opportunities Commission, Manchester.

Mahony, P. (1985) *Schools for the Boys? Co-education Reassessed*, Hutchinson, London.

Mitra, C. L. (1987) 'Judicial discourse in father-daughter incest appeal cases', *International Journal of the Sociology of Law*, Vol. 15, pp. 121–148.

Oakley, A. (1981) 'Interviewing women: a contradiction in terms', in Roberts, H. (ed.) *Doing Feminist Research*, RKP, London, pp. 30–61.

Rendel, M. (1988) 'Women's equal right to equal education', in Buckley, M. and Anderson, M. (eds) *Women, Equality and Europe*, Macmillan Press, London, pp. 185–203.

Smith, S. (1984) 'Single-sex setting', in Deem, R. (ed.) *Co-Education Reconsidered*, Open University Press, pp. 75–88.

Stanworth, M. (1981) *Gender and Schooling: A Study of Sexual Divisions in the Classroom*, WRRC, Hutchinson, London.

Stenton, D. (1957) *The Englishwoman in History*, George Allen & Unwin, London.

Statistics of Education 1972 (1975), Vol. 6, *Universities*, Department of Education and Science, HMSO, London.

Statistics of Education 1979 (1981a) Vol. 1, *Schools*, Department of Education and Science, HMSO, London, Table 21.

Statistics of Education 1979 (1981b) Vol. 2, *School Leavers CSE and GCE*, Department of Education and Science, HMSO, London, Table F.

Statistics of Education 1986: Teachers in Service, England and Wales (1989) Department of Education and Science, HMSO, London, Tables B129 and B140.

Statistics of School Leavers CSE and GCE 1986 (1987) Department of Education and Science, HMSO, London.

Statistics of Schools 1987 (1988) Department of Education and Science, HMSO, London, Table A 19/87.

Taylor, H. (1985) 'A local authority initiative on equal opportunities', in Arnot, M. (ed.) *Race and Gender: Equal Opportunities Policies in Education*, Pergamon Press and Open University, Oxford, pp. 123–135.

Tobias, S. (1978) 'Women's studies: its origins, its organisation and its prospects', *Women's Studies International Quarterly*, Vol. 1(1), pp. 85–97.

University Statistics 1987–88 (1988a) Vol. 1, *Students and Staff*, USR/UGC, Cheltenham, Table 1.

University Statistics 1987–88 (1988b) USR/UGC, Cheltenham, Table 29.

Walby, S. (1989) 'Theorizing Patriarchy', *Sociology*, Vol. 23(2), pp. 213–234.

Waters, M. (1989) 'Patriarchy and Viriarchy', *Sociology*, Vol. 23(2), pp. 193–211.

Weiner, G. and Arnot, M. (1987) *Gender under Scrutiny: New Inquiries in Education*, Hutchinson and Open University, London.

Whyld, J. (ed.) (1983) *Sexism in the Secondary Curriculum*, Harper & Row, London.

Wolpe, A. M. (1977) *Some Processes in Sexist Education*, Women's Research and Resources Centre Publications, London.

Wright Mills, C. (1959) *The Sociological Imagination*, Penguin Books, Harmondsworth.

Zweig, F. (1952) *Women's Life and Labour*, Gollancz, London.

CHAPTER 11

Human Rights and Multiculturalism in Canadian Schools

Keith McLeod

It is now two decades since the policy of multiculturalism was announced in the Canadian House of Commons on 7 October 1971. During that time there has continued to be considerable debate regarding the policy; in the same period multiculturalism has been increasingly implemented, broadened and defined. Have the policy and the implementation been a success? The answer will depend in part on what specific actions, changes, analysis, developments, events, or programmes we look at and what criteria we use to measure the 'success'. In this chapter I shall briefly examine the development of the policy itself, and I will analyse how multiculturalism has had an impact upon education and schooling. Multiculturalism within the context of Canada is an aspect of human rights, and multicultural education can be seen as an aspect of human rights education. The political, social, cultural, and economic issues which multiculturalism addresses within the context of politics, schooling, health, or welfare have to do with many of the same aspects of human dignity, fairness, and responsibilities that we traditionally associate with human rights. Multiculturalism, as will become increasingly clear, is also the recognition that Canadian society is pluralistic ethnically, racially and culturally.

In the context of an analysis of human rights and human rights education, it is my contention that multicultural education has been instrumental in developing awareness, sensitivity, and the implementation of human rights and human rights education regarding ethnicity, race, religion, national origin, citizenship, and such associated rights as equality before the law. Multicultural policy in Canada, or awareness and acceptance of pluralism, has grown in Canada hand in hand with the concern for human rights, and human rights legislation (see McLeod, 1985). Multiculturalism must be seen within the context of human rights and it will be recognized that in turn multiculturalism is part of human rights in a pluralistic society. Human rights is also associated with the concept of multiculturalism in two other ways. First, human rights, in part, places limits upon cultural pluralism; I shall cite the instance of sexual equality. Within Canada human rights legislation specifies that men and women are to be equal not only in law but also in economic and social treatment. The cultural background of many ethnocultural groups in Canada was not based upon the equality of the sexes; however, within the context of overall Canadian culture, all must now accommodate to this provision of human rights. It becomes a limitation on 'my' right to exercise 'my' cultural heritage. Secondly, while Canadian society is historically based upon the idea of individual rights, multiculturalism implies that there are group or collective rights. These are still somewhat vague and ill-defined, perhaps, but they are there nevertheless. Undoubtedly, the Canadian courts and social and cultural practice will increasingly define the parameters. Let me suggest, immediately, that there is no suggestion that individual rights and responsibilities will cease to be primary; rather they are tempered and interpreted within a broader context, a pluralist context. In a very real sense, though, as I have stated earlier, multiculturalism is also supportive of individual personal rights.

DEFINING MODELS OF PLURALISTIC SOCIETIES

Sociologists and anthropologists have analysed pluralistic societies and derived three broad umbrella concepts or theories of social and cultural relationships: dominant conformity, melting pot, and cultural pluralism. These have been succinctly summarized by an American scholar, (Newman, 1973).[1] Dominant conformity is seen as $A + B + C + D + \ldots = A$, where A is the ethnic group with the greatest power. The melting pot is seen as $A + B + C + D + \ldots = X$ or a new culture. Cultural pluralism is seen as $A + B + C + D + \ldots = A' + B' + C' + D' + \ldots$; the superscript has been added to indicate that in the process of immigrating, migrating, or associating with other cultures, the original cultures changed. One, of course, could make the same claim with reference to dominant conformity; the dominant group is bound to change by the sheer effort or process of assimilating or attempting to assimilate the subordinate.

A great deal has been written on each of the above concepts and in this brief chapter I have no intention even of summarizing the analyses and debates. I merely wish to acknowledge the concepts and the literature and to provide the most essential background. One interesting phenomenon of the application of the three concepts is that within the context of political and cultural debate people seem to think the adoption or prevalence of one precludes aspects of the other two theories, processes, or concepts being present. In cultural practice I would suggest that aspects of all three theories are often present in a pluralistic society. For example, at the same time that some persons are emulating those whom they see as superordinate, others are collectively evolving new cultural practices or norms, and still others are respecting similarities and differences. The foregoing does not diminish the role or importance of overall national cultural trends or policy, but merely recognizes social and cultural reality. There are many other aspects of the adoption and implementation of multicultural national policy that are impossible for me to deal with here, such as what in fact constitutes a culturally pluralistic society. Is it a matter of percentages? Of awareness and sensitivity? What relationships exist among ethnicity, race, and religion? Another aspect of multiculturalism is the question: When do groups of people cease to be 'minorities' within the context of a culture and when does the reality of cultural pluralism begin? I can only suggest that the answers to these questions are not wholly quantitative but somewhat qualitative.[2]

EVOLUTION OF THE CONCEPT OF MULTICULTURALISM

Before going on to discuss multicultural education, and particularly for the benefit of international readers, I should outline more definitively the Canadian concept of multiculturalism. This is, perhaps, especially important in that since the term was coined it has come to be used in many other countries and in other contexts (Bullivant, 1981).

When Canada's multicultural policy was announced in 1971, the prime minister outlined three main aspects: firstly, that there was no official culture in Canada; secondly, that there must be creative exchanges or relationships among the various cultural groups; and thirdly, that all immigrants to Canada should have access to learning one of Canada's two official languages. From the beginning multicultural policy was to be seen within the context of official bilingualism, the two *link* languages. It was also to be seen within the context of the actual ethnic and racial diversity, and within the context of the fact that immigrants must be given opportunities to adjust. The concept of multiculturalism has developed. At first the emphasis was on lifestyle: on opportunities to demonstrate cultural affinities. One result was that there was criticism that too much emphasis was being placed on 'song and dance' and lifestyle. Nevertheless, in this early period, and despite the criticisms, this kind of symbolic multiculturalism was very important in smoothing the way, and introducing Canadians in general to a positive view of pluralism. In the second phase, the implementation and development of multiculturalism featured greater attention to cultures as 'ways of life'. Much more attention was given to language retention and to other aspects of cultural retention and development, including the increasing presence of the various cultures in mainstream institutions. There was also beginning to be an increasing number of questions as to whether all persons were being given equal opportunity. In the third phase, in the 1980s, multicultural policy has emphasized not only equality of opportunity but also equality of outcome and equality of success. There has been increasing attention to access and participation. Much of this has been summed up by the concerns for 'equity' (e.g. Saskatchewan Human Rights Commission, 1985; Multiculturalism Canada, 1985; Canadian Public Health Association, 1988; Children's Aid Society of Metropolitan Toronto, 1982).

It must be noted that international events have also influenced multiculturalism in Canada. Concern about race relations in the United States have spilled across the border and there have been increasing demands in the late 1980s that multiculturalism must emphasize race relations. To some this has meant the twinning of the terms 'multiculturalism and race relations', even though race relations were a part of the multicultural policy from the beginning. A much stronger criticism has come from left-wing political sources; there has been an increasingly strident expression of the view that anti-racism is what matters and that multicultural education is outdated and must be replaced by 'anti-racist education'. Another explanation of the origin of this trend to emphasize racism in this way may be the experience and writings of the British. In Britain the human relations issues seem to have focused upon colour and racism: those who are not 'white' are 'black' and the terms racism and anti-racism are used frequently, probably because of the lack of belief in Britain that it is culturally pluralistic, and partly because of the lack of response in Britain to multiculturalism compared to charges of racism and the idea of anti-racism (Gundara et al., 1986; Skutnabb-Kangas and Cummins, 1988). However, in Canada general support for the policy and implementation of multiculturalism continues and the principle is now incorporated into a written portion of the Canadian Constitution (1981), and the policy has been made statutory (1988). The 1981 additions to the Canadian Constitution also featured a Canadian Charter of Rights and Freedoms; in a very real sense this Charter has given support to the concept of social, economic and cultural equity.

The changes within Canadian society and culture, and related policy in the past and present generations, have resulted in a new basis or set of assumptions for Canadian culture and society. These have been or are being constitutionally enshrined in the provisions for Aboriginal Rights, the Official Languages Act, Multiculturalism, Human Rights, and Citizenship. Each of these supports pluralism in one way or another.[3]

The Canadian Multicultural Act of July 1988 included an updated outline of the policy:

It is hereby declared to be the policy of the Government of Canada to:
(a) recognize and promote the understanding that multiculturalism reflects the cultural and racial diversity of Canadian society and acknowledges the freedom of all members of Canadian society to preserve, enhance and share their cultural heritage;
(b) recognize and promote the understanding that multiculturalism is a fundamental characteristic of the Canadian heritage and identity and that it provides an invaluable resource in the shaping of Canada's future;
(c) promote the full and equitable participation of individuals and communities of all origins in the continuing evolution and shaping of all aspects of Canadian society and assist them in the elimination of any barrier to such participation;
(d) recognize the existence of communities whose members share a

common origin and their historic contribution to Canadian society, and enhance their development;

(e) ensure that all individuals receive equal treatment and equal protection under law, while respecting and valuing their diversity;

(f) encourage and assist the social, cultural, economic and political institutions of Canada to be both respectful and inclusive of Canada's multicultural character;

(g) promote the understanding and creativity that arise from the interaction between individuals and communities of different origins;

(h) foster the recognition and appreciation of the diverse cultures of Canadian society and promote the reflection and the evolving expressions of those cultures;

(i) preserve and enhance the use of languages other than English and French, while strengthening the status and use of the official languages of Canada; and

(j) advance multiculturalism throughout Canada in harmony with the national commitment to the official languages of Canada.[4]

It will quickly be recognized that the policy is a commitment by Canadians not only to rights but also to freedoms and responsibilities. The policy, in the generic sense, has been increasingly implemented by the federal government as well as the ten provinces since 1971. The federal statute of 1988 referred to above is but another step not only in policy development but also in implementation, for the same Act declares that all federal institutions shall not only ensure equal opportunity in employment and advancement but shall also promote policies, programmes, and practices that will enhance awareness and response to diversity, pluralism, or 'multicultural reality'.

APPROACHES TO MULTICULTURAL EDUCATION

In order to explore multiculturalism within the context of education and schooling I shall have to turn specifically to the provincial level within the Canadian federal system, as constitutionally the provinces have sole jurisdiction over education. Culture, on the other hand, is an area of open jurisdiction, as neither the central government nor the provinces have any written or exclusive constitutional jurisdiction in the area. In order to be able to be specific I shall usually use the most populated and diverse province of Canada, Ontario, as my major example. However, before looking at the specifics of Ontario let me look at the general approaches to multicultural education that have been characteristic of Canada.

In a previous analysis of the state of multicultural education I adopted a typology in order to characterize the general approaches to multicultural education (McLeod, 1981). Three categories emerged from the analysis.

1. *Ethnic-specific* approach – by this I mean those who approach or plan for multicultural education on the basis of specific ethnocultural perspectives. This approach tends to focus upon cultural retention or the

cultural perpetuation or development aspect of the multicultural policy. It is also clear recognition that in order to have cultural sharing there must be something there to share. Examples of this perspective range from language programmes, black heritage programmes, and ethnocultural programmes and events to the more entertaining folk events.

2. *Problem-oriented* approach – this includes those persons and groups whose fundamental orientation to multiculturalism is responding to problems. Immigrants and immigrant integration are seen as problems which evoke the responses of reception centres, interpreter programmes, and immigrant services. Similarly, racism may be seen as a critical issue which leads some to focus upon anti-racism as an aspect of multiculturalism. For others intergroup relations may be seen as the paramount issue, so intercultural or intergroup programmes are developed.

3. *Cultural/Intercultural* – this is a more general approach to multicultural education: it is where multiculturalism is an ethic underlying education or the total school programme. It includes concern for cultural and linguistic continuity and development, issues related to ethnic and race relations, cultural sharing, immigrant integration, aboriginal rights, bilingualism, and human rights. It is a more comprehensive commitment socially and culturally; it is an approach which is based upon the definition of multiculturalism which includes or incorporates culture in the general sense as well as in the ethnocultural sense; it includes attention to ethnic, racial, linguistic, and religious diversity or pluralism.

Although these are the characterizations or the typology that I have used frequently, other characterizations have been used in the Canadian context.[5] For example, some have referred to the museum approach – seeing ethnic cultures as some kind of historical remnant; the song and dance approach, emphasizing what are regarded as superficial or symbolic cultural features; the anti-racist approach, focusing upon racism which is often interpreted as structural inequities; the values approach, the view that attitudes and values are the foundations for behaviour, action and discrimination; the cross-cultural communication approach, where discrimination and inequities are viewed as due to lack of communication and understanding; the training approach, which tends to view discrimination, especially racism, as a pathology which has to be treated; the intercultural approach, which suggests that group relations is the crucial issue; the linguistic approach, where culture and language are regarded as inseparable, and where cultural survival depends upon language maintenance. As will readily be observed, many of these characterizations or approaches could be included within the three more general approaches I suggested. The point must also be made that many of these so-called approaches are associated with some group of supporters who wish to rationalize or legitimize their position or maintain their territory (Mallea, 1989). The essential issue, however, that we must focus upon, is whether the underlying assumptions, the aims and objectives, of an approach or group or a programme are consistent with valid definitions of multiculturalism – and to what extent. For example, an English as a Second Language programme for immigrants that is predicated upon substituting English for the original language would be regarded as inconsistent with multicultural-ism. If the programme was additive, or aimed at adding a language, it *would* be predicated upon multiculturalism. In a society such as that of Canada, which receives many immigrants, the distinction is very important.

ONTARIO – POLICY, PRACTICE, EDUCATION

In some senses Ontario typifies many of the issues and approaches that have been outlined in the previous section. Ontario was the first political jurisdic-tion in Canada to initiate legislation to protect persons from discrimination. In the early 1940s legislation was put into place to protect 'minorities' from discrimination in contracts, housing, and work. This 'minority' legislation soon evolved into 'human rights' legislation; a Human Rights Commission was established to enforce the legislation when it was pulled together to form the Ontario Human Rights Code (McLeod, 1985).

Following the 1971 federal policy, the Ontario provincial government announced a provincial multicultural policy. Some activity was promoted in education; for example, the aims and objectives of elementary schooling were revised to reflect a multicultural perspective. The first course in cross-cultural education was offered by a faculty of education, as part of a pre-service teacher-education programme in 1972. Curriculum support documents for teachers began to be initiated by the Ontario Ministry of Education, and a Heritage Languages Program to sustain and support mother tongue retention was initiated in 1977. Attempts were also made to improve the quality and availability of English as a Second Language courses for immigrants. It might be added parenthetically that many of these changes were taking place at the same time as the vast increase was made in the availability of French language education for both Francophones and non-Francophones in Ontario. Steps were also being taken to deal with race relations and to provide cultural support to students from the black community. This was especially true after the government adopted a race relations policy in 1983; the policy complemented the multicultural policy.[6]

In 1985 a new government came to power. It reaffirmed the race relations policy and went on to outline a multicultural strategy. In the field of edu-cation, the Liberal government called together a committee to organize a provincial conference on multicultural education that was held in March 1986. This conference was stimulated in part by the work of the Ontario Human Rights Commission, which had slowly but surely been working on developing a generic multicultural education policy which local education authorities, boards of education, could adopt. School board trustees, teachers, teacher educators, Ministry of Education personnel, and community rep-resentatives met and examined and analysed multicultural education issues. At the end of the conference, the Minister of Education committed himself to provincial action. What the action would be was left open.

By September 1987 a follow-up report, *The Development of a Policy on Race and Ethnocultural Equity*, had been developed by the Provincial Advisory Committee on Race Relations (Provincial Advisory Committee on Race Relations, 1987). The select committee was appointed to address race relations at a very critical time in Ontario's history. A large number of 'visible minorities' had entered Canada since the revision in the immigration policy of 1966; significant numbers of people from the Caribbean, Africa, and Asia had moved to Ontario, particularly Toronto. For example, whereas 'visible minorities' constitute about seven per cent of the Canadian population, in Toronto at present they make up about 15 per cent of the population.

Anti-racist proponents were prominent and vocal on the committee and the result was that the report for Ontario education adopted this approach. Multiculturalism, the report states, was too culturally orientated, and too fragmented; it paid insufficient attention to values, and ignored colour differences or race. Such changes, however, scarcely do justice to the considerable achievements of those developing policies and programmes. However, the following quotation gives an idea of the report's line of argument:

> However, multicultural education, as interpreted and practised over the last decade, has demonstrable limitations. Changes have often been fragmented in content and lacked clarity, continuity and coordination. Initiatives have often relied upon untested assumptions about culture and the process of cultural transmission. Content often focuses on such material and exotic dimensions of culture as food, dress, and holidays, instead of linking these to the values and belief systems which undergird cultural diversity.
>
> Important factors shaping cultural identity, such as racial, linguistic, religious, regional, socio-economic, and gender differences have often been ignored. Not least among these problems has been the expectation that teachers from the dominant culture could easily teach about highly complex cultures.
>
> Too often well-intentioned educators have sought to ignore colour differences. 'Pretending to be colour-blind in the face of the hardships encountered by young Asian, Native and Black youngsters, and professing not to perceive any differences in treatment, is still tantamount to sidestepping the problem.' [Thornhill] Gradually, questions have been raised about the merits of this multicultural approach. Many believe that multicultural initiatives have not adequately addressed racial discrimination and inequities which are systemic within the policies and practices of educational institutions.
>
> Parents, community spokespersons, volunteers, and professionals have repeatedly asserted the fundamental problems limiting the education of achievement of many racial and ethnocultural students result from discrimination by race rather than diversity of culture. As one parent stated in the foreword to a school board policy on race relations: 'The issues facing the

colour of my skin are more pressing than those facing my culture.' (Provincial Advisory Committee on Race Relations, 1987, p. 37)

In fact, Multicultural education, and those who had been involved in its formulation and implementation, had from the beginning addressed race relations and racism. However, the report is dismissive of their efforts, whilst going on to argue that anti-racist education is the only true multicultural education.

> School boards can play a central role in eliminating racism in society, if anti-racist educational policies are developed and implemented. Such policies for schools should be developed in concert with efforts to bring other areas of Ontario society closer to equity.
>
> The goal of anti-racist education is to change institutional policies and practices which are discriminatory, and individual behaviours and attitudes that reinforce racism. Its premise is that cultural diversity is not the cause of the denial of equal educational opportunity to students from certain racial and ethnocultural groups.
>
> Anti-racist education does not negate the value of multicultural education. Rather, it is education that is truly multicultural, in a truly equitable multiracial society. It acknowledges the existence of racism and forthrightly seeks its eradication within schools and in society at large. (Provincial Advisory Committee on Race Relations, 1987, p. 39)

Some ramifications of the denigrating of multiculturalism and singularly emphasizing racism and anti-racism have already appeared. Some have isolated racial issues from general multicultural policy and support; others have suggested that racial issues are something for the visible minorities to deal with. The net effect could be seriously diminished or fractured support for pluralism if these divisions continue and become more general.

Despite the tone of the report, multicultural education has continued to develop: it has continued to address cultural and linguistic issues as well as racial issues. People are addressing questions having to do not only with symbols, and attitudes and values, but also with structures and institutions, including structural issues related to economics, access, and participation. This continuity will become increasingly evident as we examine more specific areas of education and schooling, namely administration, teachers, curricula, teaching strategies, students, and parents and communities. By examining each of these in turn we shall have a deeper sense of the meaning of multicultural education and of its implementation. One interesting phenomenon is that although the Ontario government has adopted both multicultural and race relations policies, the Ontario Ministry of Education has not adopted an overtly stated multicultural education policy despite its current efforts to encourage the 125 local boards of education in the province to adopt policies.

ADMINISTRATION

Of the some 125 boards of education in the province there are now over 40 boards with explicit multicultural education policies. A recent report for the Ministry of Education also indicates that some 25 other boards are currently contemplating or developing policies.[7] The policies tend to cover much the same aspects despite the variety of nomenclature: they are variously called multicultural, race relations, ethnic relations, or other combinations thereof. They usually include: an explicit statement of support for multiculturalism and multicultural education; a statement on the importance of leadership by the trustees and school administrators; a commitment to revising and revamping the curricula so that pluralism is reflected in the programmes and the resources used; a statement committing the school jurisdiction to using fair and appropriate means of assessment and of placement of students in various programmes and streams; a commitment to providing for staff development and to fair and just personnel policies and practices; there is almost inevitably a section on developing positive school–community relations; and usually some kind of statement or commitment to counter discrimination, racism, or racial and ethnocultural harassment. The recent report for the Ontario Ministry of Education indicates that the boards that adopt policies that concentrate on dealing with racial harassment are also the boards that are less likely to plan for ameliorative programmes. It would seem that the less strident the vocabulary, the more positive the approach. The most committed boards do not leave the implementation of the policy to chance but rather include implementation guidelines and a commitment to providing the human and financial resources needed to fulfil the policy.

There is little doubt that where one or more of the school board trustees (in Ontario they are elected) take up the cause of pluralism, the chances of commitment and action increase. There is also no doubt that where the chief executive officer of the board, the director, takes up the cause, the results are positive. Another aspect that has increased the chances of a good policy is where the community has been directly involved in developing the policy. Community involvement is often done through initial hearings with follow-up meetings to develop awareness and commitment; eventually a final draft of the policy is submitted to the public for comment and suggested changes. Policies are often officially adopted at board meetings which the public has been encouraged to attend.

As part of the administrative support, Ontario boards in their policies or as part of the implementation process have often appointed a person within their bureaucracy with the responsibility to oversee implementation and development. These multicultural or ethnic and race relations workers have extensive responsibilities: they assist principals and teachers in dealing with discriminatory incidents, provide for staff development, work with communities and community representatives, advise on curricula and resources, assist with personnel policies and practices, and promote special programmes, including those that encourage student leadership in multicultural education. Sometimes the boards also establish school–community relations offices. The staff in these are usually responsible for outreach into ethnic and cultural communities that are cut off or remote from the school and teachers.

At the school level much has depended upon the school principals (head-teachers). Where they have taken up the cause of multicultural education the relationship between the school and community has improved, teachers have received assistance, students have received support, and parents have been better informed and more involved. Principals encourage multicultural implementation in a variety of ways, for example through finding the means to send multilingual information to parents, and to reallocating personnel and resources for staff development, and through involving parents and the community in the school. The ultimate aim is to improve students' performance and success by working with parents and the community.

In conclusion, it is fair to say that collectively the trustees and the administrators are responsible for the commitment, the direction and implementation of policy, and the appropriation of human and financial resources that will not only negate ethnic and racial discrimination but which will also enhance cultural identity and development and positive human and group relations. The willingness not only to admit that bias or discrimination existed but also to exert influence and allocate resources to support cultural pluralism and positive human relations has been a major step forwards. It is a step which jurisdictions both provincial and local have yet to make. There is little doubt that much remains to be done. Some educational authorities have been slow in committing themselves to extensive implementation of multicultural education.

CURRICULUM

Curriculum change in Ontario, as elsewhere in Canada, has had its origins in community influence, professional ethics and concerns, and development elsewhere, such as in the United States. Curriculum change has varied in nature and focus: in some instances it has been linguistic and cultural in emphasis, while in other instances it has been ethnic-specific, anti-discriminatory, anti-racist, human rights, or human relations orientated.

Early attempts at curricula change in the elementary school (grades 1–8) tended to be based upon the general concern that the curricula should reflect the children's cultures so that they could identify with the school, the content, and the attitudes and values. The obverse side of the coin was that educators became increasingly concerned that there was a cultural gap between the community and parents and the school, that the school was reflecting and reproducing knowledge that was alien to the child and the family's culture. Children were being educated away from their language and culture.[8] In the mid-1970s, as a result of a consultation process, multicultural objectives were incorporated into the elementary school provincial guidelines which provide guidance and a sense of direction to teachers. Ontario elementary school education is based upon a progressive, child-centred philosophy of education. Elementary teachers were often more adaptable and ready to adjust the content to the children's backgrounds. Teachers organized units and learning experiences where cultural, ethnic, racial and religious diversity were a fundamental underpinning or assumption. Teachers increasingly consulted with community representatives and invited people of diverse origins into their classrooms. A broader range of cultural knowledge was legitimized in the schools and classrooms. Gradually there emerged a set of criteria that have become increasingly characteristic of multicultural curriculum development:

1. Multiculturalism must be integrated into the total school programme and into all aspects of school.

2. There must be a balance of similarities and differences so that ethnic relations are not exacerbated by an overemphasis on differences so that differences could even be seen in the context of similarities, and so that students could be taught skills and attitudes in terms of coping or working with differences.

3. The resources which students use must be unbiased or sensitive and where materials with a bias are used, the bias, the stereotypes, or the discrimination (by commission or omission) must be dealt with and the students taught how to recognize and deal with it personally and collectively.

4. Special days, occasions, programmes, and activities are important but in order for them to have more lasting effect they must be integrated in some way into the regular programme.

5. Within the curriculum content, the levels of intellectual and of moral reasoning of the students must be taken into account.

6. The teaching of content must be accompanied by teaching appropriate skills (which together constitute the cognitive domain), and there must also be appropriate attention to teaching for the affective domain (attitudes and values).

7. In teaching for the affective domain or even the cognitive domain it is not simply a matter of 'teaching about' human relations, human rights, or human and group identity and self-esteem, but of using teaching methods and strategies that are more appropriate, that focus upon relating the cognitive and the affective, that make issues more personal, and that build upon the positive.

Beyond the above kinds of criteria, teachers have also developed increased understanding that the community context, the teaching methods, and peer relationships are very crucial to successful multicultural education.[9]

Associated with the changes in curricula have been changes in the role of languages in education. Ontario in 1977 adopted a Heritage Languages Program whereby on community request mother tongue or heritage languages could be taught for two and a half hours a week at weekends or after school hours, or during the day where the school day was lengthened by half an hour. Thus the students from several classrooms in a school could be brought together to be taught, for example, the Greek, Chinese, Portuguese or Italian languages. The programme proved to be a significant immediate success. Within two years some 50,000 students were studying some 50 languages.

By the late 1980s there were some 100,000 students studying some 80 languages. Again the change has resulted in a positive reinforcement of the children's cultures and improved their sense of identity and security. As of 1989 the government legislated that school boards must respond to community requests.[10]

What will happen to the Heritage Languages Program in the future is an open question. It may remain a 'community request'-based programme. Another possibility is that it could become the basis of a languages programme for all children in the elementary schools. In any case there is evidence that the programme has improved opportunities and access to education, and assisted students by making school more culturally appropriate or relevant to the children.

At the secondary level in all provinces there has been much less success in adjusting the curricula. The areas that have received the greatest attention are history and social science. Courses in Canadian society and history now usually incorporate the multicultural heritage. In addition, the courses in literature now sometimes include books on a broader range of cultural topics. In Ontario for a few years, an optional grade 10 history course that focused upon 'Canada's Multicultural Heritage' was promoted by the Ministry of Education; however, this course has now been integrated into the general Canadian history courses.

As I indicated earlier, the Ministry of Education in Ontario in 1975 revised the elementary school curriculum guide by including multicultural objectives. In 1977 the Ministry also published the document *Multiculturalism in Action: Curriculum Ideas for Teachers*. In that same year the Minister of Education established a committee to develop guidelines that would assist authors and publishers to avoid bias and discriminatory references and omissions in learning materials. *Race, Religion and Culture in Ontario School Materials* was subsequently published after many revisions in 1980. Another curriculum support document, *Black Studies: A Resource Guide for Teachers, Intermediate Division*, was published in 1983 to help teachers to be aware of cultural content that could be used in assisting students to recognize the participation and the diverse roles and contributions of people from the Canadian and international black communities.[11]

Thus the curriculum pattern in Ontario is one of support documents for teachers, adjustment of curricular objectives and content, and the specific inclusion of ethnocultural and race relations objectives. The elementary schools in Ontario and elsewhere in Canada now better reflect the multicultural reality. Resources and materials are chosen with greater care so that racial diversity and many cultures are portrayed. A serious deficiency exists in secondary education despite efforts to change. Secondary education in Canada is traditional and content-orientated, and there has been considerable resistance to changing the cultural content.

TEACHERS AND TEACHING STRATEGIES

There are two key aspects to the roles and functions of teachers that must be examined: the teacher as exemplary person, and the teacher as methodologist or strategist. The concept of the teacher as exemplary person means that one should first and foremost bring to teaching an 'open mind'. It is unlikely that any person will have grown up without some bias, cultural preferences, or even prejudicial attitudes and values. These may be religious, cultural, racial, or ethnic or they may be related to other areas covered by human rights. The most important intellectual endeavour is for the teachers to recognize their own bias and prejudices. Recognition is the first and most fundamental step in being able to come to terms with oneself and with people from other cultural, racial or religious backgrounds (see Morrison, 1980).

Teachers who are secure about themselves, and their own identity, are less likely to diminish others; teachers who are reflective are less likely to reinforce structural inequities and institutionalized discrimination. The reflective teacher (which is increasingly becoming a catchphrase for teachers who continually analyse their assumptions and practices) should further enhance multicultural education. In Canadian and Ontario education the aware and sensitive teacher is expected to set standards of behaviour and be exemplary in how they treat children of diverse backgrounds. This exemplary conduct is crucial to the educative process of teaching attitudes and values, or what is referred to in pedagogy as the affective domain.

Another aspect of the role of teachers, associated with their ethical and professional standards, is the codes of ethics of their professional organizations which in greater or lesser detail eschew discriminatory practices and support human rights. One of the most detailed ethical statements on anti-discrimination is in Saskatchewan; one of the shortest is that in Ontario, which simply states that:

(a) That a society in which all people may participate equally with equal access to opportunity is a basic tenet.
(b) That discrimination against any person be opposed with vigour.
(c) That teachers, because of their influential position in the development of attitudes, pursue a leadership role in the opposition of discrimination.
(d) That teachers avoid discrimination in their work places by acting to eliminate all forms of discrimination that may appear in areas such as:
  (i)   the delegation of responsibilities in the school,
  (ii) school programs,
  (iii) curricula,
  (iv) the use of instructional materials,
  (v)   the use of language, and any other areas in their work place which reinforce or perpetuate any form of discrimination. (Ontario Teachers' Federation, 1984)

The teacher as methodologist or strategist, research increasingly indicates, is a crucial aspect of teaching. In short, it is not just a matter of what you teach but how it is taught, or – more aptly – how it is learned. Research on techniques and strategies in Canada and the United States has indicated that it is possible to teach for the affective domain. The research has indicated that simply teaching 'content' will not always result in the appropriate human rights attitudes. Ingrained prejudices, community circumstances, or family bias may prevent or inhibit positive attitudes to human relations or human rights in the student. Teachers in classrooms also have to take into account the research which indicates that children start learning attitudes and values towards groups as early an age as three and that attitudes and values are difficult to change. There is often a resistance to change – the values are emotionally held.[12] However, research on contact theory, principle testing, classical conditioning and identification theory in relation to teaching and learning also indicates that when the following criteria are characteristic of the learning situation the possibilities of learning or developing positive attitudes and values are enhanced. Many of these criteria, as will be quickly recognized, are also characteristic of what is generally referred to as 'good pedagogy'. In any event, in extrapolating from the research the following appear to be some of the significant characteristics of the learning situations (e.g. environment, methods, strategies, students, context) that are conducive to attitudinal change or the development of positive human relations:[13]

1. Experiential – the more real the situation and the more actively involved the students, the greater are the possibilities of change.

2. Enjoyable or satisfying – the research indicates that situations that are enjoyable are more likely to have a positive result on attitudes. Although there may be apprehension and even some discomfort at first, if the end result is satisfying the change may be made and be 'permanent' or long-lasting.

3. Personal – the more involved personally the persons or students are, the more they are in the position where they personally relate or identify with the victim, case, or situation and the greater the likelihood of positive change.

4. Common goal – when students or persons who are of different ethnic, racial, and/or cultural backgrounds work together towards a common goal, the chances of positive relations are enhanced.

5. Equal status – the chances are further enhanced when the persons of different backgrounds are of equal status. This equal status may be in terms of social class, or power, or position. It may simply be that they are all students in the same grade or of about the same age.

6. Continuous and ongoing – many projects and educational activities in the area of human and group relations tend to be of short duration or episodic. Classical conditioning or even behaviour psychology tells us that the more continuous or ongoing the motivation, value and attitude clarification, and the critical thinking process, the greater is the possibility of change. Most teachers understand the relationship between this factor and teaching when they relate this idea to their use of positive reinforcement.

7.   Exemplary educators – teachers, other school personnel, and parents, and community educators will enhance positive attitudinal development and positive human and group relations through their own *overt* behaviour and activity.

8.   Community support – as suggested in the previous point, the greater the community support, the greater the chance of effect; the more pervasive the support, the greater the chance of impact.

9.   Across the curriculum and school programme – again, the more frequent the opportunities are and the more consistent the learning environment is in terms of positive human and group relations, the greater the likelihood of success. It is not a matter of dogmatic expostulations but of exemplary patterns of behaviour and positive encouragement, and positive ethics, in all subjects and in all parts of the educational programme.

10. Setting limits – nevertheless, the chances of enhancing positive attitudes are also improved where it is quite clear that discriminatory behaviour is unacceptable. Ethnic and racial as well as other forms of discrimination must meet with immediate disapproval.

11. Levels of reasoning – it is important in the context of teaching for values and attitudes that the level of moral reasoning and of critical thinking and reasoning of the students be taken into account; it enables the teacher to use appropriate materials and reflective techniques.

The above concepts are based upon the cultural–intercultural educative model, that is, where the underlying assumption is that we can educate people regarding human rights and behaviour. There has been an increasing tendency among 'trainers' to use a therapeutic model or to approach ethnic and race relations and attitudes and values as a pathology that needs treatment. The educative model is philosophically appropriate to public education and to child and human development. The educative model not only addresses the individual but also encourages institutional and structural change. The human thought and action become part of peoples' social, economic, and political life or part of their commitment to rights and freedoms. The educational system changes. At the same time educators and society must be aware that in the socialization and cultural reproduction processes in any society there is failure, there is sometimes lack of achievement, and there are those who do not learn or who for a variety of reasons do not achieve what society has deemed good.

The Universal Declaration of Human Rights, the Canadian Charter of Rights and Freedoms, Human Rights Codes and our concepts of social justice and human dignity all sanction tolerance and positive human and group relations. It is a matter of cultural and social reality that ethnic and race relations must be provided for – that all people must be provided with opportunities, experiences, and examples by which they can learn. The Canadian teacher, by example and by appropriate methods, is being increasingly asked to participate in the process. The community has mandated multiculturalism and human rights.

STUDENTS

There are several ways in which students have been involved in the development and implementation of multiculturalism and human rights education in Canada. In particular I shall outline examples of student initiatives, peer relationships and support systems, student exchanges, peer counselling, and multicultural–multiracial leadership camps.

It was initiatives from students in secondary schools that led to some of the first cultural and identity support systems for the students. Students, to counteract the lack of cultural support, awareness, and sensitivity in schools, began to organize school clubs – Italo-Canadian student clubs or the black or Caribbean student groups. In some instances this frightened both teachers and administrators, especially those who were already suffering discomfort because of their lack of knowledge and understanding of the students and their culture. In some instances teachers' conscious or unconscious deprecation of students and their community's culture resulted in severe hostility. Students responded. Pedagogical reflection upon the needs and the requests of the students, however, led some schools and teachers to support the organizational efforts of students; they encouraged them to express their culture not only through club activities but also in the wider school setting. The only stipulation was that the clubs were to be open to any student.

The clubs and student participation provided cultural and identity support to the minority students. Students were able to come together and discuss mutual problems and issues. In a very real sense these associations or groupings provided some of the first examples of the legitimation of the cultural knowledge the students had acquired at home or in the community. Teachers not fearful of expanding their horizons and the subject content began to relate the culture and activities to their classrooms. In some instances schools began to 'celebrate' the diversity through ethnocultural activities and even community programmes. Although some of these activities come under the scrutiny of critics for their 'superficiality' (they were criticized for making human relations and multiculturalism a song and dance affair), the activities provided an initial basis for intercultural and interracial contact and understanding. In a very real sense the schools and teachers and community were recognizing the diversity or pluralism. In many schools these clubs or associations still exist and help provide a basic level of support and understanding.

These clubs and support systems have also operated within communities, and within ethnocultural organizations and structures, for a long time. For example, among the 'older' immigrant groups in Canada there have been Ukrainian, Scottish, Jewish, Irish, German and Chinese youth groups. Some youth groups have also worked within mainstream community organizations; for example, there are Boy Scouts groups within the Polish-Canadian community structure. There have also been numerous music, literary and arts groups within ethnocultural community groups. Such groups and activities have provided major assistance in human and group relations and intercultural understanding. As such they have played a fundamental practical role in avoiding intergroup misunderstanding and conflict. The obverse side is that such groups are a classic example not only of people exercising their rights and freedoms but also of mutual self-help and responsibility.[14]

Peer support has been recognized as a means of mutual aid. Peer relationships among students have sometimes been given sanction within the classroom, especially in relation to immigrant students. Teachers have often opted for 'buddy systems' by which students become responsible for introducing and assisting a newly arrived student. In some instances the students may have mutual linguistic capabilities, in other instances they may not. Such informal systems, especially when legitimated by the teacher, provide a basic system for contact and they smooth the process for both the immigrant student and the receiving students.

However, teachers have gone beyond 'buddy systems' in utilizing peer teaching. Teachers have had students from various cultural backgrounds teach not only them but the class. It may be a few words of a language, it may be cultural patterns and knowledge. Teachers have also been cautioned not to place too much pressure on students to be the 'experts' on their ethnic group. In some instances a student's own knowledge may be fragmentary and undeveloped. Nevertheless, such teaching opportunities may help immigrant students to integrate well into the school and larger community. Opportunities to demonstrate knowledge of their group may be very crucial in assisting students to maintain their sense of self-esteem and self-worth.

At the secondary school level, students' councils have been encouraged to help set standards of behaviour, to encourage participation, and to reflect the student body in their activities and programme. This encourages democratic participation and mutual respect of human rights. In some instances the student body has given support to interschool programmes and exchanges not only with students in other Canadian communities but also with students in other countries. Such support broadens students' cultural and racial perspectives. In the case of international exchanges there has been some success not only in developing broader perspectives but also in developing perspectives on global living. There have, however, also been some misguided efforts. Students competing on a national basis at international gatherings have in some instances produced friction and some hostility instead. Why organizers of student athletic and cultural exchanges continue to stress national teams and international *competition* is difficult to understand in the light of the research on human relations.

There have also been some problems among students when teams from schools with a particular racial mix meet school teams with a different ethnic and racial mix. The physical education teachers or instructors may not have prepared their students, and sometimes the first reaction to frustration in competition is an ethnic or racial slur. The same has happened internationally even in professional sport.

There have been extensive student exchange programmes in Canada that have been based upon exchange between students in French and English Canada. These have helped to develop understanding and they have promoted the mutual learning of the two official languages. Most recently there has been one trial student exchange based upon multicultural criteria. Students were selected on the basis of their intercultural and cultural interests. The two groups were both very diverse ethnically, racially and culturally. The programme for the students included developing awareness, sensitivity, mutual respect and support. The focus was on co-operation and co-operative activities.

Another feature of Canadian educational development has been the multi-cultural/multiracial leadership camps. These leadership camps that some of the large urban boards have developed have attempted to promote peer leadership, multi-ethnic and multiracial understanding and co-operation, intercultural skills and co-operation, as well as self-identity and self-esteem. The camps are held outside the formal school setting at a centre or a 'camp'. They usually last from one to three days. The students are encouraged to discuss the human rights and group relations in their community and in the school environment. They are given opportunities to develop skills in dealing with kinds of discriminatory behaviour; leadership skills are taught and students are given an opportunity to develop understanding of their families and communities. In some instances, such issues as interreligious, intercultural and interracial dating, family perceptions, parental reactions, and community values and attitudes are examined. As with other issues the students have an opportunity to develop skills, knowledge, attitudes and values.[15]

An old phenomenon and a new form of human relations education is 'peer counselling'. Students have been assisting one another for generations; however, students are now being offered assistance in learning how to assist and care about others – how to understand, and how to help and what it is like to be the one with the problem. Helping skills for most people are learned behaviour. Students are given opportunities to not only develop self-understanding, but also to assist others to understand themselves, their parents or family. They are helped to learn how to cope with other peers, and to work more effectively in school. Some studies indicate that peer counselling can be particularly effective during adolescence. Students do turn to one another for assistance, often more readily than they turn to parents or teachers.

To conclude this discussion on students I would like to make the point that increasing emphasis is being placed upon student involvement and student-based or student-centred activities to complement the work of teachers and administrators. I shall refer to several sections from a board of education multicultural policy statement in order to highlight the importance that is placed upon student participation. The board 'condemns and does not tolerate any expression of racial or cultural bias by its trustees, staff, or students'; the board 'reaffirms its commitment to develop and promote racial harmony among its students, staff, and the community, and to provide education that is antiracist and multicultural'; the board 'will continue to develop curricular and co-curricular programs that provide opportunities for students to acquire positive attitudes toward racial, cultural, and religious diversity'; the board 'will attempt to ensure that schools in their day-to-day operations, and co-curricular activities identify and eliminate those policies and practices which, while not intentionally discriminatory, have a discriminatory effect'; the board recognizes that 'in order to ensure equal access and opportunity for achievement of their full potential, students from racial and cultural minority groups may require special considerations with respect to (a) reception, (b) assessment, (c) placement, (d) programming, (e) monitoring, (f) meaningful communication with parents/guardians'. The focus of policy is very clearly student orientated and designed to enhance achievement.

Moreover, among the guiding principles set out in the multicultural policy of this board, the first reads that they 'will strive to maintain a student-centred approach which places the development of student potential as the first priority' (p. 19). The board also commits itself: to support multicultural clubs when requested by students and/or staff, to provide opportunities for students in all schools to participate in multicultural leadership camps and to strengthen the leadership programmes. The board also states clearly that discriminatory behaviour by students will not be tolerated (Board of Education for the City of Scarborough, 1988).

THE COMMUNITY

In one sense it is fitting, in the final analysis, to address the role of the community in some specifics. As I have alluded to earlier, community action in Canada has been the basis for the development of human rights legislation and multicultural policy. In a very real sense, the community has been the first and foremost underpinning of human rights and human relations. It was community political action which brought about anti-discriminatory legislation; it has also been community-based political action which has brought about the recognition of pluralism. In the democratic sense of community responsibility, policy must be set by the community. Legislation is the manifestation of the commitment. The international community has brought about the various Declarations on Human Rights, and in Canada human rights and the recognition of pluralism have been codified in human rights and multicultural legislation and constitutional provisions.

At the local community level in education, boards of education adopt or support multicultural education policy. In the province of Ontario, as I have indicated, out of some 125 school boards some one-third have policies and another third are in the process of developing policies. However, when we analyse community participation in multicultural education in Canada, the extent of the participation ranges well beyond policy. The roles of the community can be seen in the context of (1) initiation (policy and commitment but also programme initiation), (2) support, (3) implementation, (4) administration and (5) evaluation.

1. *Initiation* includes not only the initial development of multicultural policy but also activities and programmes for cultural retention and development, and human rights and human relations. It was the various ethnocultural groups who for many years before multicultural policy

resisted unicultural nationalism and developed programmes for human rights and cultural retention: language classes, cultural programmes, libraries, literacy societies, writing clubs, and educational societies. They also encouraged human rights and human relations as did other community groups such as Women's Institutes, labour unions, the Canadian Red Cross and religious groups. Many ethnic groups initiated their own programmes and activities.[16]

2. The community has also been the basis of *support*. Again, even before the adoption by the governments of policies and programmes, the same community groups referred to above were also allocating some of their financial resources, as well as their volunteer time, to human rights and human relations. This willingness to fund human rights and human relations has now also become a feature of the government sector – all the provincial governments as well as the federal government fund human rights commissions which not only arbitrate and mediate but often also educate. Similarly, multicultural/human rights education within the mainstream public schools is now supported and funded. It is also true that some mainstream institutions, including some in the field of education, have only progressed as far as the community has pushed and provided the support.

3. In the *implementation* aspect of human rights and human relations education, the community has also played a crucial role. Within a multicultural society it is important not only to be able to exercise cultural retention and development but also to be ready and able to mix and to share cultures within mainstream institutions. There are other aspects to implementation and the community. Community representatives become resource persons in the school, explaining and demonstrating their culture to students so that they develop an understanding of other cultures. In addition, community centres, such as Sikh temples and Italo-Canadian cultural centres, and even family homes, have accepted persons who wish to learn. Members of the community have also continued to participate on school committees. There have been some notable instances of where, when the community base has been absent, that implementation of human rights and human relations education has failed or faltered. The willingness and readiness of communities to ensure that there is not just policy but also implementation has been enhanced where there has been involvement in the planning.

4. The *administrative* aspect of the community in multiculturalism involves two issues: the involvement of the communities in overseeing the carrying out of programmes, and the involvement of increasingly broad representation in the educational control. At the national level in Canada the umbrella organization of ethnocultural groups, the Canadian Ethnocultural Council, has taken an administrative role in overseeing multicultural development. At the level of the provinces, in some instances provincial governments and departments have sought community participation in administering programmes. Local boards of education have sometimes maintained a community consultation process to advise them

on administration. In another area, boards have also used formal community liaison departments to develop links with groups with whom they have had tenuous relations.

Increasingly, there has been a trend to also examine who the administrators are. Do they reflect or represent the community? Are groups participating in control? Why are school trustees, school board personnel and even principals still coming from too few groups or from only some cultural backgrounds? Questions such as these relating to fair administrative access and promotion are being answered through community scrutiny of hiring and promotion practices.

5. The community, or the communities, are in the final analysis the ultimate *evaluators* of multicultural education. Some people have stated that the continued discriminatory practices and ethnic and racial discrimination are evidence that we have not sufficiently implemented multicultural education. However, that view must be tempered by caution. Various values have been legitimated for centuries even by laws and through religious codes, yet the values are still being violated. There is agreement that there is still much to be done in responding to the requests of the community and the communities for language education, anti-discriminatory education, fairness and equity, openness and access. One aspect of democratic participation is continual ongoing assessment and evaluation by the community.[17]

CONCLUSION

Multicultural education in Canada is an aspect of human rights education. The issues involved are the same in multicultural education as they are in other aspects of human rights and education, for example for the disabled or handicapped, or for women. As with all these groups and the issues involved, human rights education must be for all, not just a group that is at disadvantage. Multicultural education in Canada has been a response to and in turn has helped to create a more humane and human-rights-conscious society where there is a desire for equity and fairness for all, where there is consciousness not only of equality of opportunity but also of equality of outcomes. It is a recognition that where there are differences there is pluralism and where there is pluralism we must educate it (Fisher and Echols, 1989).

NOTES

1 See also the work of Milton Gordon, Michael Banton, Pierre van den Berghe and Philip Mason on pluralism and human relations.

2 I would refer readers to the writings of several Canadians, Jonathan Young, Howard Palmer, Vandra Masemann, Dean Wood, John Mallea, Enid Lee,

and to reports such as Special Committee on Visible Minorities in Canada Society (1984) and Standing Committee on Multiculturalism (1987).

See, for example, Saskatchewan Human Rights Commission (1985), Multiculturalism Canada (1985), Canadian Public Health Association (1989) and Children's Aid Society of Metropolitan Toronto (1982).

3 The interrelationships of these foundations of modern Canadian society have really not been explored. In McLeod (1989), some aspects of a modern concept of citizenship education in a multicultural–bilingual context is explored. In Ray and D'Oyley (1983), some writers explore human rights issues related to education with particular reference to access and participation.

4 The Multiculturalism Policy of Canada, Excerpts from the Canadian Multiculturalism Act, July 1988.

5 See the writings of Jonathan Young, Vandra Masemann, Enid Lee, John Mallea and Dean Wood; an interesting study by Paul Anisef (Anisef, 1986) also helps clarify approaches and perspectives.

6 See, for example, Cummins (1981), *TESL Talk* (1979), McLeod (1984) and various issues of *MC, Multiculturalism/Multiculturalisme*, a Canadian journal printed by the University of Toronto Press.

7 The study was done for the Ministry of Education by Vandra Masemann and Karen Mock.

8 See Toronto Board of Education (1976). For a Canadian study of cultural and linguistic factors see Breton et al. (1980).

9 Curriculum studies in Canada have been done, for example, by Jack Kehoe, Frank Echols, Ahmed Ijaz, Walter Werner, Richard L. Butt, and Keith A. McLeod. One of the most noted American writers is James Banks, and in Britain James Lynch. The Canadian Human Rights Foundation is currently testing some elementary school materials.

10 On the subject of heritage language education see the writings of Jim Cummins, Marcel Danesi and Rebecca Ullmann, the research of Sonia Morris, the historical research of Keith A. McLeod, and Masemann and Cummins (1985).

11 The most recent document of the Ontario Ministry of Education is Ontario Ministry of Education (1989).

12 The classic study is that of Gordon Allport (Allport, 1954).

13 See Allport (1954), and in the Canadian context this analysis is based upon works of Jack Kehoe, Ahmed Ijaz, Walter Werner, Richard Butt and Frank Echols; the work on cooperative learning techniques has also been taken into account. Internationally, the works of James Banks, Shlomo Sharan and Lawrence Kohlberg are important. Increasing attention is being given in Ontario and Canadian schools to cooperative learning.

14 See the reports and manuals done for the Boy Scouts of Canada.

15 See Burke (1982). Dr M. Burke has been one of the leading educationalists in the field of multiculturalism and is at the Ontario Ministry of Education.

16 The community United Nations Associations in Canada as well as the League of Human Rights of B'nai Brith have also been very active.

17 See Special Committee on Visible Minorities in Canadian Society (1984). There are several cities that have municipal committees working in the area of ethnic

and race relations; there are also many volunteer organizations including the Canadian Council for Multicultural and Intercultural Education.

REFERENCES

Allport, G. (1954) *The Nature of Prejudice*, Doubleday, New York.

Anisef, P. (1986) *Models and Methodologies Appropriate to the Study of Outcomes of Schooling in Ontario's Multicultural Society*, Ministry of Education, Ontario.

Breton, R., Reitz, J. G. and Vallentine, V. (eds) (1980) *Cultural Boundaries and the Cohesion of Canada*, The Institute for Research on Public Policy, Montreal.

Board of Education for the City of Scarborough (1988) *Race Relations, Ethnic Relations and Multicultural Policy*, Board of Education for the City of Scarborough.

Bullivant, B. (1981) *The Pluralist Dilemma in Education: Six Case Studies*, George Allen & Unwin, London.

Burke, M. E. (1982) 'The Ontario Multicultural, Multiracial Student Leadership Program', in *MC, Multiculturalism/Multiculturalisme*, Vol. 1, No. 1, pp. 21–24.

Canadian Public Health Association (1988) *Ethnicity and Aging*, Canadian Public Health Association, 1565 Carling Avenue, Suite 400, Ottawa K1Z 8R1.

Children's Aid Society of Metropolitan Toronto (1982) *Task Force on Multicultural Programs*, Final Report, Children's Aid Society of Metropolitan Toronto, 33 Charles Street, Toronto M4Y 1R9.

Cummins, J. (ed.) (1981) *Heritage Language Education, Issues and Directions*, Ministry of Supply and Services, Ottawa.

Fisher, D. and Echols, F. (1989) *Evaluation Report on the Vancouver School Board's Race Relations Policy*, School Board of the City of Vancouver, Vancouver.

Gundara, J., Jones, C. and Kimberley, K. (eds) (1986) *Racism, Diversity and Education*, Hodder & Stoughton, London.

McLeod, K. A. (1981) 'Multiculturalism and multicultural education: policy and practice', in *Eighth Yearbook*, Canadian Society for the Study of Education, Saskatoon, Saskatchewan.

McLeod, K. A. (1984) *Multicultural Early Childhood Education*, OISE Press, Toronto.

McLeod, K. A. (1985) 'Multiculturalism and Ontario', in *Two Hundred Years: Learning to Live Together*, Bicentennial Conference Proceedings, Government of Ontario, Toronto, pp. 94–114. See also the article by Cannon Purcell in the same volume.

McLeod, K. A. (1989) *Canada and Citizenship Education*, Canadian Education Association, Toronto.

Mallea, J. R. (1989) *Schooling in a Plural Canada*, Multilingual Matters, London.

Masemann, V. and Cummins, J. (1985) *Cultural and Linguistic Diversity in Canada*, Multiculturalism Canada, Ottawa.

Morrison, T. R. (1980) 'Transcending culture: cultural selection and multicultural education', in McLeod, K. A. (ed.) *Intercultural Education and Community Development*, University of Toronto, pp. 8–16.

Multiculturalism Canada (1985) *Education: Cultural and Linguistic Pluralism in Canada*, Government of Canada, Ottawa.

Newman, W. M. (1973) *American Pluralism: A Study of Minority Groups and Social Theory*, Harper & Row, New York.

Ontario Ministry of Education (1989) *Changing Perspectives: A Resource Guide for Race and Ethnocultural Equity*, Junior Kindergarten – Grade 12 OAC, Ontario Ministry of Education.

Ontario Teachers' Federation (1984) *We the Teachers of Ontario*, Ontario Teachers' Federation, Toronto, p. 21.

Provincial Advisory Committee on Race Relations (1987a) *The Development of a Policy on Race and Ethnocultural Equity*, Ministry of Education, Ontario.

Ray, D. and D'Oyley, V. (eds) (1983) *Human Rights in Canadian Education*, Kendall/Hunt, Dubuque, Iowa.

Saskatchewan Human Rights Commission (1985) *Education Equity: A Report on Indian/Native Education in Saskatchewan*, Saskatchewan Human Rights Commission, Regina.

Skutnabb-Kangas, T. and Cummins, J. (eds) (1988) *Minority Education*, Multilingual Matters, Clevedon.

Special Committee on Visible Minorities in Canadian Society (1984) *Equity Now!*, House of Commons, Canada.

Standing Committee on Multiculturalism (1987) *Multiculturalism: Building the Canadian Mosaic*, House of Commons, Canada.

TESL Talk (1979), Vol. 10, No. 3. See H. Troper, pp. 7–15 and K. A. McLeod, pp. 75–90.

Toronto Board of Education (1976) *We Are All Immigrants To This Place*, Toronto Board of Education, Toronto.

CHAPTER 12

Teaching Human Rights: Classroom Activities for a Global Age

David Shiman

INTRODUCTION

Somewhere someone clamours for self-determination, fights for free elections, or seeks political asylum. Somewhere a child dies of malnutrition in her mother's arms, disappears into the hands of a death squad, or sleeps in an alley under a cardboard box. Somewhere students mobilize for democracy . . .

Events such as these present an enormous challenge to teachers sensitive to human rights concerns[1] and eager to help students make sense of this complex world. They require an educational response which strives to raise student *awareness* of human rights conditions around the world, promote their *understanding* of the forces which create these conditions and those which can change them, and encourage their *action* rooted in a humane conception of justice and human dignity.

The rationale underlying this three-pronged approach to human rights education is more expansive than that normally offered for instruction in traditional content areas. True, it contains all the traditional characteristics of academic study: knowledge to be acquired, communication and cognitive skills to be developed, and attitudes to be formed. But it also encourages students to reflect on what their human rights learning means for them personally and to translate their understanding and concern into value-based action.

The following pages present a perspective on human rights education rooted in the belief that active learning is the best preparation for active citizenship in a democracy. The chapter begins with a brief discussion of the academic and action dimensions of this approach to human rights education. It then presents a rationale for building human rights education on the principles embodied in the Universal Declaration of Human Rights. Finally it offers descriptions of curriculum activities from which concerned teachers might draw. Although these are written with an American classroom in mind, many are adaptable to classrooms in other cultural settings.

HUMAN RIGHTS EDUCATION: THE ACADEMIC DIMENSION

Human rights education presents important concepts, skills and perspectives which any young person should encounter while attending school. Students need to grapple with questions related to ethnocentrism, universalism, relativism and conflict, and to examine perspectives other than their own. They should be able to place human rights issues in a global framework and recognize their relationship with environmental concerns and those of war and peace. They should understand that human rights problems manifest themselves differently in different cultural contexts and that they do not occur only 'out there', in foreign lands, but have local and national dimensions as well.

One might say that human rights education helps students to develop a repertoire of skills and concepts to include in a 'mental tool box'. Students can carry this 'box' from one context to another and draw upon it to construct frameworks for understanding human rights issues in their different forms. An instructional unit about South African apartheid should, for example, challenge the student to acquire much more than just knowledge about it. The activities should develop student understanding of pluralism, institutional racism and violence, distribution of power and resources, class system, self-determination, and international law which can be applied beyond the South African situation (Kohler, 1978). The unit should also challenge students to grapple with conflicting conceptions of freedom, justice and equality. The students will then have tools needed for understanding slavery, the American civil rights movement, sex equity, North–South dialogue, and seemingly permanent crises such as those in the Middle East and Northern Ireland.

Human rights education is multidisciplinary in nature and touches every dimension of the human experience. Concepts such as justice, responsibility, conflict, equality, liberty and freedom are neither discipline- nor age-specific. Therefore there is no educational reason to confine their study to social studies or any other single subject area. Human rights education should be infused into the curriculum in a variety of content areas and should utilize the different resources and perspectives available in the school.

To reinforce the point that subject areas other than social studies have much to contribute, let me briefly discuss the humanities, which can provide a powerful, personal lens through which to explore human rights themes. English teachers can draw on writers such as Nadine Gordimer, Richard Wright, Margaret Atwood, J. M. Coetzee, Elie Wiesel, Franz Kafka, Harper Lee, John Steinbeck, Maya Angelou, Langston Hughes and Alice Walker to engage students in the study of justice-related questions. These authors can reach the heart in ways that tables, graphs, and statistics cannot. Teachers can also draw on writers from among the winners of the Coretta Scott King and the Jane Addams Children's Book Awards (Jones, 1988). Furthermore, they can organize letter-writing campaigns on behalf of political prisoners adopted by Amnesty International which can be both human rights action and lessons in grammar.[2] Finally teachers can introduce their students to matters of freedom of expression and censorship by having them examine situations as varied as censorship in their own school library and book burning in Nazi Germany.

Art and music often express the human striving for dignity and justice. Art teachers can expose their students to Francisco Goya, Ben Shahn, Jacob Lawrence, Kathe Kollwitz and Dorothea Lange, who reflect on poverty, oppression, justice and hope in their special ways (Conrad, 1988). Music teachers can bring the life and work of Bruce Springsteen, Woody Guthrie, Paul Robeson, Billie Holiday, Pete Seeger and Marian Anderson into the classroom. Students can be challenged to articulate their own concerns and hopes for humankind through the creative arts.

Teachers sensitive to human rights hope that student exposure to and examination of human rights conditions around the world will activate their sense of human dignity and empathy. If students understand the concepts and make the concerns their own, they are on the road to becoming active citizens in this global community.

HUMAN RIGHTS EDUCATION: THE ACTION DIMENSION

Historically the American school has been a place of preparation for life rather than participation in it. Many classroom teachers might not have either the training, skills or inclination to educate in the manner suggested here. The American public, in fact, is wary of schools and teachers actively promoting certain values and declaring themselves for certain causes. They have preferred an institution which quietly reinforces traditional value systems and plays a fairly conservative role of promoting controlled gradual change in the social, political and economic order. In the present debate surrounding educational excellence, for example, there has been a heavy emphasis on academic learning and a neglect of the sort of action learning suggested here.

However, there are dangers in teaching human rights at a distance. When educators teach about world hunger and the deaths of 40,000 human beings per day from hunger-related causes as a content area fact like a formula in chemistry or a program in computer science, they are telling their students that hunger is a problem worthy of study but nothing more. When learning units are presented on homelessness, political prisoners or the denial of freedom of religion, without student opportunities for action, teachers affront sound pedagogical practice by failing to integrate theory and practice when the chance to do so is present. Finally, and most important, if they focus exclusively on the academic, teachers deprive students of the opportunity to affirm personal beliefs through rational, value-based action.

Teaching human rights should reflect a commitment to educational practices consistent with democratic principles. This requires that teachers not present students with a world view to absorb, but involve them in creating one of their own. They must be non-partisan and promote the fair and objective study of human rights issues. They must encourage their examination from a variety of perspectives. And finally teachers must help students identify their own paths for action and not present them with a prescribed list of human rights organizations with which they might work or actions they might undertake.

BUILDING ON THE UNIVERSAL DECLARATION OF HUMAN RIGHTS

This approach is rooted in principles found in the Universal Declaration because this document is the most widely recognized international standard for a just world. The Declaration asserts that every human being by the fact of his or her existence is entitled to the basic political, civil, social, economic and cultural rights included in the 30 articles. These are rights of specieshood, one might say, which *everybody, everywhere* deserves. This Declaration affirms the belief that we are all part of the human family and are all entitled to these basic rights regardless of who we are or where we happen to be born.

Those who advocate the Universal Declaration have sometimes been accused of ethnocentrism and cultural imperialism. Critics assert that this document is a Western construct unreflective of conceptions of rights rooted in communitarian principles prevalent in the non-Western world or in alternative views of the role of the state (Schwab, 1981; Donnelly, 1984; Pollis, 1982).

The fact that the Universal Declaration is rooted in conceptions of liberty, justice and equality found in the writings of John Locke, Thomas Jefferson, Thomas Hobbes and Jean Jacques Rousseau does not undercut the legitimacy of the ideas themselves (Winston, 1989). A strong argument can be made for the near 'universal' nature of these rights. Most governments have signed the Universal Declaration or a similar one affirming these rights, and individuals and groups of people in every corner of the world strive to obtain them (Donnelly, 1984; Canadian Human Rights Foundation, n.d.). Demonstrations for democracy and other forms of political activism by citizens in the Soviet Union, Eastern Europe and the People's Republic of China in the late 1980s are further evidence of the increasing popular acceptance of the Universal Declaration's principles around the globe.

Its widespread international acceptance means that a set of common questions about government behaviour towards its citizens and the quality of the human condition can legitimately be raised regardless of cultural context. Certainly teachers should ask students to question the claim of universality made by the champions of this Declaration. However, the Universal Declaration of Human Rights is too powerful a statement of principles to be cast aside as an instructional framework on the strength of this sort of criticism.

ACTIVITIES FOR THE CLASSROOM

Human rights education serves larger instructional goals than the mastery of skills or the understanding of concepts and perspectives. It challenges students to learn about, reflect on, care about, and act on human rights concerns.

The activities presented on the following pages should help students achieve some of the academic and action-orientated goals previously discussed. Some are adapted from my book *Teaching about Human Rights*, while others are drawn from materials on the resource list included at the end of this chapter (Shiman, 1988). Some focus more generally on human rights and the Universal Declaration; others concentrate on particular themes; and still others address specifically the challenge to act. Obviously these are not presented in their full form and many rights found in the Universal Declaration are not treated here.[3] However, I hope the cross-section of activities presented are in sufficient detail for easy adaptation.

Types of Rights Systems

Students have often never considered the question of whether or not there is a need for common rights for all human beings, regardless of who one is or where one lives, when they first encounter the idea of human rights. This activity helps students to understand different types of 'rights systems' and to decide which sort of system satisfies their definition of fairness.

To begin this activity, the teacher organizes the class for a simulation similar to the famous blue eyes–brown eyes activity described in *A Class Divided: Then and Now* (Peter, 1987; Shiman, 1979). The teacher divides the class into two groups according to some arbitrary characteristic such as eye colour or physical size. Group A receives certain rights, e.g. right to recess, hand homework in late, speak in class, receive help with assignments, because it possesses this characteristic, while Group B is denied these rights. After a day or so of unequal treatment, the teacher takes the rights from Group A and gives them to Group B and the activity is repeated. In the debriefing of this activity many issues related to fairness, discrimination and prejudice will emerge.

The teacher and students then generate a list of other characteristics such as gender, race, property, wealth or religion which have been bases for rights assertions throughout history. Students can create scenarios for what it would be like living under these different types of rights systems. Or they can study examples drawn from the history of systems such as feudalism, theocracy, slavery, Nazism, caste hierarchy, and male-dominated 'democracies'. In either case they can compare their findings with their interpretation of what life would be like under a rights system based on the Universal Declaration.

This activity should challenge the students to sharpen their definition of fairness and to reflect on the sort of rights system under which they would like to live. They should now better understand the motivations of those who act against oppressive, discriminatory systems based on non-egalitarian principles. They should also appreciate the sorts of concern which moved people to create documents such as the Universal Declaration.

Linking Learning with Action

Human rights problems are part of the daily experience of people everywhere – even where the students live. This activity suggests one way in which teachers can provide opportunities for their students to integrate academic learning with human rights activism in their own community (Shiman, 1988). It offers students a chance to translate an increased awareness and concerns into effective action.

To begin this activity, students select several rights from the Universal Declaration and conduct a community survey to discover what is being done to help achieve these particular rights. This involves identifying community needs and community groups working to meet these needs. Students should create a human rights directory which includes these groups as well as others working on related problems at the national and international levels. After gathering information on the rights situation in their community and discussing it in class, the students select one problem for their class project on human rights. Human Rights Day, 10 December, might become project decision day. During the remainder of the year, students develop and implement an action plan aimed at helping to eliminate the human rights problem through activities such as community education, fund-raising and volunteer service. They complement the action component of this project with a strong academic one involving research, reading, writing and reporting about the problem.

This activity can be adapted for use with quite a few of the other activities presented here. There are many ways in which the local and the global can be linked. The activity might become part of a school-wide service-learning project undertaken by students each year. Such a programme would exemplify an institutional commitment to the achievement of human rights. Furthermore, it would make a statement to students and community about the importance of integrating theory and practice.

Web of Justice

This activity can become part of any instructional unit built around a human rights theme. It can serve as a pre- and/or post-assessment: it provides an indication of the students' level of understanding of the issue and its relationship to other themes.

To begin the activity, the teacher selects a theme, e.g. racism, hunger, apartheid, capital punishment, or homelessness, or provides a stimulus such as a picture of an electric chair, student demonstrations for democracy in China, a Ku Klux Klan rally, or a starving child. Through a brainstorming activity, students generate a list of factors they associate with the chosen theme. When this is first attempted, teachers might offer some prompting to help students recognize that each theme or topic has political, social, economic, moral and environmental dimensions. Students might also need guidance in identifying ways in which the theme manifests itself at international, national, local and even personal levels.

After the initial brainstorming has been completed, students move into small groups, each with paper and magic marker, and create concept webs which highlight their understanding of the relationships among the items on the brainstormed list. Finally, each group presents its concept web and briefly explains the reasoning which went into its organization.

A successful activity built around the concept of hunger, for example, might produce a web which includes the following themes: malnutrition, foreign aid, self-help, farm production and surpluses, infant mortality, civil war, desertification, disease, Africa, local food distribution centre, dependency relationships, single-crop export economies, famine and personal consumption patterns. It might also serve as a stimulus for student action. Students can identify the points on their web where their intervention/action might improve conditions locally or globally. They might then decide to organize some sort of action project.

When it is first attempted, creating a concept web can be frustrating for both student and teacher. However, students seem to enjoy this sort of activity, for they are able to organize concepts in a manner which is meaningful to them. When it is repeated, they also discover how much they have learned.

Rights in Conflict

Many conflicts in the local community and larger world are rooted in competing assertions by individuals or groups of what they claim to be their rights. This activity helps students to examine these sorts of conflicts and explore alternative resolutions (Shiman, 1988).

To begin this activity, the teacher presents the class with examples of local conflicts drawn from the area newspaper. These might include articles about a child with AIDS being denied admittance to school, an indigent migrant worker being refused medical treatment at hospital, a student challenging a school dress code, or anti-abortion protesters blocking the entrance to a women's health clinic. The teacher divides the class into groups with each assigned a particular conflict. The students try to understand the issues from the perspective of each of the conflict's chief protagonists. They should identify the rights being asserted and/or denied and suggest ways in which the conflict might be resolved. If this is a rights-based conflict within their own community, the students might conduct field research to learn more about the issues involved and even consider becoming actively involved in trying to resolve the conflict.

This activity might move in other directions as well. Students might discuss instances in which they have felt (or feel) that their rights were violated and how these situations might have been (or might be) resolved. Or the activity might take an international focus, with students bringing newspaper articles to class with reports on rights clashes elsewhere in the world. Particular conflicts such as those on the streets of the West Bank, in a Brazilian rainforest, or in a courtroom where an affirmative action case is being heard, might become the focus for a 'rights in conflict' unit. Whichever approach is taken, students should begin to understand more fully the nature of rights-based conflict in the world.

Evaluating the World

This activity employs the Universal Declaration as a framework through which to analyse and evaluate the 'state of the world'. It sharpens student understanding of the articles in the Universal Declaration and helps them develop 'tools' for inclusion in their mental tool box.

To begin the activity, the teacher poses the question, 'Are we better off now than we used to be?' To answer this, the class selects rights from the articles in the Universal Declaration which it considers the best indicators of progress. The class divides into groups with each responsible for one article and generates a series of 'measures' of progress which relate specifically to its right. Each group then creates a series of questions derived from these measures which they use to examine the question about progress. Students pursue research projects and present reports to the class at a later date.

This activity involves sharpening student understanding of the human rights language in the Universal Declaration. It raises questions about identifying appropriate indicators, comparing across cultures, evaluating changes through history, clarifying 'better', and, of course, defining 'we'. It also places students in history, for they can see themselves as recipients of what has gone before and determinants of what may come . . . either by choosing to act or by choosing not to.

Universalism and Relativism

This activity addresses a theme which permeates discussions of human rights (Shiman, 1988). It centres on questions of whether there are or should be *universal* human rights. It also introduces students to the important concepts of universalism and relativism.

To begin the activity the teacher presents students with cultural practices unrelated to human rights and asks them whether or not they have objections to these sorts of practices. These include behaviours such as shaking hands with the left hand rather than the right, using seashells as money instead of paper bills and coins, or eating with one's hands rather than with utensils. After a brief discussion of these, the teacher presents students with practices which relate to rights asserted in the Universal Declaration and asks them to decide on their acceptability. The teacher poses questions such as 'Is it ever all right to: buy and sell people (Article 4); allow only certain people to go to school (Article 26); torture another person (Article 5); or not allow people to hold peaceful protest meetings (Article 20)?' Follow-up questions include: 'What if the majority wish it?', 'What if the government passes a law making it legal?', 'What if there is a national emergency?' Through discussion and debate, students will develop a deeper understanding of the complexities of these issues and perhaps move closer to clarifying their own positions.

A final step in this activity involves the presentation to students of cases which involve the assertion and/or infringement of rights. The teacher may ask students to examine actions such as the US government internment of Japanese-Americans during World War II, the imposition of press control and censorship by the Sandinista government in Nicaragua during its war with the 'Contras', or the Ethiopian government's forced removal of citizens from their famine-stricken homelands to another region where they can become productive farmers contributing to the nation's development. Students identify all rights being asserted or denied, including those found in the Universal Declaration. They then examine the merits of each case from the different perspectives and decide what action should be (or should have been) taken.

Rights and Fairness within the School

Students might begin raising more questions about fairness and justice in their school community as the topic of human rights is studied in class. This activity provides a framework which students can employ to examine their school world and understand the rights system in which they function. This somewhat risky activity can help teachers as well as students. As teachers sensitive to human rights they want to ensure a high degree of congruence between what is taught about justice in the classroom and how justly the classroom or school is organized and administered.

To begin this activity, students review the US Bill of Rights and attempt to identify school/classroom policies or practices which relate to particular rights. For example, school punishment procedures might fall under due process, school newspaper policies under freedom of press, and tracking under equal treatment or due process. Students conduct research to determine which rights they have and which they do not. They learn about court decisions which define the limits on their rights while students in school. This will lead to questions such as the following: Are they being fairly treated? Are there rights to which they are entitled by law but denied in their own school? Are there improvements which need to be made to make their school a fairer place? This sort of study can then move to a student determination of what actions they need to take to change school practices and finally to decisions on whether or not they wish to take these actions.

This activity is similar to ones included in some law-related education programmes promoted by the National Institute for Citizen Education in the Law (NICEL). The Institute publishes curriculum materials and assists educators with projects aimed at helping students understand the US Constitution, the Bill of Rights, and other laws which affect them.[4] There are even programmes with a specific human rights focus which get students out of the classroom and into their community where they learn about and work for human rights (Dreyfuss, 1987).

Rights through a Different Lens

Not all people interpret the concept of rights in the same way. This activity challenges students to understand the perspective on rights presented in the African Charter on Human and Peoples' Rights (Shiman, 1988). They will understand that this Charter reflects the history, cultural traditions, ideologies, and political and economic structures of the nations which created it.

To begin this activity students compare the Universal Declaration and the African Charter, identifying similarities and differences. They first examine the preambles to understand the rationale underlying the creation of each document. Thereafter, the students compare the articles themselves to identify those unique to the African Charter. These will include: right to existence and self-determination (Article 20); right to dispose of own wealth and resources (Article 21); and right to development (Article 22). Students then conduct research into the roots of these rights assertions and thereby gain insight into an African perspective on African history and cultural traditions.

This research activity might lead into discussions dealing with the proper relationship between political/civil and social/economic/cultural rights. The teacher raises questions such as 'Does one set of rights take priority over the other?', 'Can rights be prioritized?' or 'Are people's rights and human rights potentially in conflict?' These sorts of questions will promote a lively exchange of views and help students to understand perspectives other than their own.

Universal Declaration and US Constitution

This activity challenges students to reflect on a declaration of rights which is more comprehensive than that found in the US Constitution with its amendments. They will become aware of the similarities and differences between the Universal Declaration and the Constitution. This can lead them to reflect on what rights should be guaranteed to all Americans . . . and to all human beings.

To begin this activity, students brainstorm or the teacher presents students with a list of 'rights', including employment, clean environment, freedom of assembly, health and medical care, freedom of religion, shelter, education, and fair trial. Students are asked to decide which rights are essential for survival in a democracy. After discussing their reasons for declaring certain rights 'essential', students determine which are included in the US Constitution. The teacher then introduces them to the Universal Declaration and to the categories of civil/political and social/economic rights. The students compare the two documents, noting and discussing similarities and differences.[5]

The rest of the activity is built around an examination of two interrelated questions: 'Why does the US Constitution include political/civil rights but not social/economic ones?' and 'Should Americans be guaranteed rights such as shelter, health care, employment, and education which are asserted in the Universal Declaration but not found in the Constitution?' Students might select a right such as health care or employment and try to determine whether or not guaranteeing it is an appropriate and desirable response to the problem in their community and nation. They might study societies in which this right is guaranteed and decide whether there are any models worthy of emulation. They might also consider how such a guarantee might change their country . . . for better and for worse.

Students can also carry this academic learning beyond the classroom. Having identified the needs in their community, they might develop and implement a plan of action aimed at responding to the problem at the local level. Activity no. 2, entitled *Linking learning with action*, might be adapted for this purpose.

Examining One's Own Lens

This activity focuses on factors which influence the ways in which students define human rights. It is important for students to recognize that their perceptions and thoughts about rights and justice have been substantially influenced by other forces. Until they do so, they cannot begin the important task of 'naming their world', of developing their own definitions and determining what is important for themselves (Freire, 1972).

To begin this activity the teacher asks students to identify ten human rights: and writes them on the chalkboard. The teacher then introduces the class to the Universal Declaration and the categories of political/civil and social/economic/cultural rights. The students use these categories to compare their list to the Universal Declaration. If, as is expected, most rights identified by the students fall under the political/civil grouping, the teacher can then pose the question, 'Why do you think you listed more political/civil rights than social/economic/cultural ones?', or more simply, 'Where did you get your ideas about human rights?' and 'Is this the view of rights you wish to hold?'

The students then begin a research activity which explores the roots of their ideas and opinions. They record statements about rights which appear in history or social studies texts, list all references to rights which appear on television news and in the press, report on the language employed by US State Department officials when discussing rights issues, interview their parents to learn their rights perspective, and survey the community to generate a citizen list of human rights. They will also list those rights guaranteed by the US Constitution. Most likely, students will see a pattern emerge in which there are repeated references to political/civil rights to the neglect of others. Even when problems such as hunger, homelessness, and inadequate medical care are mentioned, they generally will not be described as human rights issues.

They use their shared research findings to determine the degree to which they have unconsciously 'received' a particular definition of human rights without ever thinking about it. They can also consider whether or not the definition of human rights received is that which they wish to adopt. They might ask themselves, 'How different might life be for many people if

Americans and their government viewed adequate medical care or housing, for example, as human rights?' and 'What would be the corollary to voter registration drives for adequate medical care?'

This activity might raise student awareness of issues related to the management and control of knowledge. It should help students better understand how one's perception and definition of a problem influence the actions one takes to solve it. They might ask more questions about the lenses they wear to view the world.

Hunger

There are many activities which effectively mobilize students and community to address this problem, at least on a short-term basis. Rather than select one for discussion here, I will suggest several types of activities. All of these offer opportunities for the integration of action with academic learning.

First, there is a variety of 'hunger banquet' designs which are adaptable to classroom or cafeteria.[6] The teacher places students in five groups according to either geographical area or the distribution of income of the world's population. Each group then receives a 'meal' which reflects its relative wealth. Mealtime will probably be punctuated by complaints and student 'actions' of one sort or another. At the debriefing students can give vent to their feelings and discuss their reactions to the experience. This simulation activity is an effective consciousness raiser on the problems of food resource distribution in the world. It opens doors to a variety of research activities and to meaningful class discussions of justice and personal responsibility.

Second, there are school actions aimed at raising awareness and generating funds to contribute to student-selected hunger organizations. 'Read for hunger' and 'waste reduction' projects are two such activities. The former is built around community sponsorship of students' reading activities over a period of time. The latter focuses on reducing food wastage in the cafeteria and contributing the money saved to a hunger-fighting organization. Fasting and fund-raising projects, particularly when part of an international effort such as World Food Day (16 October) or Human Rights Day (10 December), can also effectively raise student awareness of the problem and stimulate them to take action towards making conditions better.

CONCLUSION

This is an exciting time for human rights education. Populous states such as New York and California have mandated a human rights educational programme for their schools; others such as New Jersey and Connecticut recommend its inclusion in the curriculum. Elsewhere human rights enters the public school curriculum as a dimension of global education.

Action organizations such as Oxfam America and Amnesty International USA have launched educational efforts committed to integrating academic learning and action. Oxfam America, for example, produces background and curriculum materials. It also publishes *Oxfam for Kids* and sponsors a yearly 'Fast for a World Harvest'.[7]

Amnesty International USA has moved into the field of education in the past few years. Its worldwide concert tours helped to educate and mobilize many young people who now organize high school and campus groups to work for the release of political prisoners.[8] AIUSA's National Steering Committee on Human Rights Education will be producing educational materials on rights of the child, the death penalty, refugees, and the ratification of the International Covenants on Political and Civil Rights and on Social, Economic and Cultural Rights. Finally, AIUSA, in collaboration with Human Rights Internet at the Harvard Law School, now publishes *Human Rights Education: The Fourth R* twice a year. It includes curriculum activities, book reviews, and updates on conferences and human rights educational activities around the United States. Through these efforts AIUSA hopes to create a national network of teachers committed to infusing human rights concerns into their curriculum.[9]

There is a more positive climate in schools and communities for human rights education. Human rights questions are increasingly part of the public discourse and actions by state boards of education have provided an important stimulus for their inclusion in schools. However, meeting the challenge of human rights education ultimately depends on classroom teachers, not on state mandates. More than ever before, the curriculum materials teachers need are available to them. The opportunities are there for educators to challenge students to think, to feel and to act in ways which can make this world a better place to live.

NOTES

1 Special thanks to Dr Judith Torney-Purta, from whom I borrowed the phrase 'teacher sensitive to human rights' and who has influenced my work.

2 Contact Amnesty International, USA, Urgent Action Office, PO Box 1270, Nederland, CO 80466 for information about receiving Urgent Action Appeals designed specifically for young people.

3 See Constitutional Rights Foundation, 601 South Kingsley Drive, Los Angeles, CA 90005 for excellent curriculum materials on the Bill of Rights.

4 Contact NICEL, 25 E. Street NW, Suite 400, Washington, DC. 20001 about their 'Street Law' programme and textbooks and other law-related education programmes.

5 Adapted from Fernekes (1988).

6 See Shiman (1988) for one such activity. Also contact Oxfam America, 115 Broadway, Boston, MA 02116 and Church World Service, 2115 N. Charles St, Baltimore, MD 21218 for excellent resources for teaching about hunger.

7 See note 6 for Oxfam America's address.

8 Contact Amnesty International USA, 322 Eighth Avenue, New York, NY 10001 for information about these programmes.

9 To receive *Human Rights Education: The Fourth R* and join the educator's

network, write to Amnesty International USA, Educator's Network, 655 Sutter St, San Francisco, CA 94102.

REFERENCES

Canadian Human Rights Foundation (n.d.) *Let's Celebrate – The Universal Declaration of Human Rights*, Teacher's Guide, Canadian Human Rights Foundation, Montreal.

Conrad, D. R. (1988) 'Justice through the arts: the power of socially conscious art', in Thomas, T. M. and Levitt, J. (eds) *Justice: Interdisciplinary and Global Perspectives*, University Press of America, Lanham, MD, pp. 77–102.

Donnelly, J. (1984) 'Cultural relativism and universal human rights', *Human Rights Quarterly*, Vol. 1(4), pp. 400–419.

Dreyfuss, E. T. (1987) *Human Rights: High School Curriculum*, Law and Public Service Magnet High School, Cleveland, OH.

Fernekes, W. R. (1988) 'UDHR and the US Constitution', *Human Rights Education*, Vol. 1(1), p. 7.

Freire, P. (1972) *Pedagogy of the Oppressed*, Penguin Books, Harmondsworth, England.

Jones, D. B. (ed.) (1988) *Children's Literature Awards and Winners: A Directory of Prizes, Authors, and Illustrators*, Gale Research, Detroit.

Kohler, G. (1978) *Global Apartheid*, World Order Models Project, Center for International Studies, Princeton University, Princeton, New Jersey.

Peter, W. (1987) *A Class Divided: Then and Now*, Yale University Press, New Haven, CN.

Pollis, A. (1982) 'Liberal, socialist, and Third World perspectives of human rights', in Schwab, P. and Pollis, A. (eds) *Towards a Human Rights Framework*, Praeger, New York, pp. 1–26.

Schwab, P. (1981) 'Rethinking human rights in Ethiopia', *Transnational Perspectives*, Vol. 8(2), pp. 6–9.

Shiman, D. A. (1979) *The Prejudice Book: Activities for the Classroom*, Anti Defamation League of B'nai B'rith, New York.

Shiman, D. A. (1988) *Teaching about Human Rights: Issues of Justice in a Global Age*, Center for Teaching International Relations, University of Denver, Denver, CO.

Von Blum, P. (1976) *The Art of Social Conscience*, Universe Books, New York.

Winston, M. W. (1989) *The Philosophy of Human Rights*, Wadsworth Publishing, Belmont, CA.

BIBLIOGRAPHY OF CURRICULUM MATERIALS

American Federation of Teachers (1982) *International Education: Values and Perspectives on Four Human Rights*, American Federation of Teachers, Washington, DC.

Amnesty International USA, National Steering Committee on Human Rights

Education (semi-annually) *Human Rights Education: The Fourth R*, Human Rights Internet, Harvard Law School, Cambridge, MA.

Amnesty International USA (1984) *Torture by Governments*, Amnesty International, USA, New York, NY.

Anderson, C. C. (ed.) (1983) 'Beyond boundaries: law in a global age', *Intercom* No. 103 (January issue), Global Perspectives in Education, New York, NY.

Bergstrom, K. (1987) *The World Citizen Curriculum: Teaching Activities for a Global Age*, Center for Teaching International Relations, University of Denver, Denver, CO.

Bigelow, W. (1985) *Strangers in Their Own Country*, Africa Research and Publications Projects, Trenton, NJ.

Branson, M. S. and Torney-Purta, J. (eds). (1982) *International Human Rights Society and the Schools*, No. 68, National Council for the Social Studies, Washington, DC.

Center for International Programs and Comparative Studies (n.d.) *Justice around the World*, State University of New York, Albany, NY.

Center for Peace and Conflict Studies (1980) *People Have Rights: They Have Responsibilities Too: A Study Guide for the Universal Declaration of Human Rights for the Use of Young Citizens*, Center for Peace and Conflict Studies, Wayne State University, Detroit, MI.

Constitutional Rights Foundation (1982) *International Law in a Global Age*, Constitutional Rights Foundation, Los Angeles.

Croddy, M. and Maxey P. (1982) 'International Law in a Global Age: A Teacher Handbook', in *Bill of Rights in Action*, Constitutional Rights Foundation, Los Angeles, CA.

Dreyfuss, E. T. (1987) *Human Rights: High School Curriculum*, Law and Public Service Magnet High School, Cleveland, OH.

Dreyfuss, E. T. (1989) *Bringing the Declaration of Human Rights to Life: Implementation and Teaching Strategies*, Cleveland-Marshall College of Law, Cleveland State University, Cleveland, OH.

Ferguson, H. (ed.) (n.d.) *Human Rights and Citizenship*, Center for International Programs, State Education Department, Albany, NY.

Freedom House (1987) *Freedom in the World: A Curriculum Unit Prepared for Use in Global Studies*, Freedom House, New York, NY.

Harf, J. *et al.* (1980) *Global Issues: Human Rights*, Consortium for International Studies Education, The Ohio State University, Columbus, OH.

Heater, D. (1984) *Human Rights and Education in Schools: Concepts, Attitudes and Skills*, School Education Division, Council for Cultural Cooperation, Council of Europe, Strasbourg.

Human Rights Internet (n.d.) *Teaching Human Rights: Material for Primary Schools and High Schools*, Harvard Law School, Cambridge, MA.

Hursh, H. and Simmons, D. R. (1986) *World Food Day: Curriculum/Grades 4–7*, Office on Global Education, Church World Service with Center for Teaching International Relations, Baltimore, MD.

Institute for Food and Development (1984) *Food First Curriculum*, Institute for Food and Development, San Francisco, CA.

Lamy, S. (ed.) (1984) *Comparative World Issues*, University of Denver, Center for Teaching International Relations, Denver, CO.

McGinnis, J. and McGinnis, K. (1985) *Educating for Peace and Justice: Global Dimensions*, Institute for Peace and Justice, St Louis, MO.

National Council for the Social Studies (1985) *Social Education*, (September theme issue), National Council for the Social Studies, Washington, DC.

Pettman, R. (n.d.) *Teaching Human Rights*, Australian Human Rights Commission, Canberra, Australia.

Selby, D. (1987) *Human Rights*, Cambridge University Press, New York.

Shiman, D. (1979) *The Prejudice Book*, Anti Defamation League of B'nai B'rith, New York.

Shiman, D. (1986) *World Food Day: Curriculum/Grades 8–12*, Office on Global Education, Church World Service with Center for Teaching International Relations, Baltimore, MD.

Shiman, D. (1988) *Teaching about Human Rights: Issues of Justice in a Global Age*, University of Denver, Center for Teaching International Relations, Denver, CO.

State of California, Department of Education (1987) *Model Curriculum for Human Rights and Genocide*, State Department of Education, Sacramento, CA.

State of Connecticut, Department of Education (1987) *Human Rights: The Struggle for Freedom, Dignity, and Equality*, Department of Education, Connecticut.

Switzer, K. A. and Mulloy P. T. (1987) *Global Issues: Activities and Resources for the High School Teacher*, Social Science Education Consortium and Center for Teaching for International Relations, Boulder, CO.

Torney-Purta, J. (1982) 'Human rights: descriptions of classroom activities', in Graves, N. and Dunlop, O. J. (eds) *Teaching for International Development, Peace, and Human Rights*, UNESCO, Paris.

Totten, S. (1985) 'Human Rights: A Unit', *The Social Studies*, November/December, 240–243.

Tucker, J. L. and King, R. L. (n.d.) *Sample Lesson Plans: International Human Rights*, Florida International University, Miami, FL.

Zander, J. (1986) *World Food Day: Curriculum/Grades K-3*, Office on Global Education, Church World Service with Center for Teaching International Relations, Baltimore, MD.

CHAPTER 13

The Challenge of Human Rights to the Education of Children with Special Needs

Caroline Roaf

INTRODUCTION

Educators have a duty to ensure that the educational system promotes equality of opportunity and outcome, to 'attack inherited myths and stereotypes and the ways in which these are embodied in institutional practices' (Department of Education and Science, 1985), and to examine the part education itself has to play in this. Much of this book is concerned with the latter, but this chapter looks at the concept of special needs and at the way in which this informs institutional policies and practices in relation to the education of those who are said to have special needs.

The starting point for the views expressed here is that the concept of special educational needs calls for some re-examination. To date, the concept has not been fully effective because it has not been clear what group, or groups, are being described as having needs. Thus the first challenge of human rights to this issue is the need to clarify the term itself. In education, it has been too readily assumed that children with special needs are disabled in some way or have 'learning difficulties', even though special needs of this kind only account for a small proportion of the full range. Children experience highly individual configurations of need based on their educational, physical, psychological, socio-economic and cultural differences. In addition, these differences vary in stability, pervasiveness, the extent to which they can be altered, and their relevance (McIntyre and Postlethwaite, 1989). Children's special educational needs cannot be met until they have been identified and unless it is known for what reason they are failing to reach the goals of education which are, or ought to be, the same for everyone. Thus the way in which the term 'special needs' is understood by an institution has a powerful effect on its policies, on the system it creates to identify, evaluate and prioritize needs, and on its practice.

'Everyone has needs' is a cry we are accustomed to hear, and we may well accept this. Nevertheless, many needs, such as the need for love or praise, are ones to which we can claim no right. In turning to the question of which needs to meet, one is, in effect, recognizing the importance of the rights dimension in the discourse on special needs. Thus 'having a need' can suggest both the denial of educational opportunity in some respect, and the infringement of rights. Meeting needs is therefore about promoting equality of opportunity and outcome. Success in this depends, however, on three things, namely: the notion of advocacy, the assertion of the rights of the individual or group discriminated against, and changes in majority attitudes, behaviours and expectations towards that individual or group.

THE CONCEPT OF SPECIAL NEEDS

In Britain, the concept dates, in its present form, from the mid-1970s and was the subject of a government report, the Warnock Report (Department of Education and Science, 1978) and an Education Act (Department of Education and Science, 1981). The Warnock Committee of Enquiry was asked 'to review educational provision for all handicapped children whatever their handicap' (Department of Education and Science, 1978, paragraph 1.1). The members of the committee recognized that they had an extremely difficult conceptual task on their hands (Department of Education and Science, 1978, paragraph 3.30) and that there was no agreed distinction between 'the concept of handicap and related concepts such as disability, incapacity and disadvantage'. Nor could they find 'a simple relationship between handicap in educational terms and the severity of a disability in medical or a disadvantage in social terms' (Department of Education and Science, 1978, paragraph 3.3). Further, they did not feel it was part of their business 'to go deeply into the factors which may lead to educational handicap', because they were 'fully aware that many children with educational difficulties may suffer from familial or wider social deficiencies' (Department of Education and Science, 1978, paragraph 1.2).

The committee recommended that the previous categories of handicap be abolished and replaced by

> the concept of special educational need, seen not in terms of a particular disability which a child may be judged to have, but in relation to everything about him, his abilities as well as his disabilities – indeed all the factors which have a bearing on his educational progress. (Department of Education and Science, 1978, paragraph 3.6)

The significance of this for the present purpose (and the reason why the Warnock Report has been quoted so extensively here), is, first, that the ten categories of handicap which were abolished were subgroups within the main group of all those disadvantaged by disabilities. Second, 'all the factors' which have a bearing on 'educational progress' are, in fact, those which relate to the different forms of disadvantage and discrimination experienced by several minority groups. Thus, the discourse of special needs developed since Warnock conceals, or masks, a number of different minority groups, of which the group disadvantaged by disabilities is but one. At the present time, the disabled are more readily recognized than formerly as a minority group sharing, in common with other minority groups, a concern for their own needs and rights and for changes in majority attitudes towards them (Cooper, 1989; Abberley, 1987). Had this been so in the 1970s, one would, I believe, have seen a much wider and more effective application of the term 'special needs'.

The Fish Report (Inner London Education Authority, 1985), which reviewed London's provision to meet special educational needs, moved the discussion on considerably by emphasizing the relative nature of handicap and the importance of teacher attitudes:

> most individual needs for additional or different provision are relative . . . to the extent that schools and colleges can and do provide for a range of individual differences in their organisation and regular programmes and in the attitudes of teachers to such differences. (Inner London Education Authority, 1985, paragraph 1.1.32)

The report explicitly recognized the interplay of factors such as social class, gender, cultural diversity and race. But in attempting a distinction between 'special educational needs' (i.e. students with disabilities and learning difficulties of various kinds) and 'special needs' (all other disadvantaged groups) its authors were once again failing to see that while no definition can be exact, and there is interplay between them all, each minority group has its own needs and rights and the concept of need cannot be the exclusive property of any one of them.

DIFFICULTIES IN UNDERSTANDING THE CONCEPT OF NEED

With hindsight one can suggest some of the reasons for the difficulties experienced in using this concept. The first concerns the rapid increase during the 1970s in the number of schools being reorganized along comprehensive lines, and the development of an ethos which recognized the importance of valuing students equally, whatever their individual differences. Some rationale for coping with these differences in the classroom and meeting an apparently unending range of individual need was becoming a matter of urgency. The Warnock Report, suggesting that about one out of every five children (20 per cent) would need special provision at some time and that one in six would need it at any one time, while alarming in terms of actual resources available, was at least reassuring as official confirmation of what teachers' own experience was telling them. The term 'special educational need' was accepted with enthusiasm along with the idea that categorization was no longer either necessary or desirable. Teachers were thus encouraged to take account of differences and to be on the watch for *individual* needs, but were at the same time effectively discouraged from analysing these in terms of *group* needs, differences and interests.

Secondly, teachers would in any event have found this difficult to come to terms with given the tension that exists between the need, for purposes of affirmative action, to categorize and to recognize individual and group differences and the need for integration and commonality. All disadvantaged groups and individuals share a common need for social justice, yet their needs may be very different, 'special' even. For teachers, the feeling that we should treat all children the same is very powerful, but a 'colour blind' or 'difference blind' approach needs to be thought through carefully. To treat children as if they were all the same may end in the kind of injustice which results from treating unequals equally. Thus whether or not distinctions in any given situation are to be made depends on whether or not the differences are *relevant* (Oxfordshire County Council, 1986).

This highly practical issue particularly concerns members of disadvantaged groups, since it is for these groups that the distinction between relevance and irrelevance may be most acutely felt. For example, for most purposes the colour of one's skin or one's gender ought to be highly irrelevant, yet when faced with a racist or sexist incident this situation is reversed. It is thus extremely important that minority group membership, as a potentially relevant difference, is noted, accepted and understood. In some schools a minority group may be represented in very small numbers or singly. In these cases it is important to recognize that these students, whether deaf, or traveller or black, have special needs which are more complex than needs arising from less stable or shorter-term individual differences. Thus, 'since so many needs arise from expressions of social, ethnic or other group prejudice and discrimination, failure to alert the school and society to these group needs is also part of the failure to meet individual needs' (Roaf, 1989).

Significantly, the whole issue of affirmative action in relation to handicap arose because the relative nature of handicap was being increasingly appreciated. Disabled people, and the parents of disabled children, were increasingly able and willing to assert their entitlement to the same educational goals as everyone else and to reach these goals alongside their peers and not apart from them. Thus the differences between people on the grounds of disability were being recognized in terms of the relevance or not of these differences and of what was required in terms of resources and attitude change to reduce their relevance. Wheelchair hoists and pavement ramps are only two of many examples of ways in which relevant differences can be made less so.

Thirdly, in the post-Warnock debate over special needs, there has been little criticism of the concept of need itself. Only recently is it beginning to be seen as inadequate on its own as a means of achieving equality of opportunity and outcome (Roaf and Bines, 1989). To state that all children have educational needs is simply to state the obvious. It does not help one answer questions such as who defines need, parents, professionals or students? Which needs are 'special'? How are they to be prioritized? Could, or ought, any to be claimed as rights? Needs approaches tend to locate problems in an individual, seen as needy or deficient in some way, rather than in a society with obligations, duties and responsibilities, and distract from the individual as rights-bearing. For children, always much neglected as an oppressed group, to be regarded as rights-bearing would be a tremendous advantage (Boyden and Hudson, 1985; Freeman, 1987).

Lastly, the 1970s saw a growing awareness of the existence of minority or disadvantaged groups and the extent of prejudice and unfair discrimination against them. Women and ethnic minorities were expressing similar concern and were finding some redress, through the Sex Discrimination Act 1975, and the Race Relations Act 1976. In education, provision made under Section 11 of the Local Government Act 1966 to meet the educational and social needs of ethnic minorities, and initiatives such as the rise of multicultural education, the emphasis on equal opportunities, and, more recently, the movement towards an anti-racist and anti-sexist education, are part of the same effort. Today, it has become increasingly clear that, although needs continue, rightly, to be identified at an individual level, unless wider societal influences are taken into account the needs analysis will be limited. Indeed, without this wider view, individual needs may not even be recognized in the first place. It is only relatively recently, for example, that the British education system began to accept the need to provide community language teaching for any community other than the Welsh and to accept that this implies a shift in majority attitudes towards those communities. Thus it seems that the full significance of the concept of need is only recently beginning to be appreciated. One area in which to explore further the idea of a developing relationship between minority needs and majority attitudes is integration.

INTEGRATION

The integration into comprehensive schools of children with special needs arising from their disabilities has been a major preoccupation for teachers, parents and policy makers for many years. However, if we rephrase this slightly to read 'the integration of children with special needs arising from their membership of minority groups', we can see that it is an area raising many problematic issues which have long felt the challenge of human rights.

'Special schools' and 'special education' are terms which relate quite specifically to handicap and its various categories. They thus offer further evidence that a rights-based view of special needs, which recognizes that each minority group has its own special needs, is one which we may have been adopting without quite realizing it. Thus one could, with equal accuracy, call any school based on the selection of students with particular characteristics in common 'special' and indeed we do attach to such schools names which indicate this 'specialness' quite clearly. So far, we have considered four main groups: class, race, gender and disability. If we were to add different religious faiths to this, and ability, we can appreciate some of the contradictions in what we observe and the ways in which segregation has been used either to maintain advantage, privilege and status, or to wrest opportunity and advantage and to maintain identity in the face of oppression. It is not surprising, therefore, that there is so much ambivalence about the notion of integration in terms of race, gender and class, as well as in its more usual association with disability.

For powerful groups, segregation at school has been one of the most important means by which they have been able to perpetuate their own privilege and advantage. For the oppressed, on the other hand, often forced into segregation by the hostility of the majority, there has been a tendency towards marginalization. There may be benefits for a few in the short term; segregated schools may act as a proving ground, showing what it is possible for a particular group to achieve, but they do little to shift deep-seated prejudices or to reduce the limitations imposed by the majority on the minority group as a whole.

There is a further difficulty in that it is not unknown for segregated schools, supposedly looking after the interest of, for example, girls or members of a particular faith, or the handicapped, to be oppressive. Thus if segregation is to promote educational opportunity, and if integration is to live up to the expectations hoped for, they must be accompanied by advocacy and appropriate policy making. Ensuring that segregated schools do not perpetuate oppressive attitudes and behaviours and ensuring that the majority is helped to view integration favourably, not as loss but as gain, remains one of the most powerful challenges of human rights to the education of *all* children, not simply those belonging to minority groups. Helping schools to appreciate, and to include in their criteria for recording achievement, the benefits to all of co-education, or of having disabled students among them, could be one way of achieving this.

THE ASSOCIATION OF 'NEED' WITH 'HANDICAP'

However, the difficulty about the close association which has developed between 'need' and 'handicap' is not only that the concept of need is required by other minority groups. It has also proved difficult to use without the implication that everyone to whom the concept applies is deficient in some way. That this connection is not merely inaccurate but is also stigmatizing shows the extent of the prejudice still felt both against the disabled as a minority group, and also against anyone identified as 'in need'.

This has been further exacerbated by the use of the phrase 'learning difficulty' in connection with having a 'special' need. According to the 1981 Education Act (Department of Education and Science, 1981) definitions,

> a child has 'special educational needs' if he [sic] has a learning difficulty which calls for special educational provision to be made for him. (Department of Education and Science, 1981, Section 1.1)

However, the Act does acknowledge that in the case of a child whose 'language or form of language' is different from that 'which has at any time been spoken in his home' (Department of Education and Science, 1981, Section 1.4), it is possible to have a 'special need' for 'special provision' without necessarily having a 'learning difficulty'.

Unfortunately, the way in which these terms have been used subsequently by educationists makes these distinctions very difficult to grasp. For practitioners, it has been all too easy to think that if special provision is needed then whether or not this is because of 'learning difficulty' is of no concern. Yet this distinction is of huge practical importance because it determines where the need is seen to lie and how resources and expertise are to be deployed. No one would think of confusing the special needs and rights of girls with those of blacks or regard their underachievement, as a minority group, as being due to 'learning difficulty'. Yet we continue to confuse disadvantage due to disability and learning difficulty with disadvantage due to social class inequality as if they were the same and would respond to the same treatment. In Britain this is a human rights issue made particularly intractable by the blanket use of the term 'special educational need' and because of ambivalence as to whether, when and how individual differences should be celebrated, ignored or compensated for.

Further, since providing for those with needs is an intensely practical, frequently urgent, business, too little time has been spent thinking about the underlying concepts and systems which shape policy and practice. The tendency to respond first to those who shout loudest and to rely on traditional ways of meeting needs remains strong. Thus it is still a significant feature of 'special' education that it serves the interest of those who want to segregate certain students from mainstream schooling rather than those who want to integrate them and that this necessarily interferes with, and distorts, attempts at an 'objective' needs assessment (Tomlinson, 1982). Thus in the supposedly pro-integration Britain of the 1980s we have little overall reduction in the number of students in segregated provision and a marked increase in the segregation of a particular group of students, namely those with 'emotional and behavioural difficulties' (Swann, 1985, 1988; Peter, 1988).

DEVELOPING THE NOTION OF ADVOCACY

We have already referred in some detail to the Warnock Report and its proposals. It also made specific recommendations for the management, including integration, of disabled students from which one may extrapolate in relation to other minority groups. One of these recommendations is that 'one person should be designated as Named Person to provide a point of contact for the parents of every child who has been discovered to have a disability or who is showing signs of special needs or problems' (Department of Education and Science, 1978, paragraph 5.13). Elsewhere in the report it is suggested (in relation to assessment) that 'parents should be made aware of their rights to request such an assessment, and . . . that this should be one of the functions of the Named Person . . .' (Department of Education and Science, 1978, paragraph 4.28).

By expanding the Warnock concept of the named person (and clarifying the question of whose interest the named person is to look after, child's or parent's, and whether the interests of each might not require them to be separately represented) and applying it to all minority groups, we are made aware of what could become a fully developed system of advocacy to protect the educational rights of all children and young people. We could then reach a better understanding of what the role and function of the special needs teacher in school might become.

Traditionally, special needs teachers ('remedial teachers' in pre-Warnock days) dealt with problems, and the emphasis was on the particular problems of the students rather than on the structure of school and society which might be creating those problems. Typically, for example, secondary school students deemed to have 'learning difficulties' were withdrawn from mainstream classes, particularly English and mathematics, were gathered together in segregated 'bottom sets' and had a restricted choice of subjects. Integration programmes involving local special schools were unusual. Today much has changed. Comprehensive schools are here to stay and the segregation/integration debate, whether in relation to gender, ethnicity, religion, handicap or ability, while still heated, is better understood and researched than formerly. Teachers working with disadvantaged students spend more of their time supporting colleagues and students in mainstream classes and play a large part in developing appropriate curricula, resources and methods. They are also more fully concerned with reshaping the organization and management of the system as a whole to take account of relevant difference and to secure access and entitlement to the full curriculum for students who might otherwise be discriminated against or excluded from it.

However, a less benign influence of the 1981 Education Act is apparent in the uncritical use, already noted, of the phrase 'learning difficulty'. Access to special provision has become dependent on identifying students with learning difficulties who are then, by implication, categorized, inaccurately, as deficient in some way, rather than on identifying minority group membership. One group of students who have been protected from this mislabelling are those of New Commonwealth origin who receive special provision targeted to meet their specific needs and to promote changes in majority attitudes and behaviours towards them. It is true that areas designated as Social Priority Areas also attract extra resources, usually in the form of slightly more favourable staffing ratios, but this assistance is diffuse and may not necessarily end up being used with the kind of precision needed to be effective. It is this lack of precision which has, as we have noted, created a situation today where, too often, teachers are unable to distinguish between disadvantage caused by disability and disadvantage caused by social class inequality. Students are not likely to be helped by teachers unable to make these kinds of distinction.

Thus the challenge for those seeking to promote educational opportunity is to balance the need to analyse group and individual differences so that provision can be made justly and fairly, with the need to recognize the importance of what is due to all. There is no paradox here: if the goals of education are the same for everyone, then positive discrimination will be needed for some. The following description of one school's attempt to develop in such a way is outlined below.

The School

Peers is an eight-form entry, coeducational school for 800 students aged 13–18, among whom are approximately 7 per cent ethnic minority students, mainly of Afro-Caribbean origin. The school serves an industrial area (designated a Social Priority Area) of Oxford City and was originally formed from the amalgamation, on the same site, of a secondary school and a grammar school. In the early 1980s, the curriculum

> differed little from that of many other schools in the country. It consisted of a compulsory core (English, mathematics, physical education and religious education), with six options. The top line of this, significantly, represented almost subject for subject the grammar school curriculum of Littlemore Grammar School in 1958, with the descending columns representing the descending academic hierarchy. At the bottom were to be found the institutionalized ideas which arose from the Newsom Report and raising of the school leaving age initiatives of the Sixties and Seventies. At the very bottom of the columns, spanning four of them, featured the vocational skills course, run by the special needs department for dissenters and dropouts in the system. (Batty *et al.*, 1987, p 170)

Developments since 1981

In the wake of Warnock and the 1981 Education Act, the school was able to appoint additional special needs staff and new accommodation was made available so that what had been the Basic Studies area was relocated and named the Special Needs Department. These changes need not, however, have made any difference. What was significant was that new approaches, encouraged by the Warnock philosophy, went hand in hand with curriculum strategies which were then being developed in the school as a whole, 'to broaden the basis upon which achievements in school could be recognised' (Moon and Oliver, 1985). An approach to the curriculum was adopted which replaced the two-year courses of study leading to the General Certificate of Secondary Education (GCSE) at age 16, with shorter units, or modules. These have been designed, and each is separately assessed, so that students can select and put together sufficient credits to achieve the same number of entries at GCSE that they would have done formerly. This approach aimed to foster an ethos and practice emphasizing student choice, autonomy and successful learning experience and recognized that the biggest group of students with special needs were those disadvantaged not by learning difficulty, but by social class inequality. Some of the characteristics of this curriculum are:

- short-term goals;
- student responsibility, autonomy and self-evaluation;
- teachers working collaboratively in teams.

Importantly, options are kept open at all stages and students can negotiate appropriate pathways through the curriculum with advice from day and subject tutors. Ultimately, students have a free choice of modules within a structure which requires all students to cover the main curriculum areas. As is consistent with this philosophy, students are randomly grouped throughout the school.

The result of several years' work on these developments is that today, teachers at Peers can state with reasonable confidence that they work within the framework which seeks to

- promote the principle of equal value;
- give all students entitlement to the full curriculum;
- ensure parity of esteem between different areas of the curriculum;
- emphasize and actively promote successful learning experiences.

Meanwhile the staff of the Special Needs Department were able to frame, in line with the overall school ethos, their principles:

- that everyone in the school community is entitled to equality of respect and concern;
- that classroom teachers and day tutors accept responsibility for all students in their care;

and their aims:

- to ensure access to the curriculum (in the widest sense) for those students who, without the support of the department and its staff, would have limited educational opportunity, a less successful learning experience, or who would be unfairly discriminated against in some way;
- to respond to needs with appropriate action whenever possible.

So much for principles and aims. How does this relate to practice? In this school these are some of the features:

- Students who would previously have been based full-time in the department now attend full-time in the mainstream. Special needs staff now spend most of their time in mainstream support.
- Learning *difficulties* are not the first focus of attention: learning *successes* are.
- 'Having special needs' is not seen as a blanket term encompassing a group of students who are then collectively stigmatized, nor are they assumed to have 'learning difficulties'.
- Terms such as 'high' or 'low' ability are not used except in relation to specific skills.

- Where an individual student has a special need because of, for example, profound deafness, or limited command of English, or emotional or behavioural difficulty, the group is also seen to have a need: to learn how to respond to such differences appropriately and to work co-operatively.

- Special needs staff see advocacy and a concern for, and knowledge about, rights and opportunities as a central part of their job. Accordingly they have been able to assemble a team (which includes staff appointed to work with ethnic minorities and a counsellor) with the skills and experience to combine the co-ordination of strategies to meet the needs and assert the rights of a wide range of minority groups with the co-ordination of whole-school policy making for rights and opportunities.

- Records of achievement encourage students in autonomy, self-evaluation and self-esteem and open up new areas in which students can experience success. They also promote strong links between a student's academic work and personal and social development.

- A code of conduct for the whole school community stresses mutual respect, the right of students to an education offering them the best opportunity to attain their potential, the duty of teachers, support staff, governors, parents and officers of the local education authority to create the circumstances for this to happen and the right of every individual at Peers to do these things without being hindered by others.

Evaluating Performance

Nonetheless, however sound the aims, monitoring, review and evaluation are essential in order to record, maintain and develop good practice and to help identify and address the problems which remain to be solved. Finding suitable and objective criteria for doing this, which look for achievement beyond that revealed by test or examination results, is difficult. To help in this, Oxfordshire schools all take part in regular cycles of self-evaluation and must address an area of prejudice as an element in their evaluation programme in each cycle. This strategy encourages the development of long-term human rights policy making and the formation of working parties and support groups as permanent elements in the education authority's structure and in its different institutions. At the present time indicators are being designed for use by local institutions to help them review and monitor their performance and to develop good practice in a number of areas, including equal opportunities. It is expected that they will eventually cover a wide range of topics and that cross-referencing will be encouraged so that, for example, a school wishing to evaluate its provision for careers education or residential education will not be able to ignore the equal opportunities dimension in these.

CONCLUSION

The issues discussed in this chapter would seem to suggest that the discourse of human rights presents a very considerable challenge to the education of children with special needs as currently understood. Summarizing these we find first that much greater clarity is needed in our accepted use of terms and concepts, coupled with an awareness that they can be used with powerful effect and with different meanings in different contexts and by different interest groups.

Secondly, the concept of rights reinforces the concept of needs, making it easier to prioritize needs and to develop a rationale for the allocation of scarce resources. Linking needs and rights also helps to shift the focus of attention from the needy individual, to the need of the majority for changes in attitude in relation to, for example, disability or social class inequality.

Thirdly, human rights perspective challenges much existing policy making on the education of children with needs and suggests an extension in the range of skills needed by specialists in this field. Thus more knowledge and experience of the ways in which prejudice and discrimination operate in society and of policy making for equality and social justice are required than has hitherto been thought necessary. The implications for special needs teachers in this approach are profound and could, and should, involve them in a change of direction which would put them at the heart of the co-ordination and implementation of human rights policy making and education. At present, those involved in special needs and those involved in equal opportunities have difficulty in recognizing that they share the same objectives and in seeing that by working together more closely they would greatly increase their mutual effectiveness. The Warnock Report (Department of Education and Science, 1978) proposed

> a general framework of special education which is much wider than the present statutory concept and within that, though an integral part of it, the means of safeguarding the interests of the minority of pupils whose needs cannot be met within the resources generally available in ordinary schools. (Department of Education and Science, 1978, paragraph 3.45)

Thus where an equal opportunities interpretation of this would highlight the concerns of specific minority groups in relation to majority attitudes and behaviours, a special needs interpretation would show how an integrated response to these concerns could be put into practice to raise teacher expectations and individual achievement.

Lastly, relationships are profoundly affected by a rights-based view of special education. In student–teacher relationships the idea of special needs teacher as advocate requires further elaboration. Self-advocacy is also important in allowing students to share in the analysis of their own needs. Starting from where they are, knowing how to be an advocate for them and how to train them in self-advocacy, autonomy and self-evaluation have always been part of good teaching and firmly on the human rights education agenda. Teacher–teacher relationships are also important. Where the notion of advocacy is suggested in relation to students, the idea of support may be more appropriate in relation to colleagues, in helping them expand the margins of what and how and who they teach.

Thus although the education of children with special needs starts with individuals, many of them profoundly and inextricably disadvantaged, its significance reaches throughout the school system in terms of curriculum, as well as through the management and organization of the institution as a whole. But it may be that it is in the ordinary day-to-day exchanges between all members of the educational system that a human rights perspective is most important. Children and young people, particularly those who are disadvantaged in some respect, can tell us more about the challenge of human rights and its complexities than anyone: they are worth listening to.

REFERENCES

Abberley, P. (1987) 'The concept of oppression and the development of a social theory of disability', *Disability, Handicap and Society*, Vol. 2(1), pp. 5–19.

Central Advisory Council for Education (CACE) (1963) *Half Our Future (Newsom Report)*, HMSO, London.

Batty, P., Moon, R. and Roaf, C. (1987) 'Changing the curriculum at Peers', *British Journal of Special Education*, Vol. 14(4), December, p. 170.

Boyden, J. and Hudson, A. (1985) *Children: Rights and Responsibilities*, Minority Rights Group, Report No. 69, London.

Cooper, D. (1989) 'Sixteen Plus: Rights Through Life', in Roaf, C. and Bines, H. (eds) *Needs, Rights and Opportunities*, Falmer, Lewes, p. 113.

Department of Education and Science (1978) *Special Educational Needs (Warnock Report)*, HMSO, London.

Department of Education and Science (1981) *Education Act*, HMSO, London.

Department of Education and Science (1985) *Education for All (Swann Report)*, HMSO, London.

Freeman, M. (1987) 'Taking children's rights seriously', *Children and Society*, Vol. 1(4), pp. 229–319

Inner London Education Authority (1985) *Equal Opportunities for All?* (Fish Report), ILEA, London.

McIntyre, D. and Postlethwaite, K. (1989) 'Attending to individual differences: a conceptual analysis', in Jones, N. (ed.) *Special Educational Needs Review*, Vol. 2, Falmer, Lewes.

Moon, R. and Oliver, L. (1985) 'Redefining school concepts of ability – the experience of the LAPP project', *Curriculum*, Vol. 6(3), pp. 40–44.

Oxfordshire County Council (1986) *Prejudice and Equality: A Discussion Paper*, Oxfordshire County Council, Oxford.

Peter, M. (1988) 'Picking up the bill for disruption', *The Times Educational Supplement*, 22 April.

Roaf, C. (1989) 'Developing whole school policy: a secondary perspective', in Roaf, C. and Bines, H. (eds) *Needs, Rights and Opportunities*, Falmer, Lewes, p. 95.

Roaf, C. and Bines, H. (1989) 'Needs, rights and opportunities in special education', in Roaf, C. and Bines, H. (eds) *Needs, Rights and Opportunities*, Falmer, Lewes, p. 5.

Tomlinson, S. (1982) *A Sociology of Special Education*, Routledge & Kegan Paul, London.

Swann, W. (1985) 'Is the integration of children with special needs happening?' *Oxford Review of Education*, Vol. 11(1), pp. 3–16.

Swann, W. (1988) 'Trends in special school placement to 1986: measuring, assessing and explaining segregation', *Oxford Review of Education*, Vol. 14(2), pp. 139–161.

CHAPTER 14

Human Rights Education and Non-governmental Organizations: A Variety of Approaches

Philippa Bobbett

INTRODUCTION

The state of human rights education in the United Kingdom in the early 1980s was reflected in Ian Lister's paper for the Council of Europe 'Teaching and Learning about Human Rights' (Lister, 1984):

> Human Rights Education has little, or no research base; examples of practice are hard to find, outstanding pioneers are lacking.

He also expressed the view that human rights education had a tendency to be, in Mehlinger's phrase, 'goal rich and content poor'.

The situation in the 1990s looks rather different. In November 1988, over 50 organizations met in London to exchange ideas and view resources on human rights education. The meeting was convened and co-ordinated by the Education in Human Rights Network, a group set up in 1987 to promote human rights education in the United Kingdom. This initiative was inspired by the work of the Council of Europe and developments in France and other European countries. The event, celebrating the fortieth anniversary of the Universal Declaration of Human Rights, included exhibitions, market stalls and workshops. Its title was the Human Rights Forum and Fair. Forty of the organizations offered workshops of practical benefit to teachers. These groups have clearly identified human rights as a concern that they share with those working in schools. The diversity of the issues addressed demonstrates that the organizations are producing teaching material relevant to the whole spectrum of human rights – civil and political, social, economic and cultural. The conference report consisted of commissioned articles written by the workshop leaders and reviews and summaries of resources and publicity materials. This chapter is based on that report (Bobbett, 1989). Although only a sample of the work that is going on in Britain at the moment, this account includes some of the most exciting developments in this field, particularly the publication of new resources. The contributions are grouped under general headings.

THE RIGHTS OF ETHNIC MINORITIES

Five organizations ran workshops on this theme. First, Brian Netto from the London Borough of Brent Education Authority directs a centre for religious education. He suggested that the values, needs and demands of the religious communities must be taken seriously when devising programmes to promote racial equality.

Secondly, the Afro-Caribbean Education Resource Project produces learning materials which reflect the cultural diversity of our society and organizes courses for teachers on this theme. Their particular contribution to the Human Rights Education Forum and Fair was to concentrate on the resources they have produced for teachers of very young children aged between three and seven. The 'I'm Special: Myself' series (Meerabux, 1984) focuses on the specialness of each child to encourage a feeling of confidence and identity. It includes an exercise in which the children look carefully at their own skin colour and are helped to mix paint to match this colour. This exercise is intended to promote positive feelings and enable accurate expression about skin colour as some children go through a period of ambivalence and defensiveness.

Thirdly, the Association for Curriculum Development acts as a national pressure group formed by the affiliation of several independent teachers' groups. It publishes materials including a journal *Contemporary Issues in Geography and Education*. Its major focus is on curriculum materials that challenge received ideas and stereotypes. It highlights the values implicit in many apparently neutral statements and materials. For instance, the anti-racist mathematics campaign has caused people to question the traditional mathematics. Far from being a value-free subject, it is shown to be a potentially controversial area.

> Many problems involve profit, loss and interest and therefore have an ideological bias. Even the traditional method of borrowing and paying back (for subtraction) uses terms that are mainly a reflection of mercantile capitalism.
>
> Europe Singh[1]

Fourth, the Cultural Studies Project is a research project that seeks to contribute towards the development of an approach which makes racism unpopular among young people in the school and the community. Cultural studies seeks to address the problem at the popular level – looking at jokes, stories and common myths through the media of drama, dance, photography and mural painting. It does not seek to replace negative with positive images directly but aims to help young people understand how 'images of self and other are important in shaping social attitudes and behaviour, images which in turn are shaped by popular culture'.[2]

Finally, the contribution of the Teachers for Travellers team is a reminder of the white–white prejudice in British society and the extent to which this ethnic group have limited access to the fundamental right to education. The Teachers for Travellers team assess the educational needs of the children, aiming to place them in a local school. They will discuss the needs of the children with the prospective teachers and support the children during their stay at the school. One of the most common problems is the prejudice of the other children, and the team work on strategies for dealing with this. Travellers value education despite having well-founded fears about the well-being and physical safety of their children in school. Few children attend secondary schools, both because the curriculum is seen to be largely irrelevant and because the hostility towards them becomes greatly increased.

The situation should be seen against a background of legislation such as the Public Order Act of 1986 which resulted in travellers being moved on more frequently from unofficial sites. The official sites in Britain cater for less than half the traveller population.[3]

INTERNATIONAL HUMAN RIGHTS – THE CONTRIBUTION OF DEVELOPMENT EDUCATION

One definition of development is that it is a process by which people work for the provision of basic human rights for all. Article 25 of the Universal Declaration of Human Rights states:

> Everyone has the right to a standard of living adequate for the health and wellbeing of himself (herself) and of his (her) family, including food, clothing and medical care and necessary social services.

The development agencies are charities working mainly in countries of the South (the Third World). They also have an educational role in the United Kingdom. Their educational work includes producing materials for schools and funding and commissioning other organizations to do so. Among them, Oxfam's Youth and Education Department has played a major role in the production and, importantly, the promotion of the use of materials. It has a regional team of education workers and advisers who promote an awareness of the interrelatedness of global and local issues such as inequality, racism and sexism. Their work is supplemented by that of nearly 50 independent development education centres across the country which provide a source of advice to schools and also to groups in the informal education sector. The Carmarthen Centre for Development Education is one such centre. The staff contribute to national initiatives such as the drafting of the development education attainment targets that were submitted to the National Curriculum Council. They also disseminate ideas and resources to local schools and write their own materials such as packs entitled *The Arctic Child* and *The Rainforest Child* for middle school children studying global environmental issues.

The Latin America Bureau has produced *Nicaraguans Talking* (Green, 1989), a pack based on 90 interviews with Nicaraguan people. The issues of human rights thread through the book, notably in the comparisons between the country before and after the revolution, the role of the United States and its view of the Sandinistas, the position of women and the land reform issue. The book is essentially activity based, containing techniques that can be used in a classroom with a human rights ethos. Such an ethos could be said to exist where there is little direct instruction by the teacher and thus no clear hierarchy of knowledge, reflecting a respect for the students' views. The activities aim to relate the experiences and views of the students. In a section on the Literacy Crusade, the students are asked to discuss with a partner the purpose of education: is it to pass exams, teach you to read and write, help you to understand how society works, or help you to get a job or perhaps how to criticize things and decide for yourself? The students make their choice of statements, also thinking of two that are not included in the list given and then rank them according to the importance they attach to them.

Another activity-based resource is the *Action Aid* pack on the Kayapo indigenous people. The students examine various dilemmas facing the Kayapo, whose environment is being threatened by developers. The resource could be used to introduce issues such as peaceful and non-violent means of resistance and land rights.

The British Defence and Aid Fund for Southern Africa Education Group has produced a number of resources on South Africa including *Journey to Jo'burg*, a novel for children, and *The Child Is Not Dead: Youth Resistance in South Africa 1976–86*, a resource for students and teachers with newspaper articles, photographs, extracts from novels, letters and leaflets. They have also produced two resource guides, *Censoring Reality: An Examination of Books on South Africa* and *Learning about Apartheid*. There is a study guide to accompany the film *A World Apart*, which is about the life of Ruth First, the white anti-apartheid activist.

One workshop took a historical event as the basis for analysing a range of broader issues. The Reading International Resource Centre has devised a course on the Holocaust, a topic which has been approached from the perspective of education for world development. The course seeks to promote an understanding of the points of similarity and difference between the Holocaust and other catastrophes to demonstrate that the circumstances which brought about the Holocaust have been present in many other combinations before and since. In a sense, the Holocaust can be interpreted as a culmination of trends in the recent history of Western Europe, in particular colonialism, militarism and rapid industrialization (Bobbett, 1989, p. 17).

Some workshops looked at international human rights issues in a broader context, taking the issues as a starting point and then relating them to case studies. The Inner London Education Authority's Development Project materials look at themes such as development, population, food, industry and aid. The course books present alternatives to widespread myths such as 'underdevelopment is caused by overpopulation', 'hunger occurs when people can't grow enough food', 'the lack of industry is caused by a lack of human and natural resources'. For instance, many people see 'overpopulation' as a major cause of poverty in the South. The students study three case studies which offer alternatives to this view, including the possibility that the world's resources are not threatened by population growth in Southern countries but by high levels of consumption in the North.

Tackling stereotypes from another perspective, Dexter Tiranti, of the *New Internationalist* magazine, ran a workshop on how photographs are used to reflect and distort reality.

> Passivity, pathos and savagery still make up far too much of the popular media's view of nations of the South. (Bobbett, 1989, p. 24)

On a similar theme, the International Broadcasting Trust presented a video called *Developing Images*, which is an interactive video resource consisting of a 28-minute video and accompanying worksheets. The video is designed to be stopped during play for discussion and activity.

> It aims to help young people understand how television current affairs and documentary programmes are made and why particular images of the Third World predominate. (International Broadcasting Trust, n.d.)

It includes an interview with Trevor MacDonald of ITN/Channel 4 News, who explains the concept of 'news value', namely stories which are easy to explain superficially and have dramatic accompanying film. This limits the range of images transmitted.

LESBIAN AND GAY RIGHTS

The Reading International Support Centre facilitated a session on lesbian and gay rights. The group examined a number of human rights documents, including the European Convention on Human Rights and the Organization of African Unity Charter of Human Rights, and found that they were all ambiguous on the subject of lesbian and gay rights. There are some signs of movement, however. The African National Congress has recognized lesbian and gay rights in its charter since 1988, for instance. The workshop participants looked at a series of situations in which teachers might find themselves within the school environment and discussed the range of responses open to them, for example:

> You are an infant school teacher. You have been doing a project on families. The gay father of one of your pupils comes in and complains that none of the pictures on the walls or stories on the bookshelves reflect his child's lifestyle. What do you do? What are the implications of what you do?

The view emerged that, without the support of local education authority and school policy, concerned teachers risk verbal and physical abuse and perhaps even their jobs if they attempt to challenge such discrimination against lesbians and gay men.

WOMEN'S RIGHTS

A number of local education authorities in Britain now have initiatives in anti-sexist education. Anti-sexism is a concern which finds expression in the work of many non-governmental organizations.

There were two organizations which represented the field of women's rights at the Human Rights Education Forum and Fair. CHANGE has produced a book called *Of Violence and Violation: Women and Human Rights* (Ashworth, 1988). It argues that women have restricted access to the four freedoms set out in the Universal Declaration of Human Rights: freedom from want, freedom from fear, freedom of speech and freedom of belief. These form the main chapter titles of the book.

Leeds Animation Workshop is a women's collective which produces animated films exploring a variety of human rights issues. *Give Us a Smile* is a film which expresses the reactions of women to situations of harassment and looks at the response of the state.

> Cartoons, of course are made up of stereotypes and notorious for racism and sexism. The workshop's films aim to break down these stereotypes and present positive images whilst still making accessible and entertaining films. (Bobbett, 1989, p. 17)

THE RIGHTS OF DISABLED PEOPLE

The workshop run by Katherine Stewart of Kingston Polytechnic examined the ways in which the experience of being visually impaired could be sensitively transmitted to sighted young people using games and fun activities. They include experiences using the four senses of touch, taste, hearing and smell. Some well-known games such as dominoes and noughts and crosses have been adapted for the blind, and brailling machines can be used for an exercise in decoding.

HUMAN RIGHTS AND THE LAW

The Law in Education Project is a joint initiative between the Law Society and the National Curriculum Council. This major project works with teachers and solicitors and produces a range of materials for 14–17-year-olds. It focuses particularly on those aspects of the law which are relevant to this age group. The project endeavours to shift the emphasis away from the study of criminal law towards the content and skills which enable young people to become aware of their legal rights. The introductory unit *Understanding the Law* is in four parts (Law in Education Project, 1988).

The section called 'Individual and Society' looks at the role of the law in society and how laws develop and change. It takes as examples the issues of mental health and abortion. The second part examines the implementation and enforcement of civil and criminal law. A road accident is used as a case study for this section. Part 3, 'Using the Law', looks at themes such as parental care and control, marriage and divorce, trespass and nuisance. The section also introduces consumer law, contract, buying and selling and those agencies which enforce these laws. Part 4 focuses on employment law, including discrimination, health and safety and unfair dismissal.

Two other organizations have made important contributions in this field. One, the Children's Legal Centre, runs a free advice centre, monitors policies and proposals which affect young people and organizes conferences and courses, pursuing selected cases and initiating research. It produces a number of leaflets which are a valuable resource for classroom use. A major concern is the right of children to be involved in decisions that affect them. The other, the National Council for Civil Liberties, aims to defend and extend civil liberties in Britain. It pursues test cases and acts as an information service and lobbying group publishing materials on a wide range of issues, including emergency legislation in Northern Ireland, racism, government censorship and the invasion of privacy.

MANAGEMENT IN SCHOOLS AND HUMAN RIGHTS

This is an area of specialism in the Education Management Unit based at the Institute of Education, University of London. Its workshop explored the issues of access to learning opportunities, access to information and access to career development and the implications for management structures if human rights principles prevail. In this instance such principles imply the attempt to recognize and develop the value of every member of the educational community. The question of time management provides a good example:

> Time management within education needs to build in opportunities for meeting and working co-operatively. In a system where time is only allowed to some members of staff, those members are effectively given the opportunity to develop ideas and strategies and their ideas and strategies will prevail. Time management involves sharing the resource of time. (Bobbett, 1989, p. 25)

APPLYING HUMAN RIGHTS PRINCIPLES IN CONFLICT SITUATIONS

A number of groups' contributions could be classified as working from the starting point of promoting creative responses to conflict. The Forum for Reparation and Mediation (FIRM) is a network of projects and individuals involved in or concerned about conflict resolution. Its particular strength is the cross-fertilization of ideas between community-based and school-based initiatives and it also draws on experience from the United States. FIRM stresses that conflict in itself is not undesirable. It can, indeed, act as a catalyst for beneficial change. The desired result is to replace negative, violent and destructive patterns with constructive and positive ones; schools can teach the skills that will enable young people to facilitate this process themselves.

Kingston Friends' Workshop has been conducting problem-solving work-shops using conflict resolution methods since 1981. The programme of experiential learning aims to explore the skills of communication, affirmation and co-operation. Effective and assertive communication can offer the young person an alternative to violence and confrontation in a conflict situation. It can help to develop active listening which leads to an enhanced understanding of the other's point of view. Co-operation is about working together to create new possibilities. Young people can be helped to see that attempts to meet their own needs as individuals may be very limiting.

Aggression can stem from insecurity and a lack of self-confidence. Affir-mation of self and others is a skill that builds confidence and engenders respect.

The Ulster Quaker Peace Education Project relates these principles to the conflict in Northern Ireland and aims to support teachers working in isolation on peace and education for mutual understanding. There is a team of trained volunteers who work with teachers and pupils on conflict resolution and prejudice reduction:

> The Ulster Peace Education Project is keen to explore ways of allowing people to build alliances whilst recognising their differences and to address issues in a non-threatening manner. The essence of this work is that in order to built alliances with members of other groups we have to take pride in our own background and recognise the degree to which we have been hurt ourselves, as members of oppressed groups. (Bobbett, 1989, p. 15)

Both the Kingston Friends' Workshop Group and the Ulster Quaker Peace Education Project draw their inspiration from the Quaker tradition of non-violence and the principles of positive peace. Peace is not interpreted to mean a state of non-war but a society based on the constant and active practice of human rights principles. The spiritual values that are at the centre of Quaker concerns, the recognition of 'God in everyone', informs the work of the Education Advisory Programme within Quaker Peace and Service. The pro-gramme offers help and advice on related issues such as peace, conflict resolution, development, environmental issues and the social skills required for greater personal awareness and affirmation, thus emphasizing the need for inner peace and development. One particular project is the Soviet/Curriculum Development Project involving the Institute of Education, the University of London and the Academy of Pedagogical Sciences in Moscow. The focus of the project is to look at the way we teach about each other's society. It particularly seeks ways of eliminating 'enemy images'.

HOLISTIC HUMAN RIGHTS

A number of organizations seek to explore the subject of human rights as a concept, an interrelated whole. Although the concerns of Amnesty International are quite specific, focusing on the release of prisoners of conscience, its education work has a much wider brief. This is reflected in the 12-unit pack *Teaching and Learning about Human Rights* (Amnesty International British Section, 1983). The first two units deal with human rights in a broad sense with a useful 'translation' for younger students into words and pictures of each article of the Universal Declaration of Human Rights. Five of the units deal with the work of Amnesty International, including the letter-writing campaign, disappearances and torture. A unit on censorship takes the form of six assignments based on British case studies.

To present this subject matter in a way that avoids the sensationalism of issues such as torture is a considerable challenge to the teacher. The possibility of the children reacting with horror and despair may be averted if sufficient emphasis is put on the struggles and successes of people who gain recognition for their rights.

Over 270 Young Amnesty groups have been set up by young people in schools and colleges around Britain. The central Amnesty International (British Section) office supports these groups by producing and distributing resources, information and ideas for use by these young supporters.

The Minority Rights Group is best known for the reports on minority (and majority) issues throughout the world. More than 80 have now been produced. Their reports cover refugees, the oppression of women, migrant workers, threatened indigenous peoples and destructive ethnic or religious conflicts. Although the reports are primarily for adults, the Education Department is able to make some of these resources and issues more accessible to young people. It produces a number of resources, videos and packs especially designed for schools. *Profile on Prejudice* (van der Gaag and Gerlach, 1985) is a secondary pack which contains a teachers' handbook with activities on labelling, stereotyping and media bias and three profiles on travellers, Palestinians and Native Americans. The Minority Rights Group has also produced a resource book for teachers called *Whose Paradise? Tea and the Plantation Tamils of Sri Lanka* (Hillier and Gerlach, 1987). As part of its schools support programme it offers advice, workshop sessions, curriculum support and in-service training.

The Centre for Global Education has a wealth of experience in different aspects of human rights education and is engaged primarily in teacher training and writing materials. It has produced a number of resources on human rights, including the resource *Human Rights – an Activity File* (Selby and Pike, 1988). The principles on which this resource is based, namely that the learning should be experiential, interactive and participatory, are outlined in the introduction to the file:

Skills orientated human rights education is often referred to as teaching/learning for human rights. Teaching/learning in or through human rights goes one stage further. The knowledge and skills objectives remain but, in addition, learning is reinforced through the very nature of the classroom climate.

Do It Justice – Resources and Activities for Introducing Education in Human Rights (Osler, 1988) is the first of a series of resources on human rights education published by the Development Education Centre in Birmingham. The resource contains reviews of over 100 books and suggests possible activities which could be based on these materials. The potential of fiction to stimulate interest in human rights is one aspect that is explored in depth. The book also contains stimulus material such as newspaper cuttings, cartoons and sketches, students' drawings and comments, poems and quotations with suggestions for use in the classroom.

The role of the United Nations documents on human rights has been important, since they are both legally binding documents and inspiring reference points for study, discussion and action. The Convention on the Rights of the Child was adopted by the UN General Assembly in 1989 and will be legally binding for those countries that ratify it.

The Save the Children Fund has had a long association with the concept of children's rights. The original 'Rights of the Child' was drafted by Eglantyne Jebb, founder of the Save the Children Fund, in 1923. It was adopted in 1924 by the League of Nations and was one of the first international human rights documents, preceding the Universal Declaration of Human Rights by some 25 years. The Convention on the Rights of the Child makes an excellent vehicle for teaching about human rights, focusing on the principles of provision, protection and participation in decision-making by children and young people. The definition of 'child' for the purposes of the Convention is a young person under the age of 18.

CONCLUSION

A large proportion of the materials available on human rights have been generated by peace and development educators and from the anti-sexist and anti-racist movements in education. Many of these initiatives have their origins in or are closely linked with the work of non-governmental organizations. All of them have been engaged in a process of reviewing their content boundaries. A clear sense of the interrelatedness of all these fields has now emerged. The content of each has become broader and overlaps with the other concerns. The methods of progressive education, such as activity-based learning, have been adopted and developed in all fields. They remain distinct from each other only in the starting point of concern and their method of analysing the issues. The result of a greater integration of these concerns should be more lobbying power and a higher public profile for the movement.

The raised profile of human rights education has occurred because of a willingness of organizations to work together. Some organizations provide a co-ordinating role, often using the term 'network' to express the desire for a channel for communication which is not dominated by any one group but is defined and shaped by those who participate. The Education in Human Rights Network is one such organization. It provides a secretariat and helps to circulate information. Initially this was voluntary effort given by members, but subsequently the Network has managed to raise funds for some limited administrative assistance. The membership of the Network includes those working in teacher training, in universities and in schools and those working for non-governmental organizations. It is this alliance that gives the Network its strength and its potential.

LIST OF ORGANIZATIONS MENTIONED

Action Aid, Hamlyn House, Archway, London N16 5PG; Tel. 071 281 4101

Afro-Caribbean Education Resource Centre, Wyvil School, Wyvil Road, London SW8 2TJ; Tel. 071 627 2662

Amnesty International (British Section), 99–119 Rosebery Avenue, London EC1R 4RE; Tel. 071 278 6000

Association for Curriculum Development, PO Box 563, London N16 8XD

Birmingham Development Education Centre, Selly Oak Colleges, Bristol Road, Birmingham B29 6LE; Tel. 021 472 3255

Brent Teachers' Centre, Gwen Rickus Building, Sladesbrooke High School, Brentfield Road, London NW10 8HE

British Defence and Aid Fund for Southern Africa, 22 The Ivories, 6–8 Northampton Street, London N1 2HX; Tel. 071 354 1462

Carmarthen Centre for Development Education, Meanllwyd, Llangynog, Carmarthen, Dyfed SA33 5JA; Tel. 026 782 278

Centre for Global Education, University of York, Heslington, York YO1 5DD; Tel. 0904 433444

CHANGE, PO Box 824, London SE24 9JX

Children's Legal Centre, 20 Compton Terrace, London N1 2UN; Tel. 071 359 6251

Cultural Studies Project, 20 Bedford Way, London WC1H 0AL; Tel. 071 636 1500 x570

Education in Human Rights Network, Westminster College, Oxford OX2 9AT; Tel. 0865 247644

Education Management Unit, 58 Gordon Square, London WC1H 0NT; Tel. 071 636 1500

Forum for Initiatives in Reparation and Mediation, 19 London End, Beaconsfield, Bucks. HP9 2HN; Tel. 04946 71177

Inner London Education Authority (Publishing Centre), Thackeray Road, London SW8 3TB; Tel. 071 622 9966

International Broadcasting Trust, 2 Ferdinand Place, London NW1 8EE; Tel. 071 482 2847

Kingston Friends' Workshop Group, Kingston Friends' Meeting House, 78 Eden Street, Kingston-upon-Thames KT1 1DJ; Tel. 081 547 1197

Latin America Bureau, 1 Amwell Street, London EC1R 1UL; Tel. 071 278 2829

Law in Education Project, 63 Charterhouse Street, London EC1H 6HJ

Leeds Animation Workshop, 45 Bayswater Row, Leeds LS8 5LF; Tel. 0532 484997

Minority Rights Group, 379 Brixton Road, London SW9 7DE

National Council for Civil Liberties, 21 Tabard Street, London SE1 4LA; Tel. 071 403 3888

Oxfam, 274 Banbury Road, Summertown, Oxford OX2 7DZ; Tel. 0865 311311

Quaker Peace and Service, Friends' House, Euston Road, London NW1 2BJ; Tel. 071 387 3601

Reading International Resource Centre 103, London Street, Reading RG1 4QA; Tel. 0734 586692

Save the Children Fund, Mary Datchelor House, 17 Grove Lane, Camberwell, London SE5 8RD; Tel. 071 703 5400

Teachers for Travellers, Ilderton School, Varcoe Road, London SE16 3LA; Tel. 071 237 1174

Ulster Peace Education Project, University of Ulster, Magee College, Northland Road, Londonderry BT48 7LJ; Tel. 0504 265621

NOTES

1 From an article written by Peter Wilby for the *Sunday Times* 1985.
2 From unpublished material provided by the Cultural Studies Project for inclusion in Bobbett (1989) (p. 18).
3 From an interview with Dennis Longmore at Teachers for Travellers, 28 February 1989.

REFERENCES

Amnesty International British Section (1983) *Teaching and Learning about Human Rights*, Amnesty International British Section, London.

Ashworth, G. (1988) *Of Violence and Violation: Women and Human Rights*, CHANGE, London.

Bobbett, P. (1989) *A Report on the Human Rights Education Forum and Fair November 19th 1988*, Education in Human Rights Network, Oxford.

Green, D. (1989) *Nicaraguans Talking: A Case Study and Learning Resource*, Latin America Bureau, London.

Hillier, S. and Gerlach, L. (1987) *Whose Paradise? Tea and the Plantation Tamils of Sri Lanka*, Minority Rights Group, London.

International Broadcasting Trust (n.d.) *Developing Images*, IBT (publicity leaflet), London.

Law in Education Project (1988) *Understanding the Law*, Edward Arnold, London.

Lister, I. (1984) *Teaching and Learning about Human Rights*, School Education Division, Council of Europe, Strasbourg.

Meerabux, H. (1984) *I'm Special: Myself*, Afro-Caribbean Resource Project/ILEA Learning Resources Branch, London.

Mehlinger, H. S. (1981) *Social Studies: Some Gulfs and Priorities*, Chicago.

Osler, A. (1988) *Do It Justice: Resource and Activities for Introducing Education in Human Rights*, Development Education Centre, Birmingham.

Selby, D. and Pike, G. (1988) *Human Rights: An Activity File*, Mary Glasgow Publications, London.

van der Gaag, N. and Gerlach, L. (1985) *Profile on Prejudice*, Minority Rights Group, London.

PART 4

CONCLUSIONS

CHAPTER 15

The Curriculum Jigsaw and Human Rights Education

Derek Heater

Curriculum jigsaws are available in two basic patterns. The simple one is composed of pieces printed in the separate colours of the 'basic school subjects'. The other, which is more complex, contains some multi-coloured shapes, the elements of which comprise relevant portions of several of the individual disciplines. Human rights education may contribute to the whole curriculum in both designs. To drop the metaphor, lest it became strained, we must consider human rights education either as featuring components of different disciplines or as a self-contained interdisciplinary block.

Although interdisciplinary learning has recently been fashionable even at secondary level, there is some evidence that traditional subject-focused curricula are being restored, certainly in Western Europe (Torney-Purta and Hahn, 1988). However, whichever curriculum style is in use, the management of human rights education requires all the care that the teaching of any multidisciplinary theme demands. If it is taught as a module, the teacher needs to have a versatile command of the diverse subject matter and make certain that all the crucial concepts and facets of the theme are incorporated. If, on the other hand, the teaching is conducted by means of separate disciplines, cross-departmental co-ordination is imperative. As a minimum, this co-ordination must ensure that human rights education is not totally lost in the interstices between the subjects; more positively, it must seek the most effective allocation of learning tasks among the providing disciplines. In the discussion which follows, the characteristic contributions of various subjects will be presented separately, it being understood that they may appear in either curricular form.

The pros and cons of teaching through separate, traditional subjects and in the interdisciplinary mode are often nicely balanced. However, in the case of human rights education, one consideration might tip the argument in favour of interdisciplinarity. It is that politics and law, central to the very concept and enjoyment of human rights and in many countries only recently introduced into schools, may be squeezed out by the consolidation of core disciplines like history, geography, literature and languages.

The need to preserve law and politics derives not merely from their particular insights and lessons. It also relates to the need for a balanced presentation of the human rights theme. It may well be argued that political theory and law are too abstract and difficult for school purposes. Nevertheless, they do provide the essential positive face of human rights: it is these subjects which deal with their designation and protection. Teachers may so easily slip into the belief that they are teaching about human rights when in fact they are teaching about their violation. Presenting material to students about arbitrary arrest, persecution, torture – the grim tally of the denial of basic rights – is relatively easy: there is, sad to tell, so much readily accessible, concrete and dramatic evidence. The teaching of this ugly side of the human rights theme certainly has its place. But the counterbalance of examples of civilized standards and behaviour is crucial if young people are to be saved from hopeless despondency concerning the human condition. A catalogue of wrongs does not add up to a child's comprehension of rights (e.g. Council of Europe, 1985).

The problem of the heavy emphasis on the curtailment of rights rather than the human entitlement to them may perhaps be most aptly illustrated by reference to literature; so let that be the first of the school subjects for discussion.

Rarely is the imaginative writer inspired by Wordsworthian bliss to celebrate the dawn of human liberty and security. Even the French Revolution, which prompted the most memorable lines of his epic *Prelude*, has left its literary mark more in the record of the curtailment of rights during the Terror. This phase has been famously depicted by Dickens in *A Tale of Two Cities* and by Anatole France in *Les Dieux ont soif* (The Gods Are Athirst). The novelist's stock-in-trade is emotion, flowing through the writer's work to the imagination of the reader. Viewing the plentiful record of human rights violations, the novelist's heart is wrung by a bitter anger or chilling fear and the pain of conscience which demands that the injustices be exposed. None has so dramatically responded to these challenges, magnified so hideously in our own century, as Kafka in *Der Prozess* (The Trial), Orwell in *Nineteen Eighty-Four* and Solzhenitsyn in his several novels. However, even when extrapolations of trends into an imaginary future have projected an increase in the quantum of human happiness, the narratives have been short on human rights: witness Huxley's *Brave New World* and Skinner's *Walden Two*. Happiness, it is clear, may be bought at the price of human autonomy as a person, the very bedrock of the concept of individual human rights. Even Bellamy, while sensing the justice of greater female equality in his *Looking Backward*, emphasizes technical organization rather than rights. The particular issue of the denial of civil rights on grounds of race finds literary expression in much American literature of fine quality and popularity from Harriet Beecher Stowe via William Faulkner to Harper Lee. Apartheid, too, has generated similar sensitive comment, most notably Alan Paton's *Cry, The Beloved Country*.

While emphasizing the portrayal of the abridgement rather than the protection of human rights, there is nevertheless no wish to deny the value of literature for teaching about the topic. Young people must assuredly understand the bleak record of human suffering as well as the codes which encapsulate the aspirations for more humane and dignified conditions. And there is nothing quite so powerful as imaginative literature for teaching the depths to which human conduct and institutions can plunge when fundamental human rights are withheld. Not all the books listed here, it is true, are suitable reading for young people – because of their length or difficulty of language and concepts. The teacher, of course, must be the judge of the most appropriate texts and the precise method of using them. Let it suffice here to record that many successful lessons have been based upon *Nineteen Eighty-Four; Cry, The Beloved Country; To Kill a Mocking Bird* and *Brave New World*.

Whatever texts are selected, the central message can be made transparently clear, namely the imperative need to reverse or prevent, depending on circumstance, the utter offensiveness of destroying the human potential for a dignified life. Orwell's genius lay in his perceiving the logical end of such behaviour. In the judgement of Irving Howe,

> The whole idea of the self as something precious and inviolable is a *cultural* idea, and as we understand it, a product of the liberal era; but Orwell has imagined a world in which the self, whatever subterranean existence it manages to eke out, is no longer a significant value, not even a value to be violated. (Howe, 1957)

Nineteen Eighty-Four thus has great pedagogical value.

The same message may be derived, if these 'adult' texts are too inaccessible for pupils, from stories written specifically for a junior readership. Here are just a handful which are written with young people as the central characters, are available in English and have proved popular over the junior to lower secondary age-range. The particular issue of race discrimination is represented by the American novel *Roll of Thunder, Hear My Cry* (Taylor, 1976, 1980). By basing the book upon the real-life experiences of her ancestors, the author has been able to write vividly about the brutal persecution of blacks in the Mississippi of the 1930s. More didactic, with an attempt at balanced arguments, is the story of a white and a black boy living under the apartheid system c. 1980: *Waiting for the Rain* (Gordon, 1987). Extremely popular books with younger readers and which sketch in the background of totalitarian rule somewhat allusively are the Danish story *I Am David* (Holm, 1983, 1965) and the English story *When Hitler Stole Pink Rabbit* (Kerr, 1971, 1974). The eponymous hero of the first escapes from a prison camp to find liberty and trust difficult to believe in. The second is set against a background of anti-Semitism and press censorship. Finally, one may recommend the adventure story *Talking in Whispers* (Watson, 1983, 1985), written 'in tribute to the work of Amnesty International' and set in the context of a tyrannical regime in Chile 'somewhere between the present and the future'.

Much of this literature is placed in precise historical settings. Cross-reference to the history syllabus would consequently be highly desirable. History, indeed, is often the heart of a human rights syllabus, both as a quarry from which exemplifications of general concepts and issues may be hewn and as an essential reminder of the need for unremitting struggle to achieve the recognition and honouring of such rights. Recommendations concerning the historical dimension of human rights education often identify three distinct approaches (e.g. Lister, 1984). These are the analysis of key documents; the study of examples of the violation of rights in modern times; and the narrative of individual and group campaigns to entrench and extend human rights. Documents commonly cited as being of seminal importance include Magna Carta, the American Bill of Rights, the French Declaration of 1789, the UN Declaration and subsequent Covenants and the European Convention. Favourite historical topics often reflect the contrast between the principles of human rights and racial discrimination and persecution: slavery, Nazism and apartheid feature prominently in syllabuses. Political oppression in Latin America and the Soviet Union is also sometimes included. Some of these topics readily suggest personalities for fruitful study: Voltaire and religious intolerance, Lincoln and US slavery, Mandela and resistance to apartheid, for example.

However, a number of pedagogical problems are raised concerning the handling of such content. The first relates again to the fact that the experience of rights has been so much rarer throughout the span of recorded history than their denial. In our enthusiasm to teach about the beneficence of the human rights ideal we must not distort the main lesson that oppression and degradation have been the lot of the bulk of humanity for most of its so-called civilized existence. True, this core message may well enhance in pupils' eyes the value of the achievements of those societies where human rights have been and are installed. This is all well and good. But, again, one must beware of overemphasizing accomplishments for nationalistic purposes. Several countries can be justly proud of setting standards. Yet Clio must strain to be true to herself and demand scrupulous honesty in truth and perspective and not allow herself to be prostituted for narrow political purposes. Thus English pupils may truly celebrate Magna Carta, Habeas Corpus and early parliamentary government, for instance. At the same time, however, they must be reminded that in the eighteenth century English merchants grew fat on the slave trade, and the English as a whole had the reputation of being the most brutal of European people. Similarly, the US Bill of Rights must be balanced by the American treatment of black people; the French Declaration by the Terror and later anti-Semitism; and the Soviet Union's concentration on the concept of social and economic rights by the Stalinist perversion of its revolutionary ideals.

History teaching must indeed bring pupils to a realization that the subject is fraught with arguments over interpretation. At even an elementary level the question of motive can be discussed. For example, did Lincoln engage in civil war to save the Union or liberate the slaves? Nor must the justly celebrated documents be studied uncritically. During their bicentennial celebrations of their Revolution in 1989 the French made great play of the Declaration of the Rights of Man and the Citizen. It was in truth an historically pivotal document worthy of study in schools. But let it not be hidden from our pupils that the concept of social rights is absent from the document and that women were so far ignored as to be denied the suffrage not only then but for another one and a half centuries after.

The classic documents should, indeed, be incorporated in the syllabus only after careful consideration. They are too long and technical in language to be studied in their entirety[1] and their meaning is distorted if wrenched from their historical contexts. Magna Carta is a feudal document; the American Bill of Rights, a response to British imperial rule; the French Declaration, a reaction to the *ancien régime*; the UN and Council of Europe Documents, retrospective defences against the obscenities of Nazism. History as a school subject is in truth no more than 'one damned thing after another' if issues of motive, interpretation and perspective are ignored. Human rights, no less than any other topic, must be treated according to these canons of scholarship.

By the same token, historians are rightly hesitant to venture too close to the present day, where, by definition, the perspective of time is lacking. In schools which make provision for courses in civics, citizenship or whatever label is applied to political studies, these are appropriate locations for the study of contemporary issues. Three aspects of human rights need to be included: the degree to which they are enjoyed in the pupil's own country; the conditions in selected other countries; and the place that the matter of rights has assumed in international relations. The importance of handling human rights education in these ways can hardly be gainsaid. None the less, the hazards cannot be ignored. These are twofold: the political delicacy of the issue and the difficulty for young people in understanding the different meanings and emphases which attach to the basic notion of rights.

It is very evident that teaching about human rights in a country where they hardly exist would be considered highly subversive by the authorities. Even in states with a firm liberal tradition problems may arise. For instance, many complaints have been voiced in Britain in the 1980s that some civil liberties have been steadily eroded and that a written bill of rights is essential to halt and reverse this trend. The government has argued that on occasion certain rights must be abridged for the sake of the maintenance of security, law and order. If teachers discuss this issue without giving due weight to the government's case, will they be accused of unacceptable bias? Nor are governments which are bent upon demanding duties or submission from their citizens the only impediment to widespread teaching about rights. Other codes of behaviour, particularly religious, may not be entirely consonant with the Western human rights tradition. For example, the programme of a teacher eager to highlight and condemn the subordinate status of women in many societies may be offensive to some Muslims.

One is soon forced in these circumstances to distinguish between different kinds of rights, such as positive and negative freedoms, civil, political, cultural, social and economic rights, and the distinction between the rights of individuals and the rights of groups. The subtleties of these distinctions and the difficulties of reconciling different priorities have caused not only internal but also international tensions and may be hard for young people to grasp.

Teaching about the Helsinki Accords may be straightforward enough. The dichotomy between the Western civil, individualist interpretation of rights and the social, collectivist emphasis expressed by many Communist and Third World countries is not so easy to comprehend. Yet the issue was a major cause of the American and British withdrawal from UNESCO.[2] Therefore, to omit these distinctions from any teaching programme is to hide from pupils the fact that the issue of human rights can be exceedingly controversial.

Socio-economic rights – such as the right to shelter, to a reasonable standard of living, to have employment at a fair wage – are obviously dearer to the hearts of many citizens of Third World countries than civil and political rights, which cannot readily be exchanged for a square meal. Human rights in this sense relate to the overall issue of development and hence warrant inclusion in development studies elements in geography syllabuses. Indeed, a Finnish authority has even asserted a straight equation:

> The concept of *basic needs* has in recent years become a key concept in development education. Basic needs are in fact the same as basic human rights. (Pietilä, 1980)

The issue of social and economic rights raises, of course, considerable controversy. If *civil and political rights* are curtailed, the improvement of that condition is an issue to be argued and fought out between citizen and government. But the efficacy of government to affect *social and economic rights*, it may be argued, is constrained by the totality of wealth and the thrust of market forces. Whether governments, or voluntary bodies for that matter, should intervene to effect greater distributive justice in the form of welfare provision domestically or overseas aid internationally is a matter of some contention. It is also a matter too important to be omitted from the school curriculum. It is interesting to notice, indeed, how the style of geography as a subject has changed over recent decades; from the rote learning of 'capes and bays', through skills and techniques, to the recent acceptance that human and consequently politically controversial issues represent much of the real stuff of the discipline. Thus urban geography must face up to the problems of inner-city or shanty-town deprivation; economic geography, the role of investment and trade in affecting standards of living; ecological studies, the link between environmental degradation and the range of human wretchedness from poverty to refugee status.

The major threats to the ecosystem, such as the depletion of the ozone layer and the 'greenhouse effect', may not at first sight seem central to human rights education. They do none the less raise a question which is rarely asked, namely the rights of future generations. Rights presuppose concomitant responsibilities; these responsibilities most assuredly include honouring the rights of others; and these 'others' must in all justice embrace those yet to be born. Burke (though no lover of abstract human rights) understood this organic relationship across the ages. 'Society', he declared 'is . . . a partnership not only between those who are living, but between those who are living, those who are dead, and those who are to be born'

(Burke, 1790). We have no right to deprive the generations to come of their right to a planet able to sustain a reasonable standard of living. Geography teachers bear a particular responsibility to convey this moral truth.

For, indeed, rights are as much a matter of ethics as of jurisprudence. The very concept of human rights is grounded in acceptance of the moral nature of the human being and of the citizen's relationship with the state; while laws which codify the principles of rights expressly uphold this fundamental axiom. To translate into curriculum terms: law and moral education have vital roles to play in human rights education.

'Law-related studies', to use the term favoured in the United States has only recently been introduced into the curricula in any systematic way, and then only in a few countries. Yet it is law which has defined historically and still in our own age does define the limits and extent of rights. One has but to consider the steady extension of women's civil and political rights over the past century to recognize that legislation has been crucial to the fight for equality, including the quite basic need of married women to assert their right to autonomous legal identity. The problems of religious and racial discrimination have also, of course, had to be tackled through legal enactments. One German specialist on political education, reporting on a UNESCO conference on human rights education, has commented as follows:

> the participants got lost again and again in the wide range of issues. These issues cannot be dealt with methodically unless the *law-related aspect* [my emphasis] of politics, that is, the subject of human rights, is taught as an integral part of social studies or political education. (Schmidt-Sinns, 1980)

Consequently, it behoves the supporters of human rights education to ensure that where law-related studies are included in the curriculum, the human rights aspects are given due prominence; for both lawyers and governments of a right-of-centre tendency are inclined to interpret such programmes as lessons in criminal law and the citizenly duties of obedience.[3]

The contributions of moral education to learning about human rights have been left to the end of this survey because the subject can speak most directly of all to the young person in the context of his or her everyday behaviour. The idea that the individual has both rights and reciprocal obligations to respect the rights of others is a central feature of moral maturation. Young children have an acute sense of what is fair, just and right in their relationships with their peers, parents and teachers. Nothing rankles more than unjust treatment. This primitive sense can be built upon for the more sophisticated concepts of rights which have been developed in political contexts.

On the other hand, moral education, more than most school subjects, rings with a thin and false tone in the pupils' ears if confined to scattered squares on the timetable. School assemblies, style of classroom teaching, the whole ethos of the school must strive to convey the same messages and certainly not contradict them. If a school indulges in unjust and degrading forms of punishment or allows racist bullying in the playground, no amount of theoretical teaching about human rights in the classroom can hope to compensate for these negative experiences.

The contribution of moral education in this broad sense to developing an understanding about human rights is particularly pertinent to the primary school. There are two reasons for this. One is that prejudice, a mentality corrosive of attitudes which support human rights, is best prevented before the onset of puberty, when attitudes tend to harden.[4] Thus the French programme for civics lessons in the elementary school is careful to include the following for 6–7-year-olds:

> acknowledgment of the rights of others, of the equality between races and sexes, of the dignity of the person. (Lyseight-Jones, 1985)

The second reason is that much of the historical, political and legal perspectives of human rights education is scarcely apposite for the younger age levels. Basic concepts such as justice, equality, discrimination, freedom and self-determination, naturally without using these words, can therefore best be taught to young pupils in a comprehensible way by reference to their own life experiences.

Indeed, the quantity of potential subject matter, the complexity of curriculum organization and the difficulties of generalizing about the human rights curriculum over a wide age and ability range all suggest that teachers need to have in mind quite broad guidelines rather than detailed content prescriptions. What should determine a syllabus is the need for students to have learned a certain body of knowledge, developed a certain style of attitudes and mastered a certain range of skills by the time they leave school. These objectives may be listed as follows:[5]

1. Knowledge of historical developments.
2. Knowledge of contemporary declarations, conventions and covenants.
3. Knowledge of some major infringements of human rights.
4. Understanding of the distinction between political/legal and social/economic rights.
5. Understanding of the basic concepts of human rights.
6. Understanding of the relationship between individual, group and national rights.
7. Appreciation of one's own prejudices and the development of attitudes of toleration.
8. Appreciation of the rights of others.
9. Sympathy for those who are denied rights.
10. Intellectual skills.
11. Action skills.

This catalogue could be considered a checklist which teachers of different age-groups and different subjects might use to ensure that all aspects of human rights education are eventually covered.

If the ideals of human rights are to have any chance of being even approximately attained, the school must impress upon its students the interdependence of the various levels: interpersonal, national and global. For as the world becomes increasingly interdependent economically and ecologically, so it must become more fully integrated in its moral standards. The distinguished American educationist, I. L. Kandel, understood this more than a generation ago as the modern movement to establish universal recognition of human rights got under way. He wrote:

> The common goals inherent in the ideal of the rights of man can only be attained as programmes of education and instruction are based on the realization that there is no national culture which does not owe far more than is usually admitted to the influence of the cultural heritage of man of all races and of all ages. It is upon this foundation that the freedoms included in the rights of man can be laid; it is the only way that the true concept of humanism as an end in education can be developed. (Kandel, 1949)

NOTES

1 An alternative is to translate the texts into simpler language. See the 'plain language version' of the Universal Declaration, in Centre for Human Rights (1989).
2 For an account of the controversy, see Maddison (1985).
3 See, for example, the work of the Law in Education Project, jointly promoted in England by the Law Society and the School Curriculum Development Council. The address is given in Chapter 14.
4 For a summary of this area of research, see Heater (1980).
5 For a fuller exposition of these objectives, see Heater (1984).

REFERENCES

Burke, E. (1790) *Reflections on the Revolution in France.*
Centre for Human Rights (1989) *Teaching Human Rights*, United Nations, New York, pp. 21–27.
Council of Europe (1985) *Recommendation No. R (85) 7 of the Committee of Ministers*, Appendix 3.2, Council of Europe, Strasbourg.
Gordon, S. (1987) *Waiting for the Rain*, Orchard Books, New York and London.
Heater, D. (1980) *World Studies*, Harrap, London, Chapter 4.
Heater, D. (1984) *Human Rights Education in Schools: Concepts, Attitudes, Skills* (DECS/EGT (84) 26), Council of Europe, Strasbourg.
Holm, A. (1983, 1965) *I Am David*, Gyldendal, Copenhagen; Harcourt, Brace & World, New York; Methuen, London.
Howe, I. (1957) *Politics and the Novel*, Horizon Press, New York, p. 237.
Kandel, I. L. (1949) 'Education and human rights', in *UNESCO Human Rights: Comments and Interpretations*, Allan Wingate, London, p. 225.
Kerr, J. (1971, 1974) *When Hitler Stole Pink Rabbit*, Collins, Fontana, London.
Lister, I. (1984) *Teaching and Learning about Human Rights*, Council of Europe, Strasbourg.
Lyseight-Jones, P. (1985) *Human Rights Education in Primary Schools* (Report DECS/EGT (85) 46), Council of Europe, Strasbourg, Appendix II.

Maddison, J. (1985) *UNESCO and Britain: The End of a Special Relationship?* Museum and Archives Development Associates, Royston, Herts, pp. 6–8.

Pietilä, H. (1980) 'Human rights – the backbone of education', *International Journal of Political Education*, Vol. 3, p. 1881.

Schmidt-Sinns, D. (1980) 'How can we teach human rights?', *International Journal of Political Education*, Vol. 3, p. 180.

Taylor, M. D. (1976, 1980) *Roll of Thunder, Hear My Cry*, Dial Press, New York; Puffin, Harmondsworth.

Torney-Purta, J. and Hahn, C. (1988) 'Values education in the Western European tradition', in Cummings, W. K., Gopinathan, S. and Tomoda, Y. (eds) *The Revival of Values Education in Asia and the West*, Pergamon, Oxford.

Watson, J. (1983, 1985) *Talking in Whispers*, Gollancz, Fontana, London.

CHAPTER 16

The Challenge of Human Rights for Education

Ian Lister

INTRODUCTION: THE 1980s

In England the 1960s were the decade of curriculum materials projects; the 1970s saw the national Programme for Political Education, with its central concept 'political literacy' (Crick and Lister, 1978); the 1980s have been a decade of new movements in social and personal education. These new movements have included education for peace and international understanding; development education; multicultural education, teaching and learning about human rights; and environmental education of the ecological variety (what the Germans call 'Ökopädagogik' (Beer, 1984)). They have also included the growth in schools of guidance and counselling, with aims derived from humanistic psychology. They all related to human rights, and their curriculum and action programmes all had human rights dimensions in them. After a decade which saw at its start the strong impulses of these new movements, and which saw at its end a national curriculum established by law, we can now recognize more clearly the possibilities and the problems of human rights for education. From the present standpoint we can also review the achievements to date.

I came to the field of human rights education (HRE) from the field of political education in 1981. The Council of Europe, a major pioneer in the HRE field, asked me to prepare a teachers' handbook on teaching and learning about human rights (Lister, 1984). I was attracted to HRE as I thought that it might strengthen, and give coherence to, the various movements for educational reform which were then active. I also thought that an understanding of human rights principles, and the ability to recognize and work on human rights issues, were a necessary part of a proper political education. In short, I thought that human rights had an enormous potential for civic education and for education generally. I also sensed the great challenge that human rights would make to curriculum, to classroom life and to schools as organizations.

When, in 1981, I reviewed HRE and the related fields as part of the homework for the teachers' handbook project, the scene seemed to be characterized by vitality, competing and overlapping enterprises, and incoherence. Peace education was already getting embroiled in a rhetorical debate, and being labelled as 'one-sided disarmament' by its New Right opponents (Cox and Scruton, 1984) (and its concern for *justice* was being forgotten). There was little *practice* of peace education in the schools (as Kevin Green, of the University of Bradford, found when he set out to research it (Green, 1986)). Development education seemed to be strong in development education centres (DECs), but not in the schools. Multicultural education was mostly still in the stage of policy formation and formulation, and it had much more to say about school management than about classroom practice (Claycomb, 1989a). However, compared with the professional commitment and some of the practice (Atlantic College (Duczek, 1984) and Groby College (Selby, 1982), for example) in peace education, and compared with the high level of formal support that had been given to development education and was being given to multicultural education, human rights education was the underdeveloped field. It enjoyed support from international organizations (such as the United Nations and the Council of Europe) but lacked support from national governments. There was little *educational* literature in the field – nearly all the literature on human rights was legal and philosophical (Spurgeon, 1986) – and the groundwork of conceptual clarification still needed to be done. There was a lack of teaching materials, guides and handbooks. Aspirations were high, but provision was low. Like other areas of the new movements, human rights education ran the risk – in the words of Howard Mehlinger (Mehlinger, 1981) – of being 'goal rich and content poor'.

If one reviews the scene today the contrasts are striking. There are conceptual guidebooks (Heater, 1984). There are a number of teachers' handbooks. Excellent teaching and learning materials have been produced by national commissions in Australia and Canada, and by Amnesty International (1984), the Jordanhill project (Dunlop, 1984) and the Centre for Global Education (Selby and Pike, 1988), among others in the United Kingdom. However, while the time of peace education might have passed, and while the time of environmental–ecological education is now with us, the time of human rights education is yet to come, and significant support from government is still awaited. We must be aware both of what has been achieved and what still needs to be achieved when we consider the present challenge of human rights to education.

THE CHALLENGE TO CURRICULUM

The aim I propose for human rights education is both modest and ambitious. It is that all students should have an awareness of the related notions of basic rights/fundamental freedoms and fair treatment/due process. These are the essence of human rights and all selection of content, planning of activities and assessment procedures should relate to them and seek to promote awareness of them. There is a challenge for modern educators to identify *content* for the curriculum. Many of those in the new movements were so concerned about *process* that they tended to devalue *content*, and the backlash has come in England in the form of the national curriculum (where content is laid out as programme of study) and in the United States in the form of E. D. Hirsch Jr (Hirsch, 1987) and his concept of 'cultural literacy'. I have written, at length, elsewhere about content for human rights education (Lister, 1984, pp. 6–14). Here, all I wish to say is that there are some major human rights documents which students ought to be aware of (but that those documents, in their pristine form, are often dry and dusty and not the bread of life in classrooms); that human rights education needs to be kept *human* and that there are admirable human rights *people* (Gandhi, Martin Luther King, Sakharov and Nelson Mandela) and moving human rights situations and stories. My inclination when working with teachers in training, and the inclination of those like Jeremy Cunningham and David Selby when working with secondary school students, has been to start from the people, the situations and the stories and then to build up analytical frameworks (categories of rights – civic and political, social and economic, and cultural; and rights concepts) to facilitate the analysis of human rights issues. Teachers and students need to practise and develop a language of human rights, and that language can proceed from everyday language – particularly from the notion of *fairness*, which is embedded in English language and culture.

Classrooms are places where language occurs, where knowledge is transmitted and exchanged, and where behaviour and work are evaluated. However, classroom *life* is the life of students and teachers. During the 1980s some case-study research of pilot projects has greatly enhanced our knowledge of students' and teachers' perspectives on teaching about human rights and teaching about development (a closely related field). We now have a clearer idea of some of the problems which need to be overcome *at the pedagogical level*. Jeremy Cunningham, in his case study of a human rights course in a secondary school (Cunningham, 1986), surveyed and analysed students' opinions on some human rights principles. He gave the students, who were 12–14 years old, a list of principles, which were all positively stated (e.g. 'Everyone must be allowed to leave their country and return to it'), and invited them to agree or disagree with the statements. Some interesting areas of uncertainty and disagreement were revealed. On the statement 'Everyone must have equal pay for equal work', 21 per cent were in the don't know category, and 7 per cent disagreed with the statement. On the statement 'No one must be tortured', 26 per cent were in the don't know category and 26 per cent disagreed with the statement. And on the statement 'No one must be arrested without being charged', 19 per cent were in the don't know category and 15 per cent disagreed. We may, or may not, be surprised by some of these findings (Cunningham was surprised – particularly on torture) but such a mapping of opinion is a useful exercise. It provides teachers with evidence (instead of hunch and supposition) on which to plan teaching. It also creates interesting material for discussion (of opinions, not of particular students' opinions). And the opinion survey can be re-run at the end of a course and the opinion pattern then can be compared with that recorded at the start of the course.

Through a series of 'True Stories', Cunningham also attempted to identify students' interest in particular human rights issues. Some social studies teachers hold strong views on starting points (start from where they are, the local and the familiar, *or* start from the exotic and the distant). Some teachers also hold strong views on what students are, and might be, interested in. These opinions may be articles of faith and/or they may be based on teachers' craft knowledge. (They are rarely based on evidence arising from consulting the students.) Cunningham's interest-mapping exercise aimed to provide evidence about students' interest which teachers and students could take into account when developing the course. The highest-interest stories were (equal first and equal third):

1. { Racism in South Africa
   { Mistreatment in Northern Ireland
3. { Racism in Brixton
   { Arbitrary arrest in the USSR

The lowest stories were:

7. Arbitrary 'arrest' in school
8. Sexism in school
9. Sexism at work
10. Censorship in school

Cunningham's findings are an enlightening combination of topics and distances. Racism was a high-interest issue (both at home, Brixton, and away, South Africa). School issues were consistently of low interest.

Judy Dyson's case-study research was on a course of development education (or Third World studies) in a secondary school (Dyson, 1986). She researched the images that 14–16-year-old students had of other countries and peoples. Her findings, like Cunningham's opinion and interest surveys, inform us about the contexts in which human rights education must work. While students accepted the United States as being similar to the United Kingdom – 'They speak the same language . . . their way of life is similar, just exaggerated' – students' images of Africa were consistently negative – 'They haven't got towns and cities. Not as civilized as us', and 'They're all starving'.

She found that: 'in every case of people identified by the pupils as "different from us", with the sole exception of the Chinese, comments on why these people were unlike us revolved around negative perceptions of life in those areas'. Indians were poor. Africans had a lot of problems. As for Brazilians – 'We're more civilized, the way we work'. (The sole exception was a response from student who had a Chinese friend and, as a consequence, thought well of Chinese people. What she thought of China is not recorded.) In research in a multi-ethnic primary school in West Yorkshire, Carla Clay-comb found that white pupils had positive images of their fellow-students from Pakistan and negative images of Pakistan – brown, while England was green; poor, dirty and disease-ridden (Claycomb, 1989b). Overall, Dyson felt that her 'research into the pupil perspective certainly did not reveal signs of any great success in reducing the distance that they put between themselves and people of the Third World'. The comments of some of the teachers working on the course reveal similar disappointments:

> The pupils lack a concept of the scale of the problems and issues . . . They don't even know the location of the countries.

> The pupils find it boring and too hard. They come with a limited set of stereotypes and keep them. It's all too distant.

> I'm disappointed that there wasn't more empathy shown for the lot of the peoples in the Third World.

In his research on the teaching of controversial issues in the curriculum, Robert Stradling identified similar problems with the teaching of Third World issues (Stradling, 1984). He wrote that one teaching problem was that of 'capturing the interest of 14–16-year-olds on issues which they perceive as having no relevance to their own lives, and on topics . . . which are both conceptually and geographically remote'.

I have selected some of the problem areas, as identified by researchers on the evidence of observed practice, as I think we need to learn from the pilot projects of the pioneers; we need to remind ourselves that teaching and learning about human rights in schools may not be an easy enterprise *at the pedagogical level*; and to be forewarned is to be forearmed.

Human rights education raises major challenges to the hidden curriculum of classroom life in many schools, in many countries. Human rights educators seek to promote teaching and learning *about* human rights; *for* human rights; and *in* human rights. These, in turn, concern knowledge, skills and classroom climate and school ethos. The common criticisms made, even in caricatured and stereotypical forms, of conventional teaching are recognizable as the life in many classrooms, in many schools, in many countries. Henry Morris, the pioneer of community-related education, said in 1941: 'Our State educational institutions and particularly our schools are classroom ridden, lesson ridden, textbook ridden, information ridden and given over to incessant didactic discourse and discursiveness.' (Morris, 1941). Carl Rogers, a pioneer of person-centred education, listed some of the following as typical characteristics of conventional education (Rogers, 1983):

- The teacher is the possessor of knowledge, the student the expected recipient.
- The lecture, the textbook, or some other means of verbal intellectual instruction are the major methods of getting knowledge into the recipient.
- Rule by authority is the accepted policy in the classroom.
- Trust is at a minimum.
- The subjects (the students) are best governed by being kept in an intermittent state of fear.

- Democracy and its values are ignored and scorned in practice.

Paulo Freire, the pioneer of education for liberation, lists similar character-istics of the kind of pedagogical practice which negates human rights (Freire, 1972):

- The teacher teaches and the students are taught.
- The teacher knows everything and the students know nothing.
- The teacher thinks and the students are thought about.
- The teacher talks and the students listen – meekly.
- The teacher disciplines, and the students are disciplined.
- The teacher chooses and enforces his choice, and the students comply.
- The teacher chooses the programme content, and the students (who were not consulted) adapt to it.

Echoing Henry Morris, Paulo Freire lamented: 'Education is suffering from narration sickness.'

For two main reasons human rights education needs to employ the activity-based methods of the new forms of teaching and learning (such as group work, problem-solving exercises, socio-drama, role play and simulation), *as well as* more conventional methods. Firstly, the key values of human rights coincide with the key values of education for democracy, and education for democratic life is promoted by democratic discourse in school life. These values include freedom, toleration, fairness, respect for reasoning and respect for truth (evidence). David Bridges, who devoted a whole book to the theme of 'Education, democracy and discussion', listed the following as the key principles of the moral culture of group discussion. (Bridges, 1979):

- Reasonableness
- Peaceableness and Orderliness
- Truthfulness
- Freedom
- Equality
- Respect for persons

These procedural values provide the ideals for those involved in human rights education. The second main reason for the use of activity-based methods is that we want to enable students not only to identify human rights issues but also to be able *to act* upon them, and to act upon them in ways which may affect outcomes. Vanguard social educators and promoters of the new vocationalism in education are both interested in 'education for capability' and relating student learning more closely to real-life situations. While the social educators face political problems which the new vocationalists do not face, both groups are confronted by similar problems *at the pedagogical level*. These include: how can school learning, and off-site, out-of-school learning, be related to 'real life' – i.e. there are questions of authenticity relating to, for example, simulations, games and job-shadowing exercises. There are sometimes questions of danger to students – as when some school students wanted to lie across railway lines in order to act upon the issue of transportation of dangerous nuclear waste. There may be some particular problems for those trying to act on human rights issues. Many human rights issues are long term, slow to change, and may seem to be intractable. Many of the human rights incidents (though not all) happen in far-away countries to which students have access only through letter-writing campaigns and the sending of parcels for political prisoners. (The railway line, in the story cited above, did have the advantage, for the students, of being down the road.) Problems in actual practice have been recorded by case-study researchers of pilot projects. Jeremy Cunningham wrote, about the course on human rights in a secondary school:

> A general criticism was that students felt themselves bombarded with values and problems. Some actually felt guilty at their powerlessness to affect a situation like Apartheid in South Africa, and had a sense that they were being taught about it 'in order to feel responsible for it'.

In her case-study research on the Peace Studies Project at Atlantic College (an international sixth form college located in Wales), Stefanie Duczek found that some of the major issues concerned with peace, development and human rights could have a depressing and dispiriting effect on students and that there was a danger that the course, instead of empowering them, might give them a sense of their own impotence (Duczek, 1984).

These problems are identified in order that they might be overcome. It is important for students to recognize progress made in the human rights field – such as the examples of the freeing of prisoners of conscience, and the extensions of human rights, where they occur. Students can be active in issues relating to poverty and hunger, and they can work for Amnesty International groups (as they do in schools already, in both the independent and the public sectors of education). In her research Stefanie Duczek found some excellent project work done by the students. One was a group project – the mounting of an informative exhibition on human rights in the world by the students for the local population.

I have said that human rights raises challenges for teachers in classrooms, for schools as organizations, and for the nature of education in society. These may be viewed as questions of democratic classrooms, democratic schools and democratic education. I have written here, mostly, about the first question. The second question – the human rights school – was raised by me, and others, in the 1980s and it is addressed, at length, by Jeremy Cunningham in this volume. Before I conclude by looking at the question (which is *the* political question) I will list arguments I have come across, and collected, during the decade *for* and *against* teaching and learning about human rights in schools. I do this as the arguments are important information for human rights educators who need to have persuasive counter-arguments for the points against.

Arguments Made Against Teaching and Learning about Human Rights in Schools

1. Human rights are too complex for immature minds (an argument also made about other activities – such as political education and economics).
2. Human rights overstress *rights* and understress *responsibilities*.
3. To teach human rights is a form of indoctrination, in which the teacher becomes a preacher (albeit of a secular religion).
4. Human rights teachers are usually more interested in social change (or in subversion) than in maintaining the fabric of society.
5. Human rights is a culture-bound conception, born in Western Europe and North America, foisted on the world in 1948.
6. There is no consensus about what it is 'to have a right', and no consensus about human rights in general. Schools should teach only those things about which consensus exists.
7. Human rights are too individualistic and private. Group rights, collective rights and the importance of the public domain are underrepresented.
8. If we arrogate to ourselves the right to pass judgement upon, and seek to interfere with, the internal administration of justice in other countries, we are in effect according the same right of judgement and interference in our own. There is no good so great that it is worth purchasing it at the price of national independence. (Extract from a letter by a politician to a schoolteacher who had invited the politician to make a statement in support of a human rights exhibition mounted by students in a comprehensive school.)
9. Human rights issues are complex, long-term, and often intractable. Teaching about them can give students a feeling of impotence, rather than enable them to act upon issues and affect their outcomes.
10. Teachers of human rights go too far. They are not satisfied with teaching *about* human rights. They want to teach *for* human rights. They want 'human rights schools' and 'human rights classrooms'. They assert women's rights, children's rights and animal rights. Some even talk of 'the rights of trees'. Ordinary citizens will not support this.

Arguments Made For Teaching and Learning about Human Rights in Schools

1. To know about basic rights and fundamental freedoms is part of the birthright, and should be part of the entitlement curriculum, of all young people. For students in the Council of Europe's member States, where human rights are not just claims and assertions but part of the legal framework, human rights should be part of students' law-related education.
2. Human rights cases and issues are *human* and can interest, and encourage, the humanity of students.
3. Human rights offer a value framework suitable for modern society

which is, typically, multicultural and multi-faith, and part of an interdependent world. Human rights are, thus, an essential element in education for modern citizenship.

4. Human rights offer to young people something *positive* to believe in and support.

5. No man or woman is an island. We are all our brother's and sister's keepers and helpers.

6. Young people have rights and responsibilities and developing an awareness of them is a proper part of education in citizenship.

7. Important organizations – such as the United Nations, the Council of Europe, and some national Human Rights Commissions – support the teaching of human rights in schools.

8. The facilitation of non-violent change is the most urgent task today – both within societies and between societies.

9. Teaching and learning about human rights can contribute to a political education which is over and above party politics.

10. Teaching about human rights affords students opportunities of active learning, working on non-partisan projects – such as when they work for Amnesty International and conduct campaigns on behalf of political prisoners or raise funds for famine relief.

HUMAN RIGHTS EDUCATION FOR ALL: THE CHALLENGE FOR THE NEXT DECADE

The final challenges of human rights for education which I will discuss are, first, the challenge at the most general level, concerning the way in which education is defined, organized and provided in society; and secondly, then the challenge at the more particular level for human rights educators in Britain today, of how we can develop teaching and learning about human rights in the schools.

At the general level human rights principles argue for the removal of barriers to equality of knowledge through education, which should be seen as an *entitlement* of citizens. The aim of policy should be to guarantee equality of access to all citizens, regardless of social background, race, gender or belief and opinion. In the United Kingdom legislation concerning racial equality and equal opportunities supports such a policy. Human rights also argues for a pluralism of provision in education – and against any monopoly of one philosophy of education or of one kind of institution. The limits of this pluralism would be set within a human rights framework.

In Britain, we have been asking ourselves 'How can we develop teaching and learning about human rights in schools?' for ten years. We have seen examples of teaching and learning about human rights in schools – such as within the Peace Studies Project at Atlantic College; within World Studies at Groby College, Leicestershire; and in the pilot project run by Jeremy Cunningham at the Stantonbury Campus in Buckinghamshire. Some work on human rights has been done within development education and teaching and learning about the Third World, and within multicultural education. Several schools have Amnesty International groups. The challenge now, with the advent of the national curriculum, is to provide something on human rights *for all school students*. The two most obvious means of this are, first, through history (a foundation subject in the national curriculum) and, secondly, through citizenship (a cross-curricular theme). The concept of 'active citizenship' enjoys the support of central government politicians from all parties, and from Prince Charles. The opportunity now presents itself for us to learn from, and build on, the practice of the past decade and to make human rights (in terms of both knowledge and skills) part of the *entitlement curriculum* of all British subjects.

REFERENCES

Amnesty International (1984) *Human Rights Education pack*, Amnesty International, London.

Beer, W. (1984) *Ökopädagogik*, Beltz, Weinheim.

Bridges, D. (1979) *Education, Democracy and Discussion*, National Foundation for Educational Research, Slough.

Claycomb, C. (1989a) *Multicultural Education: A Literature Review*, University of York, York.

Claycomb, C. (1989b) *Multicultural Education in a Primary School*, University of York, York.

Cox, C. and Scruton, R. (1984) *Peace Studies: A Critical Survey*, Institute for Defence and Strategic Studies, London.

Crick, B. and Lister, I. (1978) 'Political literacy', in Crick, B. and Poter, A. (eds) *Political Education and Political Literacy*, Longman, London, pp. 37–47.

Cunningham, J. (1986) *Human Rights in a Secondary School*, University of York, York.

Duczek, S. (1984) *The Peace Studies Project: A Case Study*, University of York, York.

Dunlop, J. (1984) *Human Rights*, Jordanhill College, Glasgow.

Dyson, J. (1986) *Development Education for the 14–16 Age-group*, University of York, York.

Freire, P. (1972) *Pedagogy of the Oppressed*, Penguin, London.

Green, K. (1986) *Peace Education in the UK*, University of Bradford, Bradford.

Heater, D. (1984) *Human Rights Education in Schools: Concepts, Attitudes, Skills*, Council of Europe, Strasbourg.

Hirsch, E. D. (1987) *Cultural Literacy*, Houghton Mifflin, Boston.

Lister, I. (1984) *Teaching and Learning about Human Rights*, Council of Europe, Strasbourg.

Mehlinger, H. S. (1981) *Social Studies: Some Gulfs and Priorities*, Society for the Study of Education, Chicago.

Morris, H. (1941) *Postwar Policy in Education*, Association of Directors and Secretaries of Education, London.

Rogers, C. (1983) *Freedom to Learn for the '80s*, Merrill, Columbus, OH.

Selby, D. (1982) *The World Studies Syllabus at Groby College*, Centre for Global Education, York.

Selby, D. and Pike, G. (1988) *Human Rights: An Activity File*, Mary Glasgow, London.

Spurgeon, C. (1986) *A Quotational Bibliography of Human Rights*, University of York, York.

Stradling, R. (1984) *Teaching Controversial Issues*, Arnold, London.

COUNCIL OF EUROPE

COMMITTEE OF MINISTERS

RECOMMENDATION No. R (85) 7

OF THE COMMITTEE OF MINISTERS TO MEMBER STATES ON TEACHING AND LEARNING ABOUT HUMAN RIGHTS IN SCHOOLS

(Adopted by the Committee of Ministers on 14 May 1985
at the 385th meeting of the Ministers' Deputies)

The Committee of Ministers, under the terms of Article 15.*b* of the Statute of the Council of Europe.

Considering that the aim of the Council of Europe is to achieve a greater unity between its members for the purpose of safeguarding and realising the ideals and principles which are their common heritage;

Reaffirming the human rights undertakings embodied in the United Nations' Universal Declaration of Human Rights, the Convention for the Protection of Human Rights and Fundamental Freedoms and the European Social Charter;

Having regard to the commitments to human rights education made by member states at international and European conferences in the last decade;

Recalling:

— its own Resolution (78) 41 on 'The teaching of human rights'

— its Declaration on 'Intolerance: a threat to democracy' of 14 May 1981,

— its Recommendation No. R (83) 13 on 'The role of the secondary school in preparing young people for life';

Noting Recommendation 963 (1983) of the Consultative Assembly of the Council of Europe on 'Cultural and educational means of reducing violence';

Conscious of the need to reaffirm democratic values in the face of:

— intolerance, acts of violence and terrorism;

— the re-emergence of the public expression of racist and xenophobic attitudes;

— the disillusionment of many young people in Europe, who are affected by the economic recession and aware of the continuing poverty and inequality in the world;

Believing, therefore, that, throughout their school career, all young people should learn about human rights as part of their preparation for life in a pluralistic democracy;

Convinced that schools are communities which can, and should, be an example of respect for the dignity of the individual and for difference, for tolerance, and for equality of opportunity,

I.   Recommends that the governments of member states, having regard to their national education systems and to the legislative basis for them:

a. encourage teaching and learning about human rights in schools in line with the suggestions contained in the appendix hereto;

b. draw the attention of persons and bodies concerned with school education to the text of this recommendation;

II.   Instructs the Secretary General to transmit this recommendation to the governments of those states party to the European Cultural Convention which are not members of the Council of Europe.

Appendix to Recommendation No. R (85) 7

Suggestions for teaching and learning about human rights in schools

1. *Human rights in the school curriculum*

1.1.   The understanding and experience of human rights is an important element of the preparation of all young people for life in a democratic and pluralistic society. It is part of social and political education, and it involves intercultural and international understanding.

1.2.   Concepts associated with human rights can, and should, be acquired from an early stage. For example, the non-violent resolution of conflict and respect for other people can already be experienced within the life of a pre-school or primary class.

1.3.   Opportunities to introduce young people to more abstract notions of human rights, such as those involving an understanding of philosophical, political and legal concepts, will occur in the secondary school, in particular in such subjects as history, geography, social studies, moral and religious education, language and literature, current affairs and economics.

1.4.   Human rights inevitably involve the domain of politics. Teaching about human rights should, therefore, always have international agreements and covenants as a point of reference, and teachers should take care to avoid imposing their personal convictions on their pupils and involving them in ideological struggles.

2. *Skills*

The skills associated with understanding and supporting human rights include:

    i. *intellectual skills*, in particular:

— skills associated with written and oral expression, including the ability to listen and discuss, and to defend one's opinions;

    — skills involving judgment, such as:

        — the collection and examination of material from various sources, including the mass media, and the ability to analyse it and to arrive at fair and balanced conclusions;

        — the identification of bias, prejudice, stereotypes and discrimination;

    ii. *social skills*, in particular:

— recognising and accepting differences;

— establishing positive and non-oppressive personal relationships;

— resolving conflict in a non-violent way;

— taking responsibility;

— participating in decisions;

— understanding the use of the mechanisms for the protection of human rights at local, regional, European and world levels.

3. *Knowledge to be acquired in the study of human rights*

3.1. The study of human rights in schools will be approached in different ways according to the age and circumstances of the pupil and the particular situations of schools and education systems. Topics to be covered in learning about human rights could include:

    i. the main categories of human rights, duties, obligations and responsibilities;

    ii. the various forms of injustice, inequality and discrimination, including sexism and racism;

    iii. people, movements and key events, both successes and failures, in the historical and continuing struggle for human rights;

    iv. the main international declarations and conventions on human rights, such as the Universal Declaration of Human Rights and the Convention for the Protection of Human Rights and Fundamental Freedoms.

3.2. The emphasis in teaching and learning about human rights should be positive. Pupils may be led to feelings of powerlessness and discouragement when confronted with many examples of violation and negations of human rights. Instances of progress and success should be used.

3.3. The study of human rights in schools should lead to an understanding of, and sympathy for, the concepts of justice, equality, freedom, peace, dignity, rights and democracy. Such understanding should be both cognitive and based on experience and feelings. Schools should, thus, provide opportunities for pupils to experience affective involvement in human rights and to express their feelings through drama, art, music, creative writing and audiovisual media.

4. *The climate of the school*

4.1. Democracy is best learned in a democratic setting where participation is encouraged, where views can be expressed openly and discussed, where there is freedom of expression for pupils and teachers, and where there is fairness and justice. An appropriate climate is, therefore, an essential complement to effective learning about human rights.

4.2. Schools should encourage participation in their activities by parents and other members of the community. It may well be appropriate for schools to work with non-governmental organisations which can provide information, case-studies and first-hand experience of successful campaigns for human rights and dignity.

4.3. Schools and teachers should attempt to be positive towards all their pupils, and recognize that all of their achievements are important – whether they be academic, artistic, musical, sporting or practical.

5. *Teaching training*

5.1. The initial training of teachers should prepare them for their future contribution to teaching about human rights in their schools. For example, future teachers should:

    i.   be encouraged to take an interest in national and world affairs;

    ii.   have the chance of studying or working in a foreign country or a different environment;

    iii.   be taught to identify and combat all forms of discrimination in schools and society and be encouraged to confront and overcome their own prejudices.

5.2. Future and practising teachers should be encouraged to familiarise themselves with:

    i.   the main international declarations and conventions on human rights;

    ii.   the working and achievements of the international organisations which deal with the protection and promotion of human rights, for example through visits and study tours.

5.3. All teachers need, and should be given the opportunity, to update their knowledge and to learn new methods through in-service training. This could include the study of good practice in teaching about human rights, as well as the development of appropriate methods and materials.

6. *International Human Rights Day*

Schools and teacher training establishments should be encouraged to observe International Human Rights Day (10 December).

Index